RELIGION IN THE MODERN WORLD

The subject of religious diversity is of growing significance, with its associated problems of religious pluralism and interfaith dialogue. Moreover, since the European Enlightenment, religions have had to face new, existential challenges. Is there a future for religions? How will they have to change? Can they co-exist peacefully? In this book, Keith Ward brings new insights to these questions. Applying historical and philosophical approaches, he explores how we can establish truth among so many diverse religions. He explains how religions have evolved over time and how they are reacting to the challenges posed by new scientific and moral beliefs. A celebration of the diversity in the world's religions, Ward's timely book also deals with the possibility and necessity of religious tolerance and co-existence.

KEITH WARD is Professor of Religious Studies at University of Roehampton, London. A Fellow of the British Academy, he was Regius Professor of Divinity at Oxford University and served as President of the World Congress of Faiths. He is the author of numerous books; most recently, *Christ and the Cosmos* (2015) and *The Christian Idea of God* (2015), both published by Cambridge University Press.

Religion in the Modern World

Celebrating Pluralism and Diversity

KEITH WARD

University of Roehampton

CAMBRIDGE
UNIVERSITY PRESS

CAMBRIDGE
UNIVERSITY PRESS

University Printing House, Cambridge CB2 8BS, United Kingdom

One Liberty Plaza, 20th Floor, New York, NY 10006, USA

477 Williamstown Road, Port Melbourne, VIC 3207, Australia

314–321, 3rd Floor, Plot 3, Splendor Forum, Jasola District Centre, New Delhi – 110025, India

79 Anson Road, #06–04/06, Singapore 079906

Cambridge University Press is part of the University of Cambridge.

It furthers the University's mission by disseminating knowledge in the pursuit of
education, learning, and research at the highest international levels of excellence.

www.cambridge.org
Information on this title: www.cambridge.org/9781108492492
DOI: 10.1017/9781108591997

© Cambridge University Press 2019

First published 2019

Printed and bound in Great Britain by Clays Ltd, Elcograf S.p.A.

A catalogue record for this publication is available from the British Library.

Library of Congress Cataloging-in-Publication Data
NAMES: Ward, Keith, 1938- author.
TITLE: Religion in the modern world : celebrating pluralism and diversity /
Keith Ward, University of Roehampton.
DESCRIPTION: 1 [edition]. | New York : Cambridge University Press, 2019.
IDENTIFIERS: LCCN 2018041845 | ISBN 9781108716840 (pbk.)
SUBJECTS: LCSH: Religions–History–21st century. | Religion–History–21st century.
CLASSIFICATION: LCC BL98 .W37 2019 | DDC 201/.5–DC23
LC record available at https://lccn.loc.gov/2018041845

ISBN 978-1-108-49249-2 Hardback
ISBN 978-1-108-71684-0 Paperback

Contents

Acknowledgements

I am grateful to my colleagues Fiona Ellis and John Cottingham, in the Centre for Philosophy of Religion at Heythrop College, now at Roehampton University, and to those two colleges and also to Christ Church, Oxford, for encouraging and providing a marvellous academic environment for my research for this book.

Introduction

THERE ARE HUNDREDS OF RELIGIONS IN THE WORLD, AND MANY of them make claims to truth which contradict the claims of other religions. I am concerned to ask why this is so, and whether this huge diversity puts all particular claims to religious truth in question, since there seems little evidence to settle which claims are true. My general conclusion will be that diversity in religion is natural and good, and that there are rational ways of discriminating between religious truth-claims.

Part I raises some questions about the nature of religion in general. Without trying to provide a definition of 'religion', I begin with a discussion of Durkheim's well-known definition, suggesting that he gives a valuable account of the behavioural aspects of religion, but undervalues the doctrinal and experiential aspects. These three dimensions – the doctrinal, experiential, and behavioural (which includes ritual, ethics, and institutional aspects) – set the framework for my own discussion.

Truth-claims clearly belong to the doctrinal dimension, but they need to be interpreted in the light of the other two dimensions, which makes them symbolic and ambiguous in many ways. I suggest that they outline ways of life in relation to a spiritual dimension, believed to be known by people of exceptional experience, and they are oriented to the production of human good and the avoidance of harm. Religious symbols are finite expressions of spiritual powers, and the symbols change and develop in unique historical and cultural contexts. The history of religions is the history of how such symbols develop as modifications of or reactions to the religious practices of their immediate past.

Part II examines the claim that there is a 'perennial philosophy' or esoteric core underlying all religions and enshrined in some primordial tradition. I show that this is not the case, and that the claim privileges the Indian school of *Advaita Vedanta*, associated mainly with the eighth-century CE sage Sankara. There are other forms of Vedanta, especially that associated with the twelfth-century Ramanuja, that are more characteristic of the devotional traditions of India. Thus, the 'perennial' view is just one interpretation of Vedanta, a form of Idealism, holding that ultimately only Spirit exists.

Idealism is itself just one major stream of religious thought, and I pick out four such streams as covering the main possible sorts of religiously significant relation between a spiritual dimension and the physical cosmos. The others are: radical dualism, separating Spirit from matter, and looking for release from the material (an example would be some forms of Theravada Buddhism); monism, identifying Spirit and matter as two aspects of one reality, and often making Spirit inseparable from matter (for instance, Confucianism, which is mainly concerned that human lives should be in harmony with 'the Way of Heaven'); and theism, seeing matter as dependent on Spirit (characteristic of the Abrahamic religions). These four streams can overlap in many ways, but they have developed historically as distinct traditions.

I examine the perennialist writings of Aldous Huxley, Frithjof Schuon, and Huston Smith, and conclude that experience alone cannot support their view, so it depends on a largely unacknowledged acceptance of one Indian tradition of revelation. It does, however, develop a sophisticated view of religion as a common quest for a supreme existent Good of wisdom, compassion, and bliss, to be attained by the overcoming of the egoistic self, leading to increasing mediation of and eventual union with the Good. I think this could in a general way characterise reflective forms of all four streams of religious thought, but it allows for many differences of detail between them. The failure of perennialism suggests that there are many partial ways of knowing the Supreme Good, none of them complete, and that a fuller grasp of religious truth still lies in the future.

Part III considers some major historical changes in human understanding that call for a revision and development of all ancient religious claims.

One very obvious change is the growth of the scientific world-view, which has completely altered conceptions of the place of humans in the wider universe. Another is the rise of critical studies of ancient texts, which has implications for any religion which claims to be based on such texts (like the Bible). I take Rudolf Bultmann as a Christian theologian who accepts both these changes, and consequently speaks of 'de-mythologising' Christian doctrines. I argue that his programme of subjectivising all ontological religious claims is unsustainable, but that he succeeds in showing that much of Scripture must be interpreted symbolically, and this leads to the existence of many variant interpretations, dependent upon the historical context and the personal experiences of the interpreters.

A further influence arising from the European Enlightenment is epitomised in the work of Immanuel Kant, who argued for full freedom of speech and belief ('Think for yourself') and for the autonomy of morals. The argument against censorship and the unthinking acceptance of ancient authority has generally been found to be compelling, although one should also be prepared to learn from the past and acknowledge that there are authorities that should be listened to. Kant's argument for moral autonomy has been more contentious. Its main point is that moral demands are categorical, objective, necessary, and achievable, and they lay down the two main ethical goals of human flourishing and happiness. All alleged revelations must be tested by these criteria for their moral acceptability.

Kant's principles ought to lead to the espousal of full equality of concern for all persons without exception, but the rise of feminist, ecological, and liberation thought in the twentieth-century shows that there remain deep patriarchal, racist, and hierarchical elements in both religious and moral thought. A consideration of feminist writing brings out how movements critical of these elements have arisen in both religious and secular contexts, and have changed the moral landscape, although they have also caused deep divisions in contemporary thinking about morality and about religion.

In part of his thought, which is often ignored, Kant also held that there is a radical evil in human nature, and so a need for something like divine forgiveness and help in order to achieve the human moral goal. This led him to postulate God, moral freedom, and immortality, and to commend a 'moral religion'. He did not wholly separate morality and religion, but insisted that the role of religion is to support and confirm our moral beliefs. Thus, in his view, religion has an important role in providing a foundation for morality, and religious and moral beliefs are intertwined. His arguments have proved contentious, but it has become widely agreed that both tolerance of the adoption of conscientiously held beliefs and the testing of religious claims against independently held moral beliefs are necessary parts of any justifiable religion.

The Enlightenment had a greater impact on Christianity than on most religions because the eighteenth-century Enlightenment was a mainly European movement. Friedrich Schleiermacher reflected the intellectual turmoil affecting Christianity by calling for a completely new approach to religious belief. Instead of being founded on a past revelation of inerrant doctrines, he proposed that authentic religious belief begins with a distinctive sort of 'intuition' and 'feeling'. This is an experience of 'the infinite' in and through finite things and events. He was one of the first scholars to see religion as a global phenomenon, and to hold that all religions are based on such intuitions, each one developing from a distinctive basic intuition associated with its founder and being part of a rich variety of religious forms, all of which are good and necessary. Slightly alarmed by his own thesis, he later held that Christianity was the most adequate form of religion. Thereby he bequeathed to his successors the problem of reconciling commitment to one particular religion with acceptance that all (or many) religions are more or less equally acceptable. Positively, he placed Christian faith firmly within a global context, and focussed on transcendent experiences, not intellectual dogmas, as the heart of religious belief.

Another element of post-Enlightenment thought is the rejection of Aristotelian philosophy and the search to replace it with a more evolutionary perspective. Hegel is a philosopher who sees religious development as a self-unfolding of Absolute Spirit, and who sees religions as 'pictorial' expressions of that philosophy. The Hegelian view is by no means accepted by all (or even by many) contemporary philosophers, but it shows one way in which some people can see religions as positing a creatively unfolding purpose of Spirit in history, with a goal yet to be fully manifested, rather than being based on a past final and complete revelation. It also illustrates how the metaphors and symbols of religious speech can be given a non-literal but realistic basis within the world-view of modern science.

Seeing religions as part of one stream of interconnected causal influences was the result of the genesis of a new historical consciousness, given classical expression by Ernst Troeltsch. He held that each religion must be placed within a changing flow of events, and that each present has an immediate past context which generates its own unique problems. There are many diverse contextual paths of religion, and they are interconnected paths of continual and unpredictable change. Nevertheless, he claimed to detect tendencies to an absolute goal in the historical process, and he thought that Christianity was the 'normative religion' which (in a revised and liberal form) set the standard of a personalist and redemptive religion. He later came to doubt this privileging of Christianity, and to commend a historically aware, open, and developmental approach to all religions. His chief contribution to the study of religions was to see them not as blocks of ahistorical truths, but as changing and developing parts of wider social processes.

I have concentrated on these five writers both because their work is of intrinsic interest and because they responded in influential ways to the new problems for religious thought posed by the European Enlightenment. Their responses are all contentious in various ways, but the problems are real. To be rationally sustainable, religions must ally with the best modern science and with textual criticism; they must accept that ancient moral rules must often be adapted to new circumstances and that they should be conducive to universal human flourishing; they must attempt to find some plausible general world-view within which religions can find a place; they must adopt an informed global and historically conscious outlook; and they should accept that conceptual descriptions of ultimate reality are not free of local and changing linguistic and cultural influences.

All these factors can function as criteria for assessing the adequacy of religious views, and they point to the need for some sort of revision to ancient religious views. Such revision can take more or less extreme forms. One influential response, seen in part in both Schleiermacher and Troeltsch, has been the development of religious pluralism, which refuses to privilege one religion as superior to or normative for others, and which tries to see all religions as authentic paths to an ultimate reality and truth.

Part IV examines the work of John Hick and Cantwell Smith, and argues that pluralism, as they describe it, is not a coherent hypothesis. Hick's claim that we know nothing of the Real-in-itself is paradoxical, since he also holds that there is just one supreme Good. It also seems that he tends to run together questions of the truth of religious propositions and questions of how one might attain salvation. I suggest that one needs to distinguish these questions, for people can be 'saved' even if they believe some false things. I argue that salvation may be inclusive – all can be saved – while truth must be exclusive – contradictions cannot both be true. Perhaps final salvation requires knowledge of the truth, but paths towards salvation do not. Thus, one should distinguish questions of final salvation from questions of ways leading towards final salvation.

It is also useful to distinguish particular truth-claims (like 'There is a God') from the complex sets of related truth-claims typically found in religious traditions. Particular truths may be scattered among religions (many religions believe there is a God), but some religions may contain, in addition, many more dubious truth-claims, some may have more, or more important, truths than others, and all religions may contain some mistakes. Thus, it may not be helpful to hold that religions as such should fit an 'exclusivist-inclusivist-pluralist' model, even though particular truth-claims may more plausibly be fitted into such a framework.

Even then, however, religious truth-claims are often poetic or inadequately phrased or indefinite in meaning, and this means that it is very difficult to say whether they exclude, include, or are compatible with truth-claims from a different tradition. It may be helpful to contrast more restrictive interpretations with more open interpretations of such claims. I consider some major disputed doctrines between Islam and Christianity, to show how more convergent, although still diverse, interpretations of important religious truth-claims are possible and helpful.

Cantwell Smith goes even further than Hick, and suggests that we should stop using the word 'religion', which divides up historical traditions into opposing blocks. We should see many symbols used in differing cumulative traditions for the Transcendent and look for a future convergence towards truly global theology. I argue that the word 'religion' is still useful in referring to religious founders and canonical Scriptures, and that there will probably always be differences in understanding the nature of the supreme values and goals of religious practice. Nevertheless, these pluralists make the interesting suggestion that religious revelations do not have to be seen as full and final, but are likely to be partial and culture-influenced. It is possible to see religious traditions as developing by understanding and reflecting in their own way the traditions of others, and that may be a way in which religions can live more peaceably and creatively together.

Most of the writers I have considered have been liberal Protestants, so in Part V I examine the work of five Roman Catholic theologians to show how thinking about religion has changed within a more conservative religious tradition. Karl Rahner held that pluralism should not exist, and that adherents of non-Christian religions might be seen as 'anonymous Christians'. Hans Kung held that Jesus is a normative standard in religion, but he wished to move the norm from the institution of the Catholic Church to God as seen in Jesus. Raimon Panikkar agreed that Jesus is historically *sui generis*, and embodied what he called 'cosmotheandric reality', the union of divine and human. But, he held that Christ has many forms and is truly known in some way in all faiths. Paul Knitter denied (although ambiguously) that Christ was normative, and asserted that no religion has a monopoly of truth, and that there is a common ground and goal of all religions. Peter Phan affirmed that all religions are paths to salvation, and that pluralism is good and divinely willed.

These Catholic thinkers show a move from a rigorous exclusivism towards accepting some form of pluralism, although even Professor Phan calls himself an 'inclusivist-pluralist', believing that, in the end, Christ is the only Saviour. They are clear that there is an absolute truth, but not so sure that just one religion grasps it fully, and aware that religious understanding often develops through critical appreciation of and interaction with different traditions.

Part VI provides a case study of one recent interaction between Christian and Buddhists. It shows both convergence and contradictions arising, and some creative re-shaping of doctrinal formulations as each tradition seeks to understand the other. It also shows how very internally diverse each tradition is, and how religious beliefs are formed within traditions of personal experience and social history, traditions which continue to change, partly as a result of the interaction of cultural and political, as well as of purely religious factors.

My conclusion is that religious diversity is not a problem. It is natural and good, and an incentive to the continuing search for a truth not yet fully understood. In a process of dialectical interaction, in which one partly embraces and partly rejects aspects of the main alternative views that seem relevant to one's own historical situation, religious understanding continually develops. Or at least one hopes it develops, as the demand – itself a major demand of religion – to seek fuller truth, beauty, and goodness exerts its influence. Religious diversity will continue to exist for the foreseeable future. What matters above all is that such diversity should be seen as a challenge to fuller understanding in our many ways of pursuing the search for a supreme objective Good, making for universal human well-being.

Part I

The Problem of Religious Pluralism

*D*AVID HUME ARGUED THAT THE EXISTENCE OF MANY DIFFERENT religions and alleged revelations in the world was an argument against the truth of any one of them.[1] If one revelation was just obviously and unquestionably true, then one could discard all others as fakes and delusions. But different religions – Islam, Christianity, Buddhism, and Taoism, to name just a few – contradict each other, and it does not seem that any of their claims to revealed truth is much more convincing than the others. Thus, each believer in one revelation seems bound to say that most alleged revelations are mistaken – all but theirs, in fact. But this is rather odd. If someone holds that most alleged revelations are false, and that no one religion is obviously more convincing than many others, the logical conclusion is that one's own revelation is probably false.

It is implausible to say that everyone else's view is wrong, and that, as far as any impartial observer can tell, my view is not better attested than theirs, and yet that mine alone is certainly true. Thus, the existence of many conflicting religions, together with the fact that no one is clearly better attested than the others, does suggest that at least no-one should assert that they *know* their view to be the truth. Religious faith becomes an option for those who like that sort of thing. But, as for truth, that is unfortunately beyond our reach in the matters with which religion deals.

That is the argument with which I am concerned. There is a problem about the diversity of religions in the world, and the problem has become much more apparent in the modern world, where many of these different faiths encounter and live alongside one another, and where deeper

---

[1] David Hume (1955), Section X, 'On Miracles', p. 129 – 'In matters of religion whatever is different is contrary'.

knowledge of the many religions of the world and a greater attention to the reasons one might have for adopting a religion have become prevalent.

There have, of course, always been many religions, and early tribal societies have known that there are other tribal rites and practices just a little way from them. But then it was possible to adopt a religious tradition precisely because it is the tradition that sets this tribe apart and gives it its special identity. In the modern world, many religions still have a tribal character. They associate a religion with a specific society – those who say that to be Indian is to be Hindu, to be Sri Lankan is to be Buddhist, or to be Irish is to be Catholic, still have a partly tribal view of religion. But tribalism in this extended sense has become more difficult in the modern world. There are more faiths the members of which intermarry and live alongside one another, and at least some of these faiths claim to have a faith which is true for everyone in the world, not just for one ethnic or national group.

Tribalism is still a strong social tendency, and many nationalist move-ments in the contemporary world claim a specific religious tradition as their own in a distinctive way. Now, however, many leading thinkers of the religions and cultures in question distance themselves from that sort of nationalism, and wish to argue for such things as tolerance of different religions, and to ask for a rational defence of religion rather than just a tribal loyalty to one form of religion. Islam may be the religion of Saudi Arabia, but is what Islam teaches actually true and rationally defensible, and do all true Saudis have to be Muslim?

In England, the Church of England is established by law as the religion of the country, and not much more than a hundred years ago access to elite higher education and political power was limited to members of that Church. In the present, although nationalist movements sometimes try to get the Anglican Church to back them, the leaders of that Church are hugely embarrassed even to be connected to such movements. There may be as many adherents in England of the Buddhist-inspired 'mindfulness' practice as there are Church-going Anglicans. The question of truth and justification has arisen in a new way.

In one sense, it is not surprising that there are many different religions. One thing that most people would agree upon is that people are capable of disagreeing about almost everything. Whether it is politics, morality, what we did on our holidays, how intelligent a person is, whether humans have free will or not, or whether toast should be crisp or soggy, one can virtually guarantee that disagreements will arise as soon as conversation begins. When it comes to matters as abstract and complex as philosophy or religious belief, therefore, it is hardly surprising that disagreements are only to be expected. If there is to be any agreement about such matters, it is likely to be only about the most general, one might say the most vacuous, points. The more detailed and particular one's opinions are, the more disagreements will arise. There seems little hope of establishing that there can be such a thing as a universally agreed philosophy or system of religious beliefs and practices. Disagreement is one of the most obvious characteristics of human life and discourse.

Since this is the case, that there are disagreements about religion is only to be expected. The idea that there could be one 'perennial philosophy' to which all rational people could assent, or one universally acceptable core of all religious belief, seems vastly improbable. Nevertheless, claims to the existence of such a thing have been made, and it is worth investigating to what extent such claims might be made to seem reasonable, and to discover more clearly why perhaps they are doomed to failure. It is also relevant to enquire what a reasonable course of action might be, in the vast numbers of cases wherein it seems impossible to establish the truth to the satisfaction of every sufficiently intelligent and informed person, if indeed we are to speak of truth in such matters at all.

On the one hand, it is natural that there should be many religious views that differ widely. Maybe every possibility for a religious view has been explored somewhere on earth. On the other hand, such diversity poses a problem for anyone who thinks that religions make claims to truth, that contradictory statements cannot all be true, and that many religious claims seem to disagree with all the others.

1

Emile Durkheim

A PROBLEM WITH STATING THINGS IN THIS WAY IS THAT RELIGIONS ARE being thought of as systems of propositions which are truth-claiming. There are indeed truth-claims made in most religions. If one worships a supreme God, one must believe that there is such a being. Yet this is not always as clear as it may seem. If one worships ancestors, is one committed to believing that the dead still exist? Or that they really eat the food that may be offered to them? Or is one honouring their memory, and holding them as ideals to be emulated? There is something about truth-claims made in religion that is very hard to pin down.

Often called the father of sociology, Emile Durkheim wrote a highly influential book on religion – *The Elementary Forms of the Religious Life* – without mentioning truth-claims at all. He defined religion as 'a unified system of beliefs and practices relative to sacred things i.e. things set apart and forbidden – beliefs and practices which unite in one single moral community called a Church all those who adhere to them'.[1]

His emphasis was on religion as a binding force, indeed the most funda- mental binding force in a 'moral community'. He did not see the idea of God as necessary to a religious community, and instead suggested the idea of 'the sacred' as the key element in religion. The sacred is not reified as any sort of objectively existing spiritual reality. It is that which cannot be rationally explained, which inspires awe, and which is worthy of devotion. It is embodied in 'sacred things', which are material objects symbolising collective ideals. Those collective ideals are social constructs, they are 'social facts', the ideals of a specific social group. The material objects on which they are fixed are 'the flags of the clan', material objects which embody the sense

---

[1] Durkheim (1963), Book 1, ch. 1.

of the community as a social reality. It is not of primary importance what the material sacred objects are. The important thing is that they symbolise the clan itself, they excite 'collective effervescence', or intense emotional states, whose function is to bind clan members together and make them feel dependent on the group and increase their communal enthusiasm.

The object which is 'the sacred' is the social reality of the clan itself, a force greater than that of the individuals who comprise the clan, and so is felt to be a 'hidden force'. That force does not exist independently of the social group; it is the mind and will of the group, as it is focussed on material sacred objects which excite the devotion of group members. Religious practices have a function, and that is to unite the group around a specific set of ideals and values.

For Durkheim, the diversity of religions is not a problem, as each group will have its own sacred objects and rituals. It is natural to groups to stand in opposition to groups other than their own, so competition and rivalry is essential to religion. If and insofar as social groups enlarge into nation states and perhaps even towards one global community, there may come to be a universal set of sacred objects and social ideals. As sociologist Kenneth Allen says, 'There is something eternal in religion that is destined to outlive the succession of particular symbols in which religion has clothed itself'.[2] But such a global idea may turn out to be impossible, and religion may continue to support a number of moral communities which gather around their own sacred symbols and rites. If social ideals and values continue to differ, there will inevitably arise a clash of religions which may erupt into violence. Thus, the function of religion is to unify societies, but its effect may well be to destroy them.

Durkheim is probably right to think that the social, institutional, and ritual practices of religion are more important to large numbers of believers than the truth-claims and personal experiences which may be the preserve of intellectuals and saints. It is always necessary to look at the social causes and effects of religious beliefs and practices if one is to understand religions. But one cannot really understand religion adequately if one ignores the claims to experience a spiritual dimension to reality, and to provide a correct interpretation of the nature of reality, which characterise religious practice.

Durkheim himself notes that the advance of science has made religion seem less important in many modern societies. This is because the scientific understanding of reality is perceived by many to be in conflict with

---

[2] Allen (2013), p. 134.

traditional religious claims. Durkheim's own purely social understanding of religion has also helped to put many traditional religious claims into question. If sacred symbols are just symbols of the moral ideals of a specific community, then it is the uncovering of those moral ideals which takes priority. There will be no supernatural or spiritual facts to discover. There will be no actual divine commands to obey. There will be no future life to look forward to, and no objective purpose for human life. What will matter is the moral values and purposes of society, which are constructed by society itself.

This may be a good thing, insofar as one can be freed from the authority of ancient customs and traditions, and free to consciously construct a more rational set of social principles in an increasingly global world. One can invent a new global religion with rituals and communities which support such a rational global ethic. This would be, in effect, Immanuel Kant's hope for the development of religion in an enlightened world. On the other hand, if one is free to construct any values and ideals one wishes, one is also freed from the constraints of any sort of independently existing morality. One is free to pursue policies of world-domination and totalitarian rule, with no religious or 'objectively moral' principles to prevent one's freely chosen course of action.

If one thinks that one's religion has the function of upholding and reinforcing the values of one's social group, then one needs to think hard about what those values are, and whether they are worth reinforcing. Durkheim's formative work in sociology should motivate believers to examine carefully and dispassionately the values their religious practices express, and how far they are effective in expressing them. It is likely that most religious groups ('churches', as Durkheim calls them) are unaware that the values their institutions express are very different from the values they think they express. Some of those institutions seem unmoved by explicit moral considerations at all, preferring obedience to ancient rules and rituals to ordinary compassion and humane kindness. The sociological examination of religion has some hard lessons to teach religious practitioners.

Nevertheless, believers would find it hard to accept any claim that a main, or maybe the only, function of their religious practice is to create a single moral community. This is certainly one aspect of religion, but it is an intrinsically ambiguous one, and it ignores the fact that religious beliefs are often counter-cultural, and capable of criticising or rejecting the norms of the wider community. It also ignores completely any claim that there is an objective, not humanly created, dimension of reality which can be an object of human cognition and a causal influence on human behaviour. If an understanding of religion is to take account of the beliefs of actual believers, the Durkheimian analysis, on its own, will fail to take account of the felt experiences of believers, regarding them as in some sense self-deceived. And it will fail to take into account the claims to truth about the nature of ultimate reality and human meaning and destiny, which are an important aspect of many religions.

A more recent sociologically oriented definition of religion is given by Christian Smith, who offers as a definition: religion is 'a complex of culturally prescribed practices, based on premises about the existence and nature of supernatural powers, whether personal or impersonal, which seek to help practitioners gain access to and communicate or align themselves with these powers, in hopes of realising human goods and avoiding things bad'.[3]

This definition avoids Durkheim's reduction of the objects of religious practice to the ideals of a specific society, and is intentionally neutral about the nature and existence of the 'supernatural powers' with which religions deal. But it retains the emphasis on social practices as primary, in opposition to theories which aim to give a more intellectual or theoretical basis for religions.

Such a sociological perspective is extremely useful in the analysis of the actual practices of religion, but, if taken as a complete definition, it could make religion seem instrumental to existing human desires (as it often is). Whereas religious views may aim to disclose a supreme existent ideal reality, to which desires *should* conform, and with which self-renouncing union is possible, this is not in itself intellectual or theoretical, but it would lead to a greater stress of the importance of special privileged experiences – 'revelations' – and the subsequent generation of developing conceptual interpretations and internal patterns of devotion, which social behaviours and practices would seek to express. Truth-claims remain primarily important to religion, although they must be seen in the context of the experiences, practices, and aims of religious life.

---

[3] Smith (2017), p. 22.

2

Myths and Symbols

THIS CAN MAKE IT HARD TO ANALYSE THE NATURE OF THE TRUTH-CLAIMS that religions make. I will explore this complex issue by considering the truth-claims made within one religious tradition that takes the Bible as its originative text. I do so to avoid talking in an over-general way about all religious traditions, as though they were all the same. Nevertheless, what I say is meant to have implications for a wider set of religious traditions, which would in the proper place need to be worked out more fully. My aim is to show that it is hard to interpret the truth-claims that are made in a religious work like the Bible, even though the Bible seems to be making truth-claims of a rather straightforward kind about a God who acts in history. Yet those truth-claims are more complex than it may at first seem, for the Bible is a collection of documents expressing many different points of view, compiled at very different times, without any one systematic exposition of dogmatic beliefs. Some Psalms apparently deny that the righteous can ever come to harm,[1] whereas the Book of Job bluntly denies that.[2] Some texts depict God as walking in a garden or riding on the clouds,[3] yet others say that no man may see God and live,[4] and it is forbidden to represent God by any finite form.[5] Some texts portray God as a ruthlessly avenging power (as in the Noah's Ark or Sodom and Gomorrah stories), while others speak of God as one who grieves for his people and seeks to redeem them from sin.[6] Some texts seem to assume that the God of Abraham is one god among many,[7] whereas the prophet Isaiah insists that there is only one God in existence.[8] This is not what a systematic treatise would do.

Nevertheless, at a rather general level, the Bible depicts God as the creator of all things, who sees the creation as good (not perfect!), who makes a

---

[1] Psalm 37, 25. [2] Job 9, 21–23. [3] Genesis 3, 8; Zechariah 9, 14. [4] Exodus 3, 5.
[5] Isaiah 40, 38–39. [6] Isaiah 54, 7. [7] 2 Chronicles 2, 5. [8] Isaiah 44, 6.

covenant with Abraham, giving a set of laws and promising human flourishing at least for those who obey the laws. Jews are to be bound for ever by covenant with this God, who makes rigorous ethical demands and who has an achievable moral goal for human lives and for creation. This might not be a systematic treatise in philosophy or theology, but it is a definitive claim about the nature of the world, a claim that it has been created for a moral purpose by a supremely good and powerful God. Further, that God has liberated one people from slavery, and revealed to them the way to that purpose (the *Torah*), and the cost of rejecting it. In the context of other ancient Middle Eastern beliefs, the assertion that there is one supreme creator God with liberating power and a moral purpose, not a set of gods arising from primal chaos, warring one with another, and using humans to further their own aims (Compare the Babylonian accounts of the origin of the cosmos[9]), is quite distinctive.

Such an account of the Bible suggests two important points. One is that the Biblical view does not arise in a cultural vacuum, as though it could have just been handed down from heaven at any moment of time and in any culture. It was formed over centuries, and in a Middle Eastern context, where there was a more or less shared general view of the nature of the world, and a number of quite closely related religious practices already in existence. The Hebrew religious view stands within, partly develops, and partly rejects a specific historical/cultural tradition.

The other is that it is the rather general belief in a moral and purposive creator who had a special role, a vocation, for the Israelites that forms the integrating concept underlying the Biblical writings. That general belief can take many particular forms, and is subject to many varying interpretations, as very diverse groups of Rabbinical scholars debate, elaborate, and meditate upon, the texts and traditions which gradually took form as the *Tanak*, the Old Testament Bible we now know, as well as the Oral traditions which were later recorded in the Talmud.

The origins of Middle Eastern religious views are still unclear, since such origins predate any written records. But it seems that there were beliefs in many gods and spiritual beings, both good and bad, to whom sacrifices were made and which were the objects of ritual cults. For instance, Marduk, god of Babylon, undergirded and expressed the power of Babylon and its King, and had, in the mythical story, overcome Tiamat, the savage mother of the gods and cosmic symbol of the salt-water sea, a force of chaos and

---

[9] Heidel (1951).

destruction, to enable a cultured city to replace more primitive forms of tribal society. Sacrifices were held to propitiate the city god, to profess loyalty to the values that god represented, and to pray for his aid in procuring the future flourishing of the city.

The Babylonian story of origins is usually said to be a myth. Myth, in this sense, is probably not just a fictional story concocted by priests for their own ends (although that remains a possibility!). It is indeed an imaginatively created story, capable of dramatic presentation. But it is meant to express some important truths about the nature of (in the case under consideration) Babylonian society, its values, possibilities, and purposes. And it is meant to present a way in which humans could relate positively to what were believed to be higher spiritual powers that ultimately governed human destiny. There was, as Durkheim saw, a moral commitment here, to a specific set of values and purposes. There was also, as Christian Smith[10] insisted, an ontological commitment to the existence of higher, quasi-personal, powers relationship which could affect one's future well-being.

Can non-physical powers governing human destiny be represented as though they were finite physical powers or persons? Consider statues of the gods in many societies, or of heroic figures from the past, to which offerings of flowers or food are often made. The later writings of the Hebrew Bible mock the 'idols' of wood and stone which the Canaanites worshipped. But the Hebrews had in their own 'Holy of Holies', a sacred space in which the Ark of the Covenant stood between two images of Seraphim. In Roman Catholic Churches one can find a container of bread before which worshippers genuflect. It would be a misunderstanding to think that the statues and the bread are, simply as physical objects, worthy of reverence. They have come to represent invisible spiritual powers, even when such powers are believed to be 'located' in the objects in some way. Such representation usually requires special ceremonies of blessing or sanctification, which consecrates them to be conveyers of sacred presence and power. The sacred presence is not the physical object in itself. As Durkheim said, the sacred is expressed in or conveyed through the object, which then becomes 'holy' or 'set apart' from ordinary use. The objects, through some symbolic act, become symbols of the sacred.

It might be possible to say – it seems that ancient Hebrew prophets did say – that the sacred symbols of other peoples were mere 'idols', useless pieces of stone without power, whereas their own sacred objects – or, in the

---

[10] Smith (2017).

Hebrew case, their imageless god who came to be especially present in the Temple in Jerusalem – were uniquely endowed with sacred presence and power. But if one looks at the array of religious practices dispassionately, it does seem more plausible to think that many diverse groups of people, even 'idolaters', are seeking to represent and locate invisible spiritual powers in specific finite objects, which come to have a representative function in their societies.

That does not mean that every such representation is of equal value, that it does not matter which objects one worships. If someone sacrifices children before an image of Moloch, that is very different from kneeling before a crucifix and asking to be perfected in self-sacrificial love. One has to ask about the nature of the spiritual power and the use to which it is put. There are vengeful and vindictive gods who require the blood of their enemies, and there are compassionate and merciful gods, who desire their worshippers to imitate them. Unfortunately, the same gods can be viewed as vindictive by some, and as compassionate by others. Gods suffer all the ambiguities of their human devotees, and no god is safe from the disordered passions of those who worship them. Even the image of Christ on the Cross, which for a St. Francis is the supreme expression God's self-giving love, can become an object of sado-masochistic devotion, giving rise to hatred of those who 'killed God'.

There are, of course, aniconic forms of religion, like Islam and Judaism and Puritan Christianity in some of their forms. But they make it even more obvious that spiritual powers are not to be simply equated with any finite physical object. Even in such forms, sacred power tends to be localised and focussed in groups or in the hearts of devotees, or in the recitation of words which are taken to be communications of spiritual power.

We may say, speaking rather generally, that spiritual powers are distinct from physical powers, but are taken to manifest themselves in or through various physical objects or practices. Those powers embody distinctive moral values and purposes, varying with the societies which worship them. The desire to participate in the moral qualities of the gods is usually an important part of worship, together with a desire to use those sacred powers in the avoidance of evil and the promotion of good. Because human conceptions of good and evil, and of a desirable way of life, vary so much, it is not surprising that conceptions of the spiritual vary, and often oppose each other, sometimes violently.

One way of understanding myths is to say that myths tell the stories of people or things who are taken to be embodiments of spiritual power. These stories do not have to be based on historical facts. They may arise from dreams or visions, or from what is taken to be an 'inspired' utterance by those who are believed to have been given knowledge of spiritual truth. Thus, the Greek myths of Demeter and Persephone, involving descents into the world of the dead and returns to the land of the living, are almost certainly not founded on historical facts. They seem to be imaginative stories based on the cycles of death and renewal found in nature. These cycles are personified and used in the Greek Mysteries to evoke in devotees a sense of renewal of life and hope in times of trouble. The stimulus for such stories is meditation on the natural world, and an attempt to place human lives in the wider context of nature, seen as an expression of basic spiritual forces. Such myths are not, and I doubt if they were meant to be, literally true accounts of events in secular history. They are symbolic portrayals of the spiritual powers which are expressed in the natural world, powers with which humans can enter into a relationship which is positive and conducive to living well.

If this is so, then an account of myths as early, but wholly mistaken, scientific explanations of why thunder roars or rain falls, is inadequate. Thunder does not sound because some human-like figure in the sky is throwing a hammer. Nevertheless, to say that thunder is the voice of Thor can be a way of giving symbolic expression to the terror and power of nature, and of evoking a sense of fear and awe, but also of respect and submission, before the hidden spiritual forces that underlie the reality in which humans live.

3

Myth and History

*T*HE WORLDVIEW THAT UNDERPINS SUCH ACCOUNTS IS ONE WHICH assumes a spiritual basis to nature and attempts to relate human lives consciously to that basis in a positive way. Complete rejection of this worldview would mean that there are no spiritual, non-physical, forces in reality, and that there is no point in seeking to relate human beings to them. Myths posit such a spiritual dimension, being seen as expressed in and through natural events or people, and as both presenting objectively existing ideals in which people can participate and having some causal power for good.

The Hebrew belief in one creator God who has a moral purpose for creation is one interpretation of such a spiritual dimension. It postulates that there is one supreme spiritual power whose fundamental nature is justice and mercy, and who wills the rule of justice and mercy in the world. In these respects this is distinctive among ancient Middle Eastern religious views, even though it is influenced by them and builds on categories of thought influenced by them. It also claims to be not only a myth, in the sense of an imaginative symbolic story or set of stories – though it contains many imaginative and symbolic elements, of which the Genesis creation story is one – but to be based on historical revelatory events. Those events are not, however, straightforward historically establishable occurrences. They must be seen as symbolic manifestations of a supreme spiritual power, that is, as 'acts of a personal God'. The symbols are not literal, empirical truths. They are spiritual truths which are believed to have been manifested or expressed in historical events. The Hebrew Bible provides an historical narrative of a conscious interaction between one group of tribes and their God. In this narrative, God takes the initiative, issuing moral commands and promising a future fulfilment for humanity. God does so through prophetic figures, above all Moses, and through a providential guidance of history. The narrative portrays humans entering into discussions, even arguments, with God; failing to obey divine commands; repenting; and intermittently trying to establish a society truly obedient to God, hoping thereby to receive the blessing of God in the form of happiness and fulfilment (*shalom*). The symbols derived from cycles of nature are largely replaced by symbols of a developing historical and personal series of interactions.

The historical account is not a record of wholly naturally explicable events, such as a modern secular historian might give. God speaks, judges, forgives, and acts in history. This action is perceived by prophets, whose minds are opened to the active presence of God, and who mediate divine wisdom and power, in prophecies and miraculous actions. Such a thing is not foreign to the activities of shamans in many tribal societies, who receive visions from the spirit world, and who can be possessed by spirit powers. But it develops the idea of one supreme Spirit who has one specific purpose for one tribal group, which is meant to be the means to bring about the well-being of all humanity. The idea of one supremely good Spirit with a developing historical purpose for the whole of humanity can be seen as a universalisation and a moralisation of cultic practices aimed at the preferential flourishing of specific tribal groups. I think it would be reasonable to see this as a rejection of more nationalistic and non-moral practices, and a development towards a potentially universal and morally concerned religious view. In other words, not all religious beliefs and practices are of equal value and rational justifiability. Reforming movements occur in particular historical contexts, and, while many believers will oppose such reforms, they can be seen by many as genuine developments of thought towards a more universally moral and spiritually enlightened outlook.

In the Hebrew Bible, God becomes the only, all-creating God (though the Genesis account still contains echoes of polytheism – 'Let us make humankind in our own image', Genesis 1, 26), whose purposes, expressed in *Torah*, define the moral conduct of the Israelites. Their God was still the God of a particular group of people, and a sacrificial cult was an important part of *Torah*. But, at least from a Jewish point of view, their laws of justice and compassion were morally superior to those of surrounding nations, and their God was the unchallenged sovereign of all creation (though the serpent in the Garden of Eden and the mysterious sea-monster Leviathan, whom God will ultimately destroy with a sharp sword, carry hints of the Babylonian *Tiamat*).

It is when the Genesis narrative of creation is placed in the context of contemporaneous Middle Eastern mythologies that its character can best be discerned. It may seem fairly clear that it is a myth in the same sense as the 'Babylonian Genesis' was a myth. And if this is so, the attempt to turn it into a literally true account of the origin of the universe is a very much later misunderstanding of its nature. Of course, this is one of the disagreements that one finds in present day Christianity, and I am indeed saying that a literal interpretation rests on a misunderstanding of the nature of myth, a lack of appreciation of Middle Eastern mythology in general, and neglect of the historical and cultural context in which the Genesis account came into being.

Nevertheless, I have to admit that this disagreement between literal and what might be called allegorical interpretations is a real disagreement, and some will argue that Genesis gives a completely correct literal account of creation. One could, after all, claim that all religious stories about the world's beginning, including American Indian, African, and other tribal creation stories, are meant literally. They just happen to be mostly mistaken, while the Biblical one is true. The disagreement is not resolvable, even though it is clear to me that some knowledge of world religions and mythology, and an understanding of the historical context of specific writings, makes the allegorical view overwhelmingly obvious. Here one appeals to the value of greater cultural and historical understanding to enable a decision about truth to be made. That is an evaluative preference, a commitment to seeing beliefs in the light of their wider cultural and historical context, which not all would share. But if one sees the range of mythical world-views that exist, that naturally tends to undermine a literalist understanding of them. And if one sees the historical process that leads to the development of new understandings of the spiritual dimension, that will help one to discriminate between broader and narrower conceptions of the spiritual dimension.

The Biblical reference to historical events as the carriers of mythical interpretation can be clearly seen in the Biblical records of Jesus' death, and the use made of it in Christian rituals, which often use some of the imagery of myth. But mythological themes are put to a different use, and they are subsidiary to the major concerns of Christian belief. Jesus dies, and rises again. It may be said that Persephone descends to the underworld and rises again, yet Persephone's story was never a historical event; what it refers to is repeated each year in the cycle of nature, and the cult makes few moral demands, but offers a magical conquest of death to a few initiates. Jesus was a historical individual who, according to the accounts in the New Testament, offered his life for the sake of others in obedience to the will of a benevolent Creator. The myth confronts the amoral powers of the natural order and offers a difficult and secret way in which initiates can escape their power. The historical story postulates a moral goal of the natural order, demands moral obedience, and promises a historical fulfilment of the moral possibilities of human life. There is a choice to be made here, and it is basically about the moral insight and rational coherence provided by diverse, but connected, religious views.

4

Historical Development

THE JEWISH IDEA OF GOD IS DISTINCTIVE AMONG ANCIENT MIDDLE Eastern religions, but it is not an isolated and totally unique and unprecedented intellectual breakthrough. It develops naturally from, though it is also partly a revolt against, more pluralistic ideas of spirits who all have different aims and represent different values, and who are largely contacted to allay particular disasters or to answer particular requests for such things as fertility or victory in battle. The Hebrew God brings unity, universality, purpose, and morality to such a scenario. In some sense, development or progress is real. Yet that development is ambiguous, since it can lead to the idea of one supremely good God who wills all people to develop their capacities freely and creatively in a universally just and compassionate society. But it can also lead to the idea of one dictatorial God who wills that all competitors should be eliminated, who prefers just one group of people above all others, and whose commands are both repressive of individual freedom and ruthlessly enforced.

The theistic world-view is capable of developing in a number of ways, and, because of its ambiguity, it evokes opposition to the very idea of God from those who value human freedom and happiness above what they see as supine conformity and servile obedience to an all-powerful dictatorship, dressed in the robes of kindness and patriarchal concern.

One can see how the truths claimed by Judaism and later by Christianity are not straightforwardly empirically decidable. They have developed in a specific historical context over many years. They are symbolic of spiritual realities which are explicitly said to be literally unimaginable – 'no man can see me and live' (Exodus 33, 20). They are ambiguous, in that they can be interpreted in many different ways, some good and some bad, and they are not just proposed as a set of doctrines which are systematically set out and have to be believed in a specific way. They are embedded in the developing history of one society, a history which is written from different points of view and usually with the benefit of considerable hindsight. The Temple rituals of ancient Hebrew faith are repetitions of symbolic forms, both verbal and behavioural, which make possible participation in a spiritual reality accessible in a specific way by one community. There are stories, legends, myths, laws, memories of dramatic historical events, songs, proverbs, and prophecies. There is a series of sacred writings which form the framework for a specific society, from which can be derived, by learned judges and scholars, diverse and continually changing recommendations for how to live well within the community (moral laws), which portray paradigms for personal spiritual experience, and which convey a rich and complex portrayal of a supreme spiritual power to which members of the community can consciously relate.

Such a complex reality cannot be adequately portrayed just as a set of propositional truths. There are, of course, propositional truths present, but they tend to be unsystematic, not well defined, often symbolic or metaphorical, ambiguous, embedded in ritual practices, formulated in terms available within a specific historical/cultural tradition, and interpretable in diverse ways. It, therefore, becomes easier to see religions (some religions, anyway) as social and symbolic complexes pointing to values, ways of life, and modes of relationship to a transcendent or spiritual dimension of human life, which enhance human well-being. Durkheim[1] clearly saw and stressed this element of religion as a way of life in relation to communal values. But he did not suppose that there actually was an objectively existent spiritual dimension of human life, with some causal power over events that happen in the physical world. Nevertheless, when one sees the social and ritual dimensions of religions, there is much less difficulty in seeing them as diverse, because human histories, personalities, and cultures are very diverse. Diversity in this sense does not entail contradiction, and it is misleading to see religions just as sets of truths which contradict other sets. Religions as such are neither true nor false. They may contain propositions which are either true or false, but it may be very difficult to see exactly how important those propositions are, and how they are to be interpreted, and correspondingly difficult to say if and how far they really conflict with propositions, especially propositions from very different cultural and historical contexts, which seem to contradict them.

In the light of all this, I suggest that any consideration of the various truth-claims that religions make must, if it is to be soundly based, be made with

---

[1] Durkheim (1963).

regard to their specific historical, linguistic, and cultural contexts. These factors may be grouped under three main headings. The first is the doctrinal, under which I include anything that might make truth-claims, especially about the ultimate nature of reality. This would involve examination of the texts or allegedly original teachings on which most religions are held to be based, and of the theologies or systems of belief that later developed from them. The second is the experiential – the nature of the personal experiences that tend to be evoked by texts and doctrines. The third is the behavioural, covering the institutions that now exist and ritually re-enact beliefs, and the moral views and practices those institutions embody. Durkheim's and Smith's[2] analyses concentrate on the third, and to some extent on the second, of these factors. Their analyses importantly affect the way in which one treats the doctrinal factor. Yet, in the end, that doctrinal factor is essential to the continued effectiveness of religious practices, and it is that factor with which I will deal.

These factors cannot be considered separately, for they intertwine and shape one another, though they exist with different degrees of importance in different religions. As I have outlined them, they reflect Ninian Smart's analysis of religion, wherein he distinguishes seven dimensions[3] – doctrinal, mythological, ethical, ritual, experiential, institutional, and material – and Eric Sharpe's similar but simpler four-dimensional division of religion into existential, intellectual, institutional, and ethical modes.[4] My division is certainly not intended to be superior to others, it is just meant to introduce the wider context into which religious truth-claims must be placed, and to throw light on the problem of commitment to a specific religious view in a world of huge religious diversity and little hope of gaining the agreement of all intelligent and informed enquirers.

---

[2] Smith (2017).   [3] Smart (1989).   [4] Sharpe (1983), pp. 93–107.

Part II

The Perennial Philosophy

I AM NOT INTENDING TO GIVE A DEFINITION OF RELIGION, BUT I think it is reasonable to say that many of the things we ordinarily call religions do share something in common. They are concerned with a spiritual dimension of reality. This is something not describable in terms of the natural sciences, something not physical, but present in and through the physical. It is described in various ways in various religions, but it (or possibly they) is usually said to be of great value and power. It is said to be accessible by humans, especially by rare individuals who are especially sensitive to that dimension, and who attract others to follow their teachings. The value of the spiritual is something in which humans can participate, and gives a purpose or goal to their lives which is felt to enhance true well-being and liberate from harm. A spiritual dimension, apprehended by exceptional individuals, relation to which can liberate from evil and enhance human well-being – this could be said to be a central core of many religions, and certainly of the major religions that flourish in the world today.

Can one go further than this, and assert that there is a more definite common core of religion, which has existed for thousands of years, a primordial tradition which underlies all the various religions that now exist? This is the claim of what Aldous Huxley[1] called 'the perennial philosophy', a term first coined by Agostino Steuco, in 1540,[2] though Huxley uses it in quite a different sense.

---

[1] Huxley (1947).   [2] Schmitt (1966).

29

5

Aldous Huxley

*A*LDOUS HUXLEY DEFINES THE PERENNIAL PHILOSOPHY AS 'THE metaphysic that recognises a divine Reality substantial to the world of things and lives and minds; the psychology that finds in the soul something similar to, or even identical with, divine Reality; the ethic that places man's final end in the knowledge of the immanent and transcendent Ground of all being'.[1] At first sight, this does seem rather like what I have called the central core of many religious traditions. But in Huxley's definition, already many things more specific and contestable are said. For instance, there is said to be only one divine Reality. That Reality is 'substantial to' – which I take to mean is the underlying substance of, the true reality of – all finite things. It is both immanent and transcendent, so it is somehow in all things and yet also beyond and greater than all things. This is a fairly widely held view, but many religious views are polytheistic, or deny that there is one supreme ultimate Reality. And many deny that the supreme Reality includes the finite universe as part of itself.

It is also a fairly widely held religious view that humans have souls, which are similar to this Reality, or even identical with it. But many religious views deny that there is a 'divine spark' within the human self, deeper than the mind, or they think of the soul as a reality independent of the divine with its own autonomy, which will never be one with the Divine.

It is a widespread religious belief that there is a final purpose in human life, which lies in knowledge of this divine Reality. But many religious views deny that knowledge, even of God, is the ultimate good; many deny that there is any life after bodily death; and many deny that there is just one final purpose for all human beings.

---

[1] Huxley (1947), p. 1.

It turns out that the clue to these factors is the *Advaita Vedanta* of the eighth-century Indian commentator on the Vedas, Sankara,[2] which holds that the one reality is *Brahman*. All finite things are parts of *Brahman*, and their separateness is in fact an illusion. A human soul is *Atman*, an 'inner Self' which is identical with *Brahman*. The purpose of existence is to realise the illusory character of one's transitory personality and mind, and achieve a state of objectless Pure Consciousness, beyond separated individuality, and dissolved in the Ocean of Being-Awareness-Bliss, which is the ultimately Real.

When this is made clear, it appears that, far from being a perennial philosophy, this is just one rather extreme form of Vedanta, disputed by the other main Indian schools of Vedanta, and that Vedanta itself is just one rather elitist (Brahminical) type of Indian religion, whose major doctrines have usually been seen as opposed to those both of Middle Eastern theism and of Far Eastern non-theistic religions.

Huxley claims that his 'Highest Common Factor' view is 'immemorial and universal', whereas in fact it is Sankara's innovative eighth-century CE philosophy which many scholars see as a Hindu 'Take-over', an attempt to mitigate the appeal of Buddhism in India by incorporating elements of Buddhist thought into the Vedanta.

The radical difference between the *Hinayana* (traditionalist) schools of Buddhism and *Advaita Vedanta* can be seen in the fact that *Hinayana* teaches '*anatta*' or '*anAtman*', which means that there is no eternal *Atman* or inner self, whereas the Upanishads teach that '*Atman* is *Brahman*', and that is the ultimate Reality. Huxley disguises that difference by suggesting that what the Buddhists deny is the existence of one enduring soul-substance in each individual. They do deny that; but they also deny that there is one eternal Self, the same in all individuals, which is identical with eternal *Brahman*, Being, Awareness, and Bliss. There is only the flow of the five *skhandas*, thoughts, perceptions, and feelings, with no underlying substance-self. There is no eternal Reality, only Emptiness (*sunyata*).

For that reason, Huxley concentrates on *Mahayana* Buddhism (which some scholars, like Richard Gombrich, think is not a proper or certainly not an original form of Buddhism at all). The *Mahayana* school does speak of a *Dharmakaya*, or cosmic body of the Buddha, and that does sound rather like an Eternal Cosmic Mind. It is an important fact that apparently opposed religious views can converge, especially when one is reaching the limits of language in speaking of spiritual reality. But the fact remains that there are

---

[2] Sankara (1962).

forms of religious thought, older than *Advaita*, which deny that there is one eternal Self, though they do speak of liberation from the wheel of suffering and rebirth. There is not just one perennial philosophy, present in all, or in all developed, forms of religion.

Huxley presents a spirituality in which, if one becomes 'loving, pure in heart and poor in spirit',[3] one may experience and immediately apprehend 'ultimate Reality'. We actually become one with the 'eternal now of the modeless Godhead'.[4] The Godhead is beyond the personal God, which is real on its own level, and it is beyond time, beyond all limitation, and beyond all speech. The ultimate aim of all human beings is to be absorbed into this Godhead, and, though few will achieve it in any one generation, eventually it is the destiny of all sentient beings.

If one thinks, as Huxley does, that devotion to a personal God is acceptable for all but a few enlightened souls, it perhaps hardly matters that our ultimate goal is said to be the complete loss of a sense of self and a realisation that one is and has always been one with an ultimate reality without qualities (*Nirguna Brahman*). Yet it may seem odd that all the positive values that have been realised in our lives in this universe have been illusory and are destined to pass away and be left behind in eternity. The contrast with a spiritual view which sees the universe as an environment in which new positive values can be realised, which sees these values as conserved for ever in God, and hopes for some sort of communal or relational being in the afterlife, is almost total.

---

[3] Huxley (1947), p. 5.   [4] Huxley (1947), p. 38.

6

Experience of the Ineffable

$\mathcal{I}$T IS HARD TO SEE HOW EXPERIENCE ALONE COULD DECIDE between these grand metaphysical views, especially since very few of us have the immediate apprehension of the divine that is being postulated by *Advaita*. It might be wise to be reticent about that of which one cannot speak, and not claim that it has given one privileged insight into ultimate truth. Many people can probably think of times at which a sense of self has been lost as one immerses oneself in a beautiful piece of music, for example. There is, one might say, only the music, and one is wholly absorbed in it. But, in fact, that remains a finite experience, which takes a certain amount of time, and which has degrees of more and less. We do not really cease to be an experiencing subject while we are 'lost in the music'. It is only that our attention is focussed entirely on the object, and there is no sense of 'possessing' or 'owning' it and keeping it to ourselves. Yet we know that there are others who lack such awareness, and that this awareness is 'ours', part of our finite experience. There can be finite experiences of something that seems to transcend time and language, but that does not imply that our finitude has ceased.

I see no reason to deny that an experience of a seemingly timeless and boundless reality is possible and desirable, at least for some. But I would be hesitant to say that such an experience shows what Reality is really like. It rather seems to show how Reality can be apprehended when one passes the limits of language and understanding, and rests in a sense of 'pure acquaintance' with an indescribable presence – which some (for instance, G. F. Stout)[1] call an 'objectless awareness'. There is perhaps an object, but it is beyond description and understanding.

[1] Stout (1911).

Consequently, I do not see why one needs to address or answer the question, 'Which is greater, objectless awareness or the sense of awareness of a personal Divine presence?' There may be that of the divine which is beyond description and understanding, and there may be that which appears to us as a personal mind-like presence. Why cannot both be true, and why must one be 'greater' than the other? The case for this is well argued by Jerome Gellman, who argues that, since God is a plenitude of being, not just a person, there will be many facets of a rich and complex divine reality, and different experiences can be experiences of different facets of the divine.[2] One can have an idea of God which is indescribable in some ways and describable as being like a personal presence in other ways.

In other words, 'Atman is Brahman' is an interpretative theory, not ascertainable by experience alone, and that theory can be described, as it is by the twelfth-century Vedantin Ramanuja,[3] a Vishistadvaita Vedantin (a qualified non-dualist), by saying that souls and matter form the body of the Lord, and in that sense 'are Brahman', although they are never just 'absorbed' into the primal One (in fact, for Ramanuja, there is no primal One, no Brahman without qualities).

Sankara's view, according to Sushanta Sen, Professor of Philosophy in Visva-Bharati University, affirms that 'whatever undergoes change ... cannot have any intrinsic value and reality of its own'.[4] The whole material world is an illusion which must be dispelled, and the Atman, 'a permanent substance which remains fixed and constant amidst all sorts of change of the body, sense-organs and the mind',[5] is identical with Brahman, the Absolute Reality beyond all attributes.

Ramanuja disagrees strongly. In Ramanuja's opinion, the world of change and time is indeed an appearance of Brahman. Being the body of the Lord, it expresses what Brahman is, and what happens in the world is certainly not just an illusion which should be dispelled. It is the self-expression of Absolute Reality. That reality is not Nirguna, without qualities, but Saguna Brahman, a Lord of infinite good and beautiful attributes. Ramanuja denies the existence of Nirguna Brahman, holding that this is a wholly fictitious concept. As for Atman, the inner self, it is true that it is part of Brahman – that is what the Upanisadic phrase, 'Atman is Brahman' means, he thinks. Nevertheless, finite selves remain distinct, depending wholly on Brahman for their existence, yet related to Brahman in a love which is found expressed in Krishna, for instance. Ramanuja says of Sankara, 'his view rests on a

[2] Gellman (1997).   [3] Ramanuja (1962).   [4] Sen (1989), p. 86.   [5] Sen (1989), p. 85.

fictitious foundation of hollow and vicious arguments'.[6] It is not the case that even all Indian Idealists (who form just one part of the rich complex of Indian religious traditions) agree that there is an Undifferentiated Unbounded.

Ramanuja's Vedanta is much closer to the theistic idea that a Creator God expresses its being in the created world, that the actions of human persons can be seen as the actions of the Lord in and through them, and that finite selves relate to the Supreme Lord in love. Naturally there are differences from Abrahamic theism, differences concerned with rebirth and with cosmology, related to the Indian historical context. But there seems little reason to call Sankara's interpretation a 'perennial philosophy', when it is only one interpretation of Vedanta among many, and when a major stream of Indian religious thought is *bhakti*, or loving devotion to a personal Lord. This stream is given a sophisticated philosophical expression in the work of Ramanuja, whose work is, if anything, more perennial in India than the paradoxical and difficult doctrines of *Advaita*.[7]

---

[6] Ramanuja (1962), vol. 48, p. 39.

[7] For an exposition of Ramanuja's view, see Lipner (1986). I also give a short account of Sankara and Ramanuja in Ward (1998), chapters 1 and 2.

7

Perennialist Critiques of Other Religious Views

D ESPITE ALL THIS, HOWEVER, HUXLEY STILL HOLDS THAT 'THE core and spiritual heart of all the higher religions is the Perennial Philosophy'.[1] Yet, he is extremely critical of some forms of higher religion, especially of *Hinayana* Buddhism and Lutheran Christianity. With regard to Christianity, he writes, 'Most of the religions and philosophies which take time too seriously are correlated with political theories that inculcate and justify the use of large-scale violence'.[2] He thinks it important to hold that the supreme Reality is timelessly eternal, and not temporal. He has not noticed that traditional Lutheran ideas of God say precisely that God is timelessly eternal.

In a similar vein, he says that 'because Christians believed that there had been only one Avatar, Christian history has been disgraced by more and bloodier crusades, interdenominational wars, persecutions and proselytising imperialism ... (than Eastern faiths)'.[3] Huxley is especially opposed to Christian doctrines of substitutionary atonement, which he regards as primitive and savage. It may be so, but it must be admitted that it, rather than the Perennial philosophy, is in fact the core and spiritual heart of much Christianity, both Catholic and Protestant. I agree that it is important to discover the causes of religious violence, and that Christians have been unduly prone to such violence, but I am not sure that a major cause has been belief in the temporality of God or the uniqueness of incarnation. It is more likely to have been the thought that salvation depends upon correct belief, coupled with the idea that differing beliefs put souls in eternal peril. Happily, the Second Vatican Council of the Roman Catholic church rejected those beliefs.[4] But I do not think they are connected with belief in one

---

[1] Huxley (1947), p. 270.   [2] Huxley (1947), p. 222.   [3] Huxley (1947), p. 229.
[4] See the discussion in chapter 26 of this book.

incarnation of God in time, a belief which can easily be combined with belief that such an incarnation saves all humans, especially those who follow their consciences sincerely, and that tolerance is a major Christian virtue.

Huxley is also scathing about those who believe in everlasting personal survival. 'Man's obsessive consciousness of and insistence on being a separate self is the final and most formidable obstacle to the unitive knowledge of God. To be a self is ... the original sin'.[5] He has in mind here one Hindu view that the sense of individual selfhood is a fall from the divine and must be overcome. But most Abrahamic religions do not accept such a view, and regard individual selfhood as a gift to be cherished for eternity. That is, they consciously reject 'the perennial philosophy'. It is not the heart and core of their religion.

Towards the end of his book, Huxley writes,

> The reign of violence will never come to an end until, first, most human beings accept the same, true philosophy of life; until, second, this Perennial Philosophy is recognised as the highest factor common to all the world religions; until, third, the adherents of every religion renounce the idolatrous time-philosophies, with which, in their own particular faith, the Perennial Philosophy of eternity has been overlaid; until, fourth, there is a world-wide rejection of all the political pseudo-religions, which place man's supreme good in future time and therefore justify and commend the commission of every sort of present iniquity as a means to that end.[6]

Unfortunately, there is virtually no prospect that most human beings will agree on any one philosophy. It does not seem true, anyway, that the Perennial philosophy is or ever was or ever will be common to all religions. There is no hope of people ever renouncing 'idolatrous time-philosophies', since they happen to think such philosophies are probably true, and one can accept that the human supreme good will lie in some future time (perhaps beyond the time of this cosmos, but still susceptible to change and development and new experiences), and totally oppose the use of violence to justify the attainment of such a good.

---

[5] Huxley (1947), p. 45.   [6] Huxley (1947), p. 229.

8

The Void and Pure Mind

*I*T WILL BE APPARENT, THEN, THAT I AM NOT CONVINCED BY THE central arguments of 'The Perennial Philosophy'. And yet I find the book to be a truly insightful and fascinating compilation of spiritual writings from a wide range of religious traditions, many of them not well known in English-speaking countries.

There are quotations from *Mahayana* Buddhism (but not *Hinayana*, of which critical comments are made), Sankara (but not Ramanuja or Madhva), Kabir and Rabi'a in the Sufi tradition (but not Muslims like Ibn Taymeya), Philo, Boethius and Dionysius, Eckhart and Ruysbroek, Zen, Taoism, Catherine of Siena, St. John of the Cross, and George Fox. However, it is very misleading to say that all these writers belong to one 'Primordial tradition'. To put the Quaker Fox together with the Catholic saint Catherine, the Buddhist Buddhaghosa with the neo-Platonist Philo, the rather questionably Catholic Eckhart with the third Patriarch of Zen, and then to put them all together in one tradition, overlooks the huge differences of religious belief and practice that exist between them. There is not just one tradition here.

Nevertheless, the selected quotations do pick out some striking similarities. The Hindu Sankara speaks of an absolute identity between *Brahman*, absolute reality, and *Atman*, the inner self, an identity beyond the subject–object distinction which can be spoken of as 'Pure Consciousness'.[1] The Taoist Lao Tzu speaks of 'the Void' and 'Quietness' as the culmination of meditative states.[2] Ashvaghosha refers to a state in which one can experience 'the perfect unity of all sentient beings', where there is 'no dualism, neither shadow of differentiation', where one experiences 'Mind's Pure Essence',

---

[1] Sankara (1962).   [2] Huxley (1947), p. 104.

having 'no lingering notions of the self'.[3] And the *Lankavatara Sutra* speaks of '*Nirvana*, the state of Suchness, absolutely transcending all the categories ... the *Tathagata*'s inner consciousness'.[4]

In these very different religions, exceptional individuals, usually after having practiced meditation and attitudes of detachment and self-forgetting, have experienced a state in which the sense of individual selfhood is lost, and one experiences a sense of pure consciousness and bliss which is indescribable in any language, where all things seem to be one, and where time itself seems to be transcended.

This state is, nevertheless, often described, admittedly inadequately, in terms of love, unity, wisdom, and bliss. It is felt as an acquaintance with what is ultimately real, which is the core of all beings. It is explicitly said to be for the few, and not accessible to or even appropriate for everyone. By definition, such an ineffable experience cannot be conceptually described. So, if one does attempt descriptions (as Pure Mind, the Void, or being-consciousness-bliss) they cannot be drawn from the experience itself. One can only describe the path to it. The indescribable cannot be described.

Does this imply that the ultimate reality is a total forgetting of individuality, a state beyond time and individual personality? Or is it rather a sort of deeply unitive love, where individuality is not lost, but one 'loses oneself' in the being of the Beloved? If all metaphors are inadequate, it seems most appropriate to say that none captures the absolute truth, but each one points beyond itself to the Unfathomable, the 'Darkness beyond Being' (Dionysius).

If there is 'a Godhead beyond God', that is not saying that God is not the ultimate reality. It is rather saying that our *concept* of God does not give us the whole story. Beyond what can be said, there is that which cannot be said. That 'more' is accessible only to those who have passed beyond all clinging to self, and all competitive clinging to one's own favourite dogmas.

But is it literally true that I am one with the Ultimate, a Pure Consciousness beyond the subject–object duality? That is a doctrine, and if the lesson of the unitive state is that all doctrines are to be set aside, it follows that no doctrine can be literally true! A doctrinal description is a way of imagining the ultimate good, in the light of an experience which, whatever it may feel like, is, as an experience, definitely not timeless (it endures for a finite time) and has not eliminated my individual personality (it is, after all, 'my' experience).

There is a tension in the descriptions of the unitive state, between saying that it is 'beyond a personal God', beyond all subject–object relations,

---

[3] Huxley (1947), p. 292.   [4] Huxley (1947), p. 208.

without any differentiation, just the Void, and saying that it is Pure Mind, good, intelligent, all-pervading, that it is bliss and wisdom. There is a tension between saying that what is experienced is 'beyond' all multiplicity and temporality, and that it is the inner reality truly expressed in temporal multiplicity (this tension is epitomised in the *Mahayana* Buddhist saying, '*Nirvana* is *Samsara*'). There is a tension between saying that one loses the self in 'the Void' (Lao Tzu),[5] and that one is 'being oned unto God in perfect charity' ('The Cloud of Unknowing').[6]

Such differences cannot, in the foreseeable future, be eliminated. What seems to be common, however, is the idea that there is a rare but tremendously important sense of an Ultimate Reality which is literally indescribable, but is more like Pure Mind, Wisdom, and Eternal Bliss than like some unconscious nullity, and that the way to it is through self-forgetting, universal compassion, and contemplative prayer.

---

[5] Huxley (1947), p. 104.   [6] Huxley (1947), p. 37.

9

The Supreme Good

*T*HAT IS PERHAPS TOO VAGUE TO BE THE BASIS OF REAL RELIGIOUS commitment, and so particular religions spell out ways of devotion, meditation, and moral practice, which relate people in specific ways to an object and goal considered to be of supreme reality and value. The ways differ; they follow different teachers in different traditions. But their goal is the supreme good, and their way is a way of self-giving altruism.

Insofar as religions embody such teaching, they agree on a particular interpretation of what I have called the 'central core' of commitment to a spiritual dimension, a rarely achieved experience of it, and a goal of liberation from harm and the realisation of some sort of well-being. The spiritual dimension becomes one reality of wisdom, compassion, and bliss. The experience becomes one of felt unity with this reality. And the goal is a fully conscious and selfless union with supreme reality. That articulation of the central core is not universally agreed. It is a very sophisticated philosophically systematised conceptualisation. It is very different from, for instance, some tribal view that there are many spirits, good and bad; that they can be experienced as terrifying or dangerous, and so need propitiation; and that the goods aimed at by religious rituals are such things as fertility and victory in war. My intention in saying this is not to denigrate tribal religions. It is just to point out that a claim that there is a primordial tradition of religion seems to be anthropologically and historically implausible. This philosophy is much too sophisticated to be perennial.

Still, the idea of one supreme spiritual reality, of the overcoming of the egoistic self, and of a goal of union with supreme goodness, is characteristic of some major world religions. So far as that is true, religions are companions, whose disagreements can inspire a sincere search for truth and goodness. This may not be a Perennial philosophy, which is something agreed by all from the earliest human history. But it is a common quest for the Good by the renunciation of self. In that quest, we may have many specific beliefs, and we may follow many different religious teachers. If we can accept others as engaged on such a common quest, we can and should respect the beliefs and practices of others and learn from them both whatever adds to our own conceptions and what mirrors our own practice in a different form.

It is probably true that a supreme Spirit would be beyond human comprehension. It does not follow that nothing true can be said of it, however inadequately, and it is at that point that different traditions say different things. As a matter of fact, I think Huxley actually claims to know too much about the unknowable – for instance, that all things are identical with it, and that it is completely beyond time and change.[1] How could we know that, if we are speaking of the unknowable?

One thing that is of value in Huxley's compendium is the realisation that there are sophisticated and profound spiritual traditions which are very different from most varieties of personal theism. Speaking of a personal God is not the only way to approach a spiritual goal, and it is salutary to realise that belief in a personal God is by many regarded as relatively infantile and over-anthropomorphic. One way of accounting for this is to say that there are two (at least two) different sorts of spiritual experience – which Ninian Smart has called the numinous (associated mainly with the Abrahamic faiths) and the mystical (emphasised more in Indian faiths).[2] Hans Kung added a third, the way of wisdom or harmony, which is characteristic of Chinese traditions.[3] Some say that one path (usually the way of personal devotion) is a lower form for those who cannot yet grasp the ultimate truth. Of course, the followers of *bhakti*, the way of devotion, would say that the experience of undifferentiated Brahman is the lower form, for people who have not realised that love is both ultimate and relational. One could also say – and this would be my choice – that the same ultimate spiritual reality is capable of being experienced under a number of aspects, since the ultimate reality is rich and complex, rather than wholly undifferentiated and simple.

It could be, for instance, that the mind of God is in some respects eternally and unchangeably self-existent, and in other respects contingent and responsive to temporal changes. Just as human persons can be perceived in different ways by different people, so the supreme reality might be perceived differently in different conceptual traditions. It would follow from this that there is a more general truth about ultimate reality – namely, that it is both personally relational and eternally self-existent. There is still an implicit

[1] Huxley (1947).   [2] Smart (1989).   [3] Kung (1993).

claim to ultimate truth. But at least this truth would allow, or even encourage, the existence of a number of ways of apprehending that truth, all of which are partial (though not just totally false, except insofar as they claim that theirs is the only way). All that is required is the postulate that Spiritual Reality is not totally apprehended in any tradition, that human apprehension is never wholly adequate, and that there is a spiritual reality which can be approached in a number of ways. Each of those ways, however, requires practical moral commitment to the Good for its own sake, to Truth as a goal of reasonable reflection, and to Beauty as a desirable and intrinsically worthwhile object of contemplation. These are ideals, the realisation of which lies in the future, as far as humans are concerned, but for religion the ideals do exist, not in human minds, but either in the mind of God or perhaps in a quasi-Platonic world of 'Forms' as values which motivate and can empower the best human thought and action.

10

Frithjof Schuon

*A*S WELL AS THE CLAIM THAT THERE IS A PERENNIAL PHILOSOPHY THAT has existed virtually unchanged since ancient times, another attempt to hold that there is such an ancient tradition is the thesis that there is a transcendent unity of religions, a primordial tradition known to a small group of initiates. The main advocate of this position, which shares much in common with Aldous Huxley's perennial philosophy, is Frithjof Schuon. His distinctive contribution is to distinguish between esoteric and exoteric forms of religion. On the exoteric level – which he also calls 'theological' – religions are very different, and are each fitted to a specific historical and cultural situation. But on the esoteric – 'metaphysical' – level they are united in a higher all-embracing reality.

The esoteric plane is the source of absolutely certain knowledge, but it is open to very few, a spiritual elite which has trained itself by moral, ascetic, and meditational practices to come to know the truth. This truth is one in which knowing 'becomes its own object', so there is no distinction of knower and known. There are no temporal distinctions, for it embraces all times. It includes everything, but in a way without differentiation or division. It is rather like Aquinas' 'Being existing of itself', which Aquinas describes as both utterly simple (without inner divisions), and also as containing all possibilities and actualities 'in a higher form'. But it differs in two main ways – it can be known by means of intellectual intuition and by the few – and it contains all actualities and possibilities. For Aquinas, the 'beatific vision' is not knowable by Intelligence or by a spiritual elite, at least during this life (except possibly for Jesus, who was uniquely divine). And, for Aquinas, the infinite excludes everything finite, even though finite things are included in it in a higher manner. It is, he says, without real relation to finite reality.

The core of Schuon's idea is that within each human life, deeper than the soul or mind, is the 'spirit', which is the divine spark within everyone, uncreated and indestructible, and identical with the ultimately Real. At this deep level, I am not separate from Ultimate Reality, but identical with it, and enlightenment, the ultimate goal of human existence, consists in my realisation of this unity.

The cosmos comes to be from that unlimited ground of being as a sort of 'descent' which happens by necessity. Every possibility inherent in the One must be realised. Souls are fractured splinters of being, which is a necessary emanation from the One. As such, finite being carries with it degrees of imperfection, and the object of the spiritual life is to return to the unity of the One. The influence of Plotinus is clear.

Religions belong to the exoteric realm, and as such they are imperfect. Within them, the One is not known or experienced as such, but appears in different ways to accommodate the differing characters and needs of various cultures and peoples.

Someone who accepts this esoteric/exoteric distinction will find the One symbolically expressed in the various religions. They are all relative and convey spiritual knowledge 'beneath the veil' of ritual symbols,[1] but their exoteric adherents will usually not realise this, and will give their own religion priority and superior truth. They will not see that each view has only qualified reality, and it is part of divine Providence that this is so, for most people cannot face the full truth of the absolute Unity of Being and its 'fall' into individuality and diversity. The divine truth has been distributed in different forms, each of which is appropriate for people at a specific stage of spiritual development. 'Pure and absolute truth can only be found beyond all its possible expressions',[2] and 'a universal Reality cannot have only one manifestation to the exclusion of any others'.[3] So many exoteric religions are necessary, but none are absolute.

Schuon holds that each exoteric religion is suited for one particular people – Christianity is for the Western world, the successor of the old Roman Empire; Islam is for the Arabic peoples; Hinduism is for Indians; and Taoism for Chinese. For them it would be wrong, at least in general, to convert to another religion, for each religion is a fractured image of the truth, and each can lead people to a more transcendent view (but not to the 'superior truth' of another religion, since all exoteric religions are to some extent illusory).

This view is pluralistic at the exoteric level, but not at the esoteric level, where truth is one, and is known with absolute certainty. The view is in fact

---

[1] Schuon (1984), p. xxxiii.   [2] Schuon (1984), p. 20.   [3] Schuon (1984), p. 21.

as exclusivist as that of the most exclusive Christian or Muslim, for it regards all those who disagree with it as existing at a lower level of spiritual ignorance. For instance, those who believe that a personal God is supreme are told that this view is perfectly acceptable for them, but only because they are incapable of understanding the truth and are spiritually immature. When properly instructed, they will see that the idea of a personal God is a symbol, which may be very helpful and even necessary for people at a low level of spiritual intelligence, of something very different and much greater, the One Reality of which all things are parts.

Schuon seems to suggest that it is proper for a European to be Christian, for an Indian to be Hindu, and for an Arab to be Muslim. In this, he is agreeing with those who think that one's religion should be decided by race or nationality. Yet that view is perhaps one of the major causes of religious violence in human history. It has led to nationalist and ethnic clashes which have been sharpened by a heightening of religious emotions, and it has markedly decreased attempts to achieve multi-religious tolerance and co-habitation. Things are much more difficult than this, in a world where Indians, Arabs, and Europeans move around the world and live alongside one another in many different countries.

Finally, it is not satisfactory to say, 'I am Christian because I am European', and even if that is largely true, it is not a reason for accepting some beliefs as true that they are held by people of the same ethnic group as myself. What is true and reasonable is that I should begin my religious life by learning the symbols, rites, and customs that I have been taught in my youth. But as I grow older, I may come across many different systems of belief, and they may put my original beliefs in question, or at the very least in a new and wider context. Many people now have access to a range of different religious ideas and practices. They sometimes have a problem of how to choose between them. But, in practice, such choices are always made from an already existing background of learned beliefs and values.

In any case, the choices might not be as decisive as they may seem. Schuon says that 'the ideas that are affirmed in one religious form ... cannot fail to be affirmed, in one way of another, in all other religious forms'.[4] If this is so, adhering to one religion is not wholly cutting oneself off from other religions, and is not a matter of choosing one out of totally contradictory assertions. It is more a matter of finding oneself attracted to the central idea

---

[4] Schuon (1984), p. 19.

or web of ideas that form the heart of a specific religion, and that modify all the other ideas by seeing them in organic relation to that central one.

Thus, Schuon suggests that Christianity is 'a way of Grace or of Love'.[5] Judaism is a way of 'Justice and Judgment', and Islam is a way of 'Unity'. Christianity, he suggests, arose as a necessary corrective to the legalism and exclusivism of a Judaism which had become perverted in some ways. Islam arose as a corrective to some Christian views of Substitutionary Atonement and a suspicion of polytheism. Judaism and Christianity were never false, for they contained in themselves the possibility of counteracting their own negative tendencies. Nevertheless, it was necessary that new religious paradigms should arise to emphasise different aspects of the symbolism contained in the exoteric forms of religion, and perhaps also to counteract the tendency of both Judaism and Christianity to claim to be absolutely and exclusively true.

Religions are 'organic unities' which develop by necessary trajectories and arise from the influence of charismatic founders and originating holy texts. For Schuon, all religions are necessary, and all need to point beyond themselves, at least for those who have ears to hear and eyes to see, to the esoteric truth which they symbolise in different ways and with different controlling paradigms. Yet, though he is in principle committed to affirming the necessity and (relative) truth of all religions, Schuon in fact does discriminate between them. He says at one point that Judaism has outlived its usefulness, and that 'Christ is the Word that inspires all Revelation',[6] which does seem to privilege one sort of religious view (a Christian one, in this case) above others. He also says that religions may become decadent or lose their vitality,[7] which also differentiates between forms of exoteric religion.

One could attempt to affirm parity of religions by saying, for instance, that the *Dharmakaya* is another equally acceptable name for the cosmic reality that inspires all Revelation, and is equivalent, when rightly interpreted, to Christ. Yet, this is only true if a specific interpretation is taken of Christ and of the *Dharmakaya*, respectively. What it seems to imply is that each religion can find its own paradigm idea reflected in other religions. The paradigms remain different – Christ is the Son of God and the *Dharmakaya* is a selfless state beyond personhood – but they could be seen as functionally equivalent. That is, they both gesture inadequately towards a higher cosmic spiritual reality that has personal and suprapersonal characteristics, and that is connected with the inner nature of humanity.

---

[5] Schuon (1984), p. 138.   [6] Schuon (1984), p. 81.   [7] Schuon (1984), p. 95.

Both these ideas exist only at the level of relative truth, which is given by the esoteric tradition, the assertion of an all-including Plenitude without qualities. But there is a suspicion that this assertion, though it seems finally important, in fact drops out as largely irrelevant, since we can say nothing about it, and any claim to have certain knowledge of it can only really say that one can experience a state in which a sense of selfhood is not present, and a great joy and calm is felt. As I have suggested, such an experience can in no way license the belief that there exists an all-including Reality which is identical with each human true Self, and which is greater and more real than any supreme personal Spirit.

What remains is a belief that there may be many forms of authentic religion, or relation to spiritual reality. If so, one can take note of the different ways in which such a relation is conceived and realise that one's own way is far from complete or adequate. Perhaps differences cannot be overcome by submerging them in one Unknowable Infinite. But it can be helpful to see that such differences may be exaggerated by misunderstandings and ignorance of others. One should seek to understand how others come to think as they do and be prepared to modify one's inherited beliefs by attending to new knowledge and insights. It is to be hoped that a certain spiritual convergence may take place as one comes to accept the piety and sincerity of many of those who hold different views.

After all, one hopes that there really is one spiritual truth, that none of us grasp it completely, and that sincere effort should bring all of us nearer to that one truth. So, spiritual convergence is a reasonable hope, but it will always be necessary to oppose views which are believed to be immoral or based on ignorance and travesty, fear, and hatred. And the acceptance of difference will be necessary as long as human knowledge remains partial and inadequate, for difference may play a positive role in inspiring the search for fuller knowledge and understanding. What some might like to see is acceptance of a common goal of truth and compassion, and the acceptance of diversity in our ways of approach to it.

11

Problems with the Esoteric View

*T*HIS, HOWEVER, IS NOT SUFFICIENT FOR SCHUON.[1] FOR HIM, THE esoteric truth does not just lie in the future, yet to be discovered. It is already known with certainty by initiates, and has been known, in fact better known, by people in ancient times. Initiates of the ancient mysteries know that there is an infinite and all-including reality, from which every possible form of being emanates with absolute necessity. All phenomena are necessary expressions of possibilities eternally present in the Unconditioned, and they will all be folded back into the Unconditioned, or, to put it more correctly, are already and eternally folded back into a non-temporal state to which initiates have access.

It is not hard to see the influence of Schleiermacher and Hegel, as well as of Plotinus and pseudo-Dionysius, in this scheme. The claim that it is an esoteric truth which underlies all exoteric religions begins to look more like an assertion of the supremacy of one view of religion, which reveals a truth that the religions themselves are unable to see. As such, it suffers from the same sort of exclusive assertion of superiority, which is just what it complains about in the case of particular exoteric religions.

Moreover, there are some features of Schuon's account which seem questionable.

I find it worrying that Schuon seems ready to accept the legitimacy of violence in religion, since violence belongs to the political, exoteric, world: since 'It was God who allowed polygamy to the Hebrews and commanded Moses to have the population of Canaan put to the sword, it is clear that the question of the morality of such conduct is in no way involved'.[2] The wars engaged in by Islam cannot be judged morally, for they are 'indispensable for

---

[1] Schuon (1984).   [2] Schuon (1984), p. 115.

the propagation of a religion'.[3] At the esoteric level, Spirit is above moral constraints, and cannot be judged by moral criteria, since all its manifestations are necessary ways of expressing the possibilities of Infinity.

Neither morality nor reason can be used to criticise religion, for this esoteric view, since Infinity is supra-moral and supra-rational – 'the amorality of the spiritual position is rather a supermorality'.[4] Schuon even justifies the form of Tantra which breaks ordinary moral rules, on the ground that it can help the intuition of a supramoral Unity which is beyond good and evil.

It is true that students of religion have to cope with the fact that religion has often been associated with and has even sponsored violence. Some early Biblical writings did recommend the genocide of Canaanites. It is hard, however, to see this as a true revelation of the supramoral will of God, or to see why, if such a thing is accepted, it should not be equally acceptable for the spread of religion and the elimination of unbelievers today (as is accepted by some). An alternative explanation is a developmental one. Early prophets shared in the moral barbarism of their times, and their belief in what God willed was consistent with their moral outlook. Yet, it was mistaken. These early forms of revelation were a mixture of moral insight – there is one God who wills justice and mercy – and moral obtuseness – justice requires killing unbelievers for the sake of the truth. There is an important lesson here, which is that claims to revelation are never infallible. They can be partial and mixed with moral obtuseness. A modern example might be the failure to see that women and animals are proper objects of moral concern, even when a certain amount of attention is paid to the well-being of both sorts of beings.

If one says that Israel should not take territory by force on religious grounds, or that Muslims should not kill apostates, one is committed to accepting some form of development in religion. Both these practices are recommended in the Scriptures of these faiths, but many believers would deny that they are applicable today. One can only understand this as a form of moral advance.

In a similar way, the acceptance of modern cosmology and biology necessitates a revision of traditional explanations of human origins and the place of this planet in the Divine plan for the universe. Schuon seems to want to leave 'orthodox' traditional moral and cosmological interpretations in place, because they are relatively true for those traditions. Because his view of Spirit means that it is indescribable, morally as well as rationally – 'Existence carries

---

[3] Schuon (1984), p. 114.   [4] Schuon (1984), p. 51.

all the qualities within itself in undifferentiated equilibrium',[5] good as well as bad – there is no place for moral or rational criticism of existing religions. His esoteric view, which begins by seeming tolerant and, therefore, morally estimable, ends by rendering itself unable to criticise any form of religion, however violent and irrational. That is a dubious benefit.

Schuon's view also leads to some unusual comments about specific religions, which do not reflect accurately what they would say about themselves. He holds that Muhammad and Christ are one, 'in their inward and Divine reality, which is identical'.[6] This is not really surprising for him, since all human beings are identical in their inward reality with God. Uniqueness is ascribed to Jesus and to Muhammad alone, in their respective traditions, because the 'theological perspective' is always 'founded on a transcendent fact appropriated exclusively on behalf of a particular manifestation of the Word'.[7] The exclusiveness is false, but is necessary for ignorant believers.

More surprisingly, Schuon holds that Muhammad and the Virgin Mary both 'incarnate a principial or metacosmic Reality'.[8] Mary and the Prophet were both created before all other things, and are 'grounds' for the reception of the Word, although the Prophet, when he utters the Qur'anic sutras, 'is directly identified with the Christ'. Mary and the Prophet symbolise the mercy of God, like the Indian goddess Lakshmi or the Chinese Kwan Yin. They all symbolise the capacity of the Infinite to dissolve all the vicissitudes of the world. As such, they can appear to believers (in visions or apparitions) as concretised forms of the Beatific vision.[9]

One can see here the way in which Schuon takes many diverse exoteric forms and interprets them as symbols of a higher reality. Schuon plays on the fact that both the Qur'an and Jesus can be referred to as the 'the Word'. Though the exoteric interpretations are quite different, if 'Word' is taken as metaphor it is possible to see them both as symbolising expressions of the mind and will of God. That in turn becomes a symbol for the Existence which is beyond all conceptual expression, but from which all concrete realities emanate. Perhaps what is really going on is the renunciation of literal interpretation in favour of metaphorical expression at successive levels of generalisation and abstraction. That, in itself, is a helpful view of much religious language. But the esoteric view leads to a re-interpretation of exoteric beliefs which is foreign to the exoteric traditions themselves. This is paradoxical, when the exoteric traditions are said to be both necessary and relatively correct. He does really mean that they need correcting in the light

[5] Schuon (1984), p. 123.   [6] Schuon (1984), p. 119.   [7] Schuon (1984), p. 120.
[8] Schuon (1984), p. 121.   [9] Schuon (1984), p. 123.

of his own religious view (which he calls, not just another religious view, but 'the esoteric' and transcendental unity of all religions). To put it bluntly, according to Schuon, the world's religions are misinterpreted by their own most scholarly and devout adherents. This view is not quite as tolerant and all-inclusive as it may at first sight appear to be.

The suspicion that the perennial philosophy, or the primordial tradition, is just one religious view among others, rather than the ancient and hidden reconciler of all religious diversity, is, I think, strengthened by the attempt of another major and widely read scholar of religion who seeks to provide a synthesising overview of world religions. This is Professor Huston Smith, the author of 'The World's Religions', an excellent and widely read exposition of religions in the modern world.

12

Huston Smith

$\mathcal{I}$N HIS LATER BOOK, *THE FORGOTTEN TRUTH*,[1] DR. HUSTON Smith too argues that there is a 'common vision' in the world's religions, a 'primordial tradition' which expresses one common truth that underlies all their different myths, doctrines, and stories. The common vision, as in Huxley and Schuon,[2] is that there is an ultimate reality from which all things emanate, the Infinite or Unbounded, the 'Being, Awareness, and Bliss' of the Upanishads. From the Infinite emanates a celestial realm, which can be called 'universal mind', the supreme expression of the divine in the manifest world. It is here that one finds a personal God, not the supreme reality, but its first expression. Here also are the Platonic Forms under the rule of the supreme Form of the Good. In accordance with the 'principle of plenitude', which decrees that 'nothing that is possible be left undone',[3] and that 'every grade of finitude must be actualised',[4] this gives rise to an intermediate realm, the 'psychic plane', of angelic and demonic beings, and also of 'etheric', 'astral', or subtle bodies of various sorts. From that realm emanates the terrestrial realm, the realm of matter which humans inhabit. In Smith's typology there is no distinct sub-terrestrial realm, since that has been subsumed into the intermediate realm, where both good and evil beings and powers exist.

Human beings have material bodies; minds or streams of consciousness; souls, the subjects, and witnesses of consciousness; and spirits, which are eternal and identical with the Infinite. This is again in accordance with the teaching of *Advaita Vedanta*, that '*atman* is *Brahman*'. The inner spirit (*atman*) is identical with the Absolute and Unbounded source of all things (*Brahman*). Humans have descended by emanation (Smith is prepared to call it creation) from the Infinite, and their ultimate destiny is to return from

---

[1] Smith (1976)   [2] Huxley (1947); Schuon (1984).   [3] Smith (1976), p. 49.
[4] Smith (1976), p. 28.

the material realm, passing through the intermediate and celestial realms, and finally realising their identity with ultimate reality, at which point they will transcend their egoic form of consciousness, the subject–object dichotomy will be overcome, and they will find themselves to be fully one with the Infinite. That Infinite can be known by mystic vision, and, by reference to William James, such a peak mystic experience is described as ineffable, unitary, joyful, and noetic.[5] It gives knowledge, although that knowledge cannot be formulated in language; it gives a sense of unity with all things; and it brings a sense of joy or bliss. It is the ultimate religious experience, and a foretaste or intimation of the final release of the ego from its finite attachments.

This is a presentation of the 'perennial philosophy' which has many resonances with the neo-Platonic thought of Plotinus, with the writings of Dionysius the (Pseudo)-Areopagite, with Sankara's reading of Vedanta,[6] with some Sufi and some Zen teachings, and with some of the teachings of Theosophy and similar more recent schools of esoteric philosophy. It is, thus, drawn from many sources, and perhaps those sources are very diverse, and do not really form one tradition at all unless they are forced into a sort of Procrustean bed. This 'primordial tradition', which Smith locates as ancient wisdom (perhaps present even in the Neolithic age),[7] is more like a cocktail of many elements, mixed together in a very personal way. This impression is amplified when one examines the range of 'esoteric' teachings that exist and differ and divide from each other, from Theosophy to Anthroposophy, from Kabbalah to Zen, and from Hermeticism to the channelled words of Seth. The primordial tradition constantly splinters into conflicting sects just like any other religion or ideology. Anthroposophy (the Rudolf Steiner school) distinguishes itself from Theosophy, the Unity Church distinguishes itself from Christian Science, and Rosicrucians differ from Swedenborgians. Even within the primordial tradition, diversity and conflict exist. What tends to unite them is a general agreement that there is one Supreme Spirit, that many worlds emanate from it, that humans have non-physical bodies which probably re-incarnate, that there are secret teachings from a number of 'seers' which the main world religions partly conceal and partly misinterpret, and that there is a purpose for human lives, which consists in a disciplined ascent to union with the Supreme Spirit.

As one reads the very varied expositions of this esoteric tradition, one becomes aware that there are many different specific expositions of it, some

---

[5] James (1960), p. 366.   [6] Sanakara (1962).   [7] Smith (1976), p. 125.

of them much more fantastic than others. Many of them contain appeals to arcane forms of numerology and prophecy – most of which differ from each other in detail – and with many competing claims to have privileged intuitions of spiritual and psychic worlds. In this respect many forms of esoteric religion are just as firmly based on inerrant revelation as any world religion. This is not really a pluralist vision, except in the sense that overt world religions are picturesque versions of the real truth, which is known to initiates who may be members of many world faiths. 'Religions', the world faiths, are mixtures of truth and falsity, and each of them is more or less equally so. But the 'primordial tradition' is absolutely true; the only difference being that it regards itself as a 'spirituality' and not a 'religion'. This is very different from a form of pluralism like John Hick's, which holds that no-one knows the absolute truth, though many religions are more or less adequate attempts to approach it.[8]

Huston Smith has a view of reality as a spiritual hierarchy, in which the material world descends from a series of spiritual worlds above it. 'In the celestial realm the species are never absent ... as earth ripens to receive them, each in its turn drops to the terrestrial plane'.[9] The higher psychic plane 'houses evil as well as good',[10] and 'the moral and affective differences that look so large in popular thought are secondary'.

The Ultimately Real is said to be wholly indescribable, and is certainly beyond the idea of a personal God. 'The world mind is the supreme expression of the divine in the manifest world',[11] but 'nothing finite can be final'.[12] One has to ask, is this really a core truth which is shared by all religions? And the answer is that it is very obviously not. Thomas Aquinas, for instance, a major theologian of the Roman Catholic faith, denied the extreme apophaticism of Dionysius, and he denied the view that the Supreme Reality could only be spoken of in negative terms. Huston Smith seems to agree with Thomas Aquinas some of the time, since he admits that some analogical terms about the Infinite, like 'good' and 'powerful', are 'more accurate than their opposites'. But this is probably true only of the relative realm of appearance, not of the ultimate reality-in-itself.

The spiritual vision is that the world of material reality is a descent from primal unity, and a return to that unity must be accomplished in the minds of spiritually enlightened people. This return is not envisaged as lying in the future – we may recall Huxley's warning that such a hope for a future Utopia is the seedbed of many harmful illusions. Any hope for temporal 'progress is

[8] Hick (1989).   [9] Smith (1976), p. 139.   [10] Smith (1976), p. 46.   [11] Smith (1976), p. 48.
[12] Smith (1976), p. 53.

an illusion',[13] and possibly 'the Golden Age of humanity' is 'somewhere around the Neolithic'.[14] Huston Smith opposes views like that of Teilhard de Chardin,[15] whom he describes as 'pseudo-Christian', quoting with apparent approval Peter Medawar's notorious review of Teilhard de Chardin's 'The Human Phenomenon' in the journal *Mind* in January 1961 that talks of 'Teilhard's alarming apocalyptic seizures'.[16]

The primordial tradition is far from being a historical, evolutionary, or developmental view of human existence. We are not progressing towards a greater grasp of truth. On the contrary, we are falling away from a primordial knowledge which we have largely forgotten. The age of Kali is upon is. Things are going to get worse. But all this is foreordained and necessarily what it is. The 'common vision of the world's religions' offers no hope of a future transfiguration of nature where it will fulfil its own potentialities. The ultimate possibility is return to the One, 'the flight of the alone to the Alone', as Plotinus put it.

This seems to me to be a very particular and not very widely held interpretation of ultimate religious truth. Its claim to be a 'common vision' is not well evidenced, though it is one stream of religious thought that has surfaced in a number of religious traditions, usually on the borderlines of orthodoxy, and not without its own internal differences and conflicts.

One major difficulty of the view, a difficulty which faces all three writers I have considered, is that Smith describes the Infinite as 'Being Unlimited, Being relieved of all confines and conditionings ... All-Possibility, the Absolute'.[17] In it all complements are united, and all contradictions resolved – even the opposition between good and evil. He quotes Chuang Tzu: 'To see all in the yet undifferentiated primordial unity, or from such a distance that all melts into one, this is true intelligence'.[18] There is perhaps a sense in which this is true. The supreme primordial being could somehow contain all possibilities of being in itself, from the very worst to the very best. It could be experienced as a unity without internal divisions or temporal change. it might indeed be described as an undifferentiated and self-complete unity which includes all qualities in itself. But the possibilities which form the content of such an undivided unity would precisely be possibilities, and it does not follow that, as Huston Smith puts it, 'nothing that is possible be left undone', that every possibility must be actualised.

---

[13] Smith (1976), p. 121. [14] Smith (1976), p. 125. [15] Teilhard de Chardin (1959).
[16] Smith (1976), p. 133. [17] Smith (1976), p. 25. [18] Smith (1976), p. 33.

The Principle of Plenitude

$\mathcal{I}$T IS POSSIBLE THAT THE SUPREMELY REAL, DISTINGUISHING between good and bad possibilities, could actualise only the good qualities in the divine being itself, to the highest possible degree, and, thus, indeed be called the 'good' and 'beautiful'. This would be a selection from the complete set of possibilities, determined by the evaluation of their intrinsic goodness. Yet, the principle of plenitude asserts that the primordial unity necessarily actualises all the possibilities which lie within it, and, in that respect, it would be a being which goes out from itself to generate a finite realm of beings, both good and bad.

It would in my opinion be horrifying to think that even the possible worlds in which many creatures suffer endlessly without relief have to be actual just because they are possible. It is more plausible to say, as Huston Smith also does, that 'every grade of finitude must be actualised'.[1] This more general formulation could be interpreted to mean that, in every possible grade of beings, only possible states of goodness, even those which are necessarily entangled with some lesser and more transient states of destruction and suffering, and which may carry with them the possibility of generating other evil states, must be actualised. There may be, in the nature of the Supremely Real itself, a necessary tendency to realise all sufficiently good potentialities within it. In an image used by Plotinus, the supremely perfect light may necessarily emanate goodness and perfection in diminishing degrees of intensity until the light fades out in the limit of the darkness of non-being. On this interpretation, it is goodness which necessarily diffuses itself in a series of 'grades of finitude'. This is one possible version of the 'great chain of being' of which Arthur Lovejoy wrote. The more

---

[1] Smith (1976), p. 28.

extreme version would insist that all possibilities, good and bad, are necessarily actualised.

Lovejoy defines this as the 'principle of plenitude' (he claims to have invented the term), the principle that 'no genuine potentiality of being can remain unfulfilled'.[2] He points out that, in this form, the principle might well be called 'the principle of the necessity of imperfection in all its possible degrees'.[3] As such, it seems to license a great deal of pessimism about the possibility of ever eliminating evil, and to justify leaving even very bad things very much as they are, since there is a very good reason for their existence, and in fact their existence is absolutely necessary. As he proceeds to analyse the principle, he claims that it has licensed two conflicting notions of the Supreme Reality which cannot be combined. They often have been combined in the history of thought, but this is simply 'the most extraordinary triumph of self-contradiction ... in the history of human thought'.[4] One idea is that of a self-sufficient perfect and changeless being who needs nothing and can be affected by nothing. The other idea is of a being who necessarily emanates from itself the world of change and time, in which there is a reason for everything being as it is, and whose prime attribute is 'infinite generativeness'.

Since these ideas are incompatible, one must go. Lovejoy chooses to reject the 'self-absorbed' and changeless being, as being too negative about the moral demands and pleasures of the temporal world. But he also rejects the hyper-rational idea that there is a sufficient reason for everything, which leads, he thinks, to complete determinism and the lack of any contingent and truly free choices in the world. He prefers what he terms 'evolutionism', a view influenced by the German idealist philosophical poet Schiller. The cosmos, he says, does not spring from a changeless and perfect all-including Being. It begins with pure potentiality, it begins as 'a colossal accident', and moves through suffering, irrational accident, trial and error, towards the 'realisation of the greatest possible fulness'.[5] The story of the universe is the actualising of being and goodness through meeting and overcoming opposition, and it is not wholly rational and necessary. The principle of plenitude has been 'the history of a failure',[6] he says, and the ghost of Plato, at least in one of its guises, has been exorcised at last.

I do not think Lovejoy is correct in saying that Plato's changeless Good actually contradicts Plato's 'Demiurge', who generates a world of time and chance. It is possible for a being to be necessary and changeless in some

---

[2] Smith (1976), p. 52. [3] Smith (1976), p. 340, note 36. [4] Smith (1976), p. 157.
[5] Lovejoy (1936), p. 326. [6] Lovejoy (1936), p. 329.

respects, and contingent and changing in others. But it is true that the 'primordial tradition' recommends a sort of Plotinian ascent to the undifferentiated One as the height of the human spiritual quest, and relegates any personal attributes of God to a lower, less real, level.

Lovejoy is probably correct in saying that the principle of plenitude, in its full force, would make all evil necessary and everything that happens strictly determined. The existence of real creative freedom and radical novelty in the world does seem to require some degree of 'openness' in nature. It is not true, however, as he seems to suggest, that if something is not determined by a sufficient reason, then it is irrational or accidental. Contingent choices are not determined, but they are not accidental or arbitrary. They may be free choices of possible futures, which means choosing some possibilities and excluding others, thereby limiting any principle of plenitude severely.

The principle may, as I have suggested, remain in a qualified sense as the necessity that many good possibilities will be realised. Lovejoy himself, on his evolutionist view, claims that in the universe there will eventually be a realisation of the greatest possible fulness of being. Thus, he seems committed to saying that there is a purpose, a goal envisaged and ultimately promulgated by the Being which is the source of all possibilities. That Being presumably is not itself a mere possibility, but an actual, intentional, and directive, though not wholly determining, source of actualities. His evolutionist view is not in fact from pure possibility and accident to full actuality, but from a primordial actuality which both envisages all possibilities and intentionally selects some of them as goals of the cosmic process. There is here a very qualified version of the principle of plenitude, specifying that some possibilities will necessarily be actualised, presumably because of their intrinsic worth, even if it takes time.

Even on this revised principle, the Primordial Being may also necessarily generate states of destruction and suffering. But such suffering does not arise by will and intention, nor does it give rise to positive enjoyment of the suffering of others. The Primordial Being from which suffering emanates, though it is the source of what we rightly call evil, cannot itself be called 'evil', for it is not the *intentional* source of the suffering of others.

Emanation can be distinguished from creation. Emanation is a necessary generation from the Primordial Being, as an overflowing from the internal necessities of its being, according to which a set of possibilities is actualised without being willed. Creation, on the other hand, might be seen as the conscious willing of many forms of goodness, and it arises from the personal aspect of the One. Such a creative will and impulse for goodness may exist throughout all the grades of finitude, even in realms far distant from the primordial One, realms which are the most remote actualisations and expressions of the nature of Being itself.

This conception of the origin of the cosmos, if it makes sense, would provide a plausible account of the existence of evil, suffering, destruction, and apparent waste in a universe which is also replete with beauty and intelligibility and happiness. It would require seeing the divine as a complex reality. The divine would have a necessary and 'impersonal' nature which would seem to be inclusive of all possibility, and to be beyond the reach of human imagination. It would also have a more 'personal' nature which is truly creative and is expressed in choices oriented towards goodness, and which are open to new futures.

On such a view, the existence of some realities which express the various 'grades of finitude' is necessary. But those grades do not, as in Plotinus, emanate from the One by necessary descent, eternal souls gradually falling through the various grades of being towards darkness and negativity. Beings rather ascend from an ocean of primal potentiality towards the Primordial Being by a creative selection and actualisation of possibilities (an echo of the *tohu va bohu*, the formless void, of the Biblical creation myth). Those possibilities which are actualised result from the gradually developing creative activity of communities of emergent souls, by processes whose features are not all pre-determined. Real creativity and mutual interaction may be found in the finite selves which are generated by the developmental processes of an emergent cosmic creation. These processes may be thought of as influenced or 'drawn' towards goodness by the Primordial Being, leading finally to the return of an estranged world to its primal source.

This return need not be construed as a 'flight from the Alone to the Alone', or a loss of self in an undifferentiated unity. Especially when seen in the light of an evolutionary or developmental view of the cosmos, it could be seen as the creative emergence of new sorts of value, which could not have existed without time and development, without struggle and persistent effort. The final goal might then not be an abolition of the illusion of time, and of a 'time-bound philosophy'. It might be the self-unfolding of the primal Being as an enduring communion of creative co-operation, a society of selves transfigured by their growing conscious interaction with the 'Self of all'.

The 'apocalyptic seizures' of Teilhard de Chardin are not as radically opposed to the perennial philosophy as the perennial philosophers think. But Teilhard de Chardin's vision of a future communion of being creatively developed from a primal source of potentiality is a different and indeed more time-bound vision than that of the perennialists, who wish for the abolition of time and a return to a primal unity beyond all multiplicity and change.[7]

There is, as Lovejoy suggests, a major dispute about the value and meaning of time, creativity, and relationship in contrast to eternity and absolute self-sufficiency, a contrast of, though not a contradiction between, a principle of creative and relational emergence with a principle of change-less perfection. The perennial philosophy of Huxley, the esoteric teaching of Schuon, and the primordial tradition of Huston Smith stand on one side of that dispute. Perhaps it was only after an evolutionary view of the cosmos developed, after the European Enlightenment, that a higher evaluation of time, particularity, relationship, and development became possible. The perennial philosophy has, however, always been just one strand of religious and philosophical thought, and, while it may express some fascinating insights into a possible religious philosophy, its claim to be the one under-lying truth behind all the various religions of the world does not seem to be plausible.

In particular, the distinction between a personal, temporal God and an impersonal, eternal Ultimate may not be such an unpassable divide. The upholders of a perennial philosophy or primordial tradition, as has been seen, subordinate the personal God to being a lower manifestation of the impersonal Ultimate. But this need not be a sharp divide. If God, the Supreme Reality, has a personal aspect, then God can be spoken of as Mind, but mind vastly unlike any human minds, which are ignorant, learn, change in temperament, and are subject to irrational passions. It is a unique Mind, knowing all that it is possible to know, and having the greatest possible power to act. It is a Primordial Mind, necessary in its existence, though contingent and creative in its actions, and beyond human imagin-ation or complete understanding. If one speaks of 'a Darkness beyond being', one may be speaking of what is beyond understanding and imagination. But there may be, and spiritual writers often speak as though there was, a personal and creative aspect to this reality.

Thus, Aquinas speaks of God as 'suum esse subsistens',[8] which is not much like a person, as we understand that term of a developing finite being essentially related to others. Yet, Aquinas' God is the Father of Jesus Christ and became incarnate in Jesus. Mahayana Buddhism speaks of 'Pure Consciousness', which is often said to be impersonal, and yet the idea of

---

[7] An excellent and much more sympathetic interpretation of Teilhard de Chardin can be found in King (1996).

[8] Aquinas (1967), 1a, 7, 1, p. 96.

consciousness implies a 'personal' or mind-like being of some sort, because consciousness is a property possessed by persons and not by things. These can be seen as two aspects of the same spiritual Reality, and we need not subordinate one to the other. Thus, Pure Consciousness and the personal creator and redeemer of the world may be two aspects of the same Divine Ultimate. The complex being of the Divine may have more than just two aspects. One can speak of relation to the Divine as a sense of union with what is beyond all conceptual thought and limitations. One can speak of it as a sense of union with a being of supreme intelligence and bliss (*sat-cit-ananda*). One can also speak of it as a personal relation to a creator and sustainer of existence. And one can speak of it as an awareness of an inner inspiring presence and power. These can all be ways in which God is, and none needs to be subordinated to the others.

14

Perennialism and Diversity

*T*HE CLAIM THAT THERE IS ONE PERENNIAL PHILOSOPHY, ESOTERIC OR primordial tradition, underlying and uniting all religions, is very difficult to sustain. Religions are just really different, and they reflect the very different values and world views of differing individuals and cultures. This, given the diversity of human personalities and histories, is only to be expected. It is not really a problem. A problem arises only when one tradition claims to possess the full and final truth about ultimate reality. From the discussion so far, I have meant to suggest that, though there are truth claims in most religions, the nature of such claims is far from straightforward. They are to a large and indefinite extent symbolic or metaphorical. The perennialists seem to be right in saying that such truths, which necessarily use concepts familiar to often very localised and sometimes idiosyncratic languages and cultures, are to some extent relative. That is, the way that truths are expressed depends on the languages, with their many layers of connotation and association, that are available to different cultures. The truths are also heavily value-laden (for instance, in some cultures personal reality is taken to be the supreme value, whereas in others the personal is thought to be unduly egoistic and individualistic) and emphasise the values that are thought to be important in different cultures. This does not mean that truth is relative, in the sense that whatever one group says is really true 'for them'. It means that the grasp of objective truths that a community has is relative to its own level of understanding and evaluation. There is an absolute truth. But any communities' grasp of it is limited by the finitude of human minds. The mistake of perennialists is to think that there is a way of escape from this form of relativity to a higher mode of absolute certainty, open only to a gnostic elite.

Perennialists may be right in saying that one important religious goal is to seek to overcome the grasping ego and achieve conscious and life-enhancing union with an actually existing supreme Good. Many major religions in the modern world would accept such a description of their own religious path. But it is probably mistaken to think that the way to this goal can be traced back to some primal and continuing, although hidden, tradition, and that the modern world has largely forgotten it. There have been enormous changes in moral and rational understanding in the course of human history, and they have made a difference to religious understanding. Some of the effects of these changes have been negative, but some have been positive, and it is important to see how such positive changes have, or should have, affected ancient religious traditions.

I conclude that there is no perennial philosophy. But there is, underlying many religions, a rather general belief in the existence of a spiritual dimension, which is often thought to be of supreme value. Humans can have a conscious relationship to it, which may deliver them from harm or enhance human well-being. This relationship can be cultivated by various spiritual techniques or rituals, both public and private. It makes moral demands, or at least outlines a correct way of living a good life, and promises the possibility of some form of moral or evaluative fulfilment. It is believed to be accessed by sensitive 'seers' or teachers, often by one outstanding teacher, and it is often said to be only fully known after the death of the earthly body.

This rather general orientation to a spiritual dimension has in the course of human history generated four major streams of religious thought, which between them encompass the main sorts of relation that may be thought to exist between physical and spiritual reality.

One stream asserts that only the spiritual really exists, and the physical is its appearance or expression. This is a form of philosophical idealism, and it is what the perennialists claim is the primordial form of ancient wisdom. It developed in the Indian subcontinent, where it continues to co-exist with more localised or tribal forms of religious practice. Despite what the perennialists say, it has many forms, but they tend to stress the importance of ascetic and meditative practice, leading to a sense of union with Absolute Spirit (*Brahman*) and release from the physical world of suffering and imperfection. It is classically expressed in the schools of Vedantic Hinduism, based on particular (and differing) interpretations of the Upanishads.

A second stream also originated in India, passing from there to many East Asian countries, and it is a form of radical dualism between matter (*prakriti*) and spirit (*purusa*). Ascetic and meditative practice is centred on the monastic community (the *sangha*), and is ultimately concerned with release from the physical. But, unlike Idealism, it opposes the spiritual to the physical, and has little or no concern with a personal creator or form of Absolute Spirit with which one might have a relationship. This is found in *Theravada* Buddhism and the Jain faith. These two streams may be said to be examples of what Friedrich Heiler called the 'mystical' path of religion, which seeks union with one Absolute Reality – though, as should be clear, there is not just one path, and not all of them would be happy to call themselves 'mystical'.

The third stream is Abrahamic theism, which posits a personal Creator with knowledge, will, and purpose, as the source of the physical. It is a prophetic stream, largely concerned with social justice and with salvation from the evils of injustice and oppression. It would belong to Heiler's 'numinous' path, as it tends to emphasise devotion to an 'other' personal being of both joyful attractiveness and dreadful power. It is unfortunately obvious that, within this stream, there are tendencies to opposition and violence which have not yet been wholly resolved.[1]

The fourth stream could be seen as presupposing a form of philosophical monism. It holds that there is only one reality, that the spiritual is the physical, or is one dimension of the physical, and does not exist without the physical. The physical, however, has a dimension of objective value (the *Tao* or the Way of Heaven in Chinese thought) which is a model of what it is to live a good human life. This is most like Hans Kung's 'wisdom' path.[2] Its teachers are sages rather than prophets or gurus, and what they teach is how to live in accordance with the hidden moral structure of the cosmos. This might be called a path of transcendental humanism, though again there are sometimes severe differences between Confucians and Taoists as to what exactly this path is.

These four streams, with their proliferating tributaries and side-channels, are explorations of the main possible forms of relationship to spiritual reality that humans have conceived. There are other logical possibilities of relationship, depending on whether spirit and matter are conceived as separable or not, self-determining or not, independently existent or not. Some are almost religiously insignificant (like hard materialism and the emergence of the spiritual, including God, from the material), and some can be seen as sub-classes of the four streams mentioned. If that is the case, the perennial philosophy can be seen to be only one tributary of one stream of religious thought and practice. Yet, these streams are not arbitrary collections of differing views. They are parts of developing historical processes of reflection and spiritual practices, with a common goal of finding human fulfilment through conscious relation to a deeper reality. If that is so, it may be that looking to find a direction to historical change that points towards the future, rather than attempting to retrieve a forgotten past, is more helpful to solving the problem of how to believe religiously in a world of so many diverse beliefs.

[1] Heiler (1932).   [2] Kung (1993).

Part III

The Critical Turn

SINCE THE SIXTEENTH CENTURY, HUMAN THOUGHT AND KNOWLEDGE HAS changed and expanded significantly. These changes impact upon religious beliefs which were largely formulated long before that time. In the following section, I will consider some of these major changes, and the way in which they affect traditional religious beliefs.

The greatest change in human understanding of the world has occurred because of the rise of scientific method and the consequent discoveries that new technology has made possible. New scientific knowledge affects all traditional religions to some extent, but I will begin by considering its impact in Europe, where new challenges to ancient religious beliefs were most keenly felt. In Judaism and Christianity, the Biblical account of a six-day creation not too long ago, and a cosmology that placed the earth at the centre of the universe, with stars as lamps hung on the dome of the sky, had been widely accepted. Even when the Bible was not taken as a source of information about the beginning and size of the universe, philosophical efforts like those of Aristotle, impressive though they were, assumed a universe very different from the one modern science has revealed. It was a universe in which everything had a purpose (final causes), in which things had essential and unchanging natures (formal causes), and in which all effects had to have causes which were like but greater than their effects. All these Aristotelian assumptions were to be put in question by the development of a more mechanistic view of natural causality, the idea that material things do not have unchanging essential natures, but develop by gradual and mostly continuous change, and the widespread acceptance of a view that the greater does emerge from the less, and that new qualities come into being gradually in the course of cosmic evolution. A whole world view was changing, and religions had to decide what response to make to this.

The impact on religious views might, nevertheless, not have been very great, since it was widely accepted that large parts of the Bible were metaphorical. Augustine, for example, did not think that the 'six days' of creation were actual days, or even that they were periods of time.[1] He saw them as picturesque ways of making logical distinctions between kinds of entity – rocks, plants, animals, and humans, for example. But the translation of the Bible into various languages, and the ability to distribute it widely among populations, gave rise to more literal interpretations of the texts.

At the same time, the rise of critical interpretations of the Biblical texts began to make people suspect that there were factual and moral errors in what was held to be 'the word of God'. The Protestant Reformation had in effect undermined the authority of the Roman Catholic Church as an interpreter of Scripture for many Christians. Most early Protestants wanted to base their faith on the Bible, but no longer viewed the Catholic magisterium as a reliable interpreter. So individual interpretations of the text, differing from each other in many ways, led to the existence of many different accounts of what the Bible actually said.

Protestants might not have wanted to say that there were mistakes in the Bible, but they certainly did want to say that there were mistakes in the interpretation of the Bible by large numbers of its readers. One could avoid accusations of factual error by appealing to metaphor. One could avoid accusations of moral error by saying that new times and circumstances had changed the applicability of written moral principles. Christians were virtually compelled to say this, in view of the fact that large sections of the *Torah*, the Old Testament law, were rendered obsolete by Paul's teaching. Paul had said, 'The letter kills, but the spirit gives life' (2 Corinthians 3, 6), and so there was precedent for replacing ancient written laws by later amendments of them (remember that Jesus said, 'You have heard ... but I say to you)'.

This gave rise to more occasions for dispute, since it was not clear which bits of written law were to be ignored. Calvin said that the ritual and hygiene laws could be ignored, but such a distinction would not be acceptable to a Jew, and it is not explicitly said even in the New Testament. The Ten Commandments were often taken as still in force, even though about half of them are in fact more ritual than what we might call moral. Keeping the Sabbath holy is the most obvious case. Early Christians did not hesitate to change the day from Saturday to Sunday, to ignore most of the specific rules

[1] See Augustine (1982), Book 1.

in the Old Testament about how to keep the Sabbath, and Calvin himself taught that no special holy days should be kept at all, since they were all vain ceremonies.[2] It might be good, Calvin thought, to give servants a day off once a week, and to keep time for Church services, but there is no specifically religious reason for keeping a Sabbath. It turns out, however, that even Calvinistic Presbyterians disagree with Calvin about this, and rigorous Sabbath day exclusion of all secular activities often became a mark of Protestant piety. To this day there are still highly charged arguments about moral matters which are founded largely on Old Testament texts, and those arguments often hinge on whether they have moral authority for Christians or not.

What the Protestant Reformation brought about, even if it did not mean to do so, was a new questioning of authority, a more critical approach to sacred texts, and a new problem of how far and in what sense texts which were framed in the context of an obsolete and mistaken world-view could be taken as sources of eternal and inerrant truth. These new factors were not confined to Protestant Christianity, and the Roman Catholic Church also had to deal with them, and in more recent years has done so very effectively.

---

[2] 'Christians, therefore, should have nothing to do with a superstitious observance of days': Calvin (1989), Book 2, Ch. 7, para. 31, p. 341.

15

Rudolf Bultmann

*T*HE PROBLEM OF THE OBSOLETE WORLD VIEW OF THE BIBLE IS serious. Many of those who give a completely negative interpretation of the Bible do so because they think it rests upon a view of the cosmos and the place of humans within it which is incompatible with modern, scientific-ally influenced, thought. Religion, or at least Christian and Jewish religion, is, to put it bluntly, obsolete, and the Biblical view of a flat earth at the centre of the universe, constantly troubled by the actions of angels and demons, replete with miracles and monstrosities of all sorts, and governed by a supernatural Dictator, is a myth which no scientifically instructed mind can stomach. As the theologian Rudolf Bultmann put it, Christian faith needs to be rescued from this myth if it is to survive. It must be de-mythologised, but, if it is de-mythologised, will anything worth-while be left?

Bultmann's definition of 'mythology' is, however, rather too broad. He writes that mythology 'believes that the world and human life have their ground and their limits in a power which is beyond all that we can calculate or control'.[1] But Immanuel Kant, to take just one classical philosopher, believed that, and I do not think he can be accused of having a 'mythology'. Just about all theists believe that too, but they would regard this as a simple statement of truth, not at all mythological.

Bultmann goes on to say that 'mythology speaks about this power inadequately ... as if it were a worldly power'. Again, 'myths give worldly objectivity to that which is unworldly'.[2] Most writers would agree that God is spoken about inadequately, and that we need to use concepts taken from our experience in this world to speak of a divine being who is greater than this world. There is hardly any alternative. This is just the classical doctrine of

---

[1] Bultmann (1960), p. 19.   [2] Bultmann (1960), p. 19.

analogy, taken in a rather vague sense. If all statements about God are taken literally (that is, in their primary meaning, as applied to finite objects), that is a theological mistake. To say 'God is a rock' is false in its primary meaning, but it can well be true in a metaphorical sense, meaning that God is durable or steadfast.

What Bultmann really has in mind is partly the world-view of ancient cultures, which do not know about other galaxies or about the place of earth in the universe, or the evolution of humans on earth. That worldview is false, and needs to be replaced by a modern scientific worldview. He also has in mind a literal interpretation of heaven and hell as 'above' or 'below' the ground. That, also, can be shown today to be literally false. But the mistake there is basically the mistake of taking metaphors as literal truths. The mistake is easily rectified by taking talk of 'above' and 'below' as metaphorical – and it is reasonable to suppose that they have always had such an interpretation in the minds of sophisticated believers.

It is true that we must eschew obsolete views of the universe, and we must not take metaphors literally. But this is not 'de-mythologisation', if that is what he describes as the re-interpretation of mythological statements in completely non-objectifying terms.

One of Bultmann's concerns is how to interpret what we assume is the eschatology of Jesus. I do not think we can be sure what Jesus' thoughts about the end of the world really were. The New Testament certainly ascribes some statements about the 'end of the age' to him, and does not make clear in what sense or to what degree such statements should be taken as symbolic or metaphorical. Bultmann seems to assume that they were taken literally, and he calls that a 'myth'. I rather think that, on a literal interpretation, most of those statements are not just mythical; they are literally false. We have to interpret them as symbolic if we are to read them as true, but that is nothing new. The question is, what do they symbolise?

Bultmann suggests that one element is a claim that 'this world is temporal and transitory . . . in the face of eternity'.[3] 'Men have turned it into a place in which evil spreads and sin rules'.[4] Thus, the world falls under the judgment of God. But Christians hope for bliss after death, for existence in a 'transcendent world . . . where man reaches the perfection of his true, real essence'.[5] I think this is an excellent reading of Gospel metaphors about the end. But he then calls this view mythological, so that it, too, needs re-interpreting. However, I do not think these are myths, which I have earlier

---

[3] Bultmann (1960), p. 23.   [4] Bultmann (1960), p. 26.   [5] Bultmann (1960), p. 30.

characterised as imaginative personifications of natural forces or of human ideals. They are statements, intended to be true, about this life and the afterlife. Descriptions of the afterlife are inadequate and metaphorical, phrased in highly symbolic terms. But statements about transitoriness, sin, judgement, and eternal bliss are not myths. They are either true or false.

It becomes clear that, what Bultmann means by de-mythologisation is the denial of any objective truth to such statements. They are, he says, actually telling us 'to be open to God's future', and to be ready 'for the unknown future that God will give',[6] or to achieve 'freedom from anxiety in the face of the Nothing'.[7] This freedom is 'obedience to a law ... which man recognises as the law of his own being'.[8] Claims to objective truth are re-interpreted as what may be called the adoption of existential attitudes.

What is wrong with this programme is that existential attitudes are made appropriate and reasonable only by being correlated with objective facts. If I am to have hope for the future, I must believe that it is possible that what I hope for can happen. If I am to adopt an attitude of freedom, I must believe that I am not totally constrained by physical or spiritual powers. In general, if my inner attitudes are to be appropriate, they assume that external reality is of a specific sort. Otherwise they will be self-delusions (however psychologically helpful such delusions may be for some).

Bultmann says very insightful things about the appeal of scripture and of Christian preaching. He says that the message of scripture must not be bound to an ancient worldview which is obsolete. Preaching is not primarily about a worldview (he sometimes, in my view correctly, calls it a worldview, not a myth), either ancient or modern. It is a 'personal message', addressed to the 'hearer as a self'.[9] As we go through life, we may become keenly aware of the demands of morality, and of our inability to escape from our own pride, greed, and hatred. If we hear the Gospel message, we may become convicted of sin, or at least of our own moral and personal failures, and of the need for forgiveness and a renewal of life. This is a deeply personal matter, concerned with how we see and evaluate our own lives and responsibilities. It is at such a point that we may hear the message that a new life in the Spirit is possible for us, and we may seek such a life. In a similar way our life-experience may give us a sense of the transience and emptiness of such things as fame and luxurious wealth. We may then hear a message that there is a transcendent and enduring source of goodness, and we may respond by

[6] Bultmann (1960), p. 31.   [7] Bultmann (1960), p. 77.   [8] Bultmann (1960), p. 41.
[9] Bultmann (1960), p. 36.

committing ourselves to that possibility. We seek to exchange anxiety and attachment for freedom and commitment to the good.

These are not matters of committing ourselves to anything so grand as a world-view or a particular philosophy. They are matters of assessing our lives as inadequate or misdirected in some way and responding to the possibility that we can be 'saved' from such inadequacy by commitment to an enduring goodness, which will open up our own true selves. These are what might be called existential concerns, concerns about what it is like to exist as a human being, and how we can learn to live well in a world that is beset by hatred and ignorance.

What Bultmann does not point out is that such existential concerns are not particularly Christian. They are even more explicit in Buddhism, which does not speak of a God. Heidegger, whose existential analysis Bultmann does refer to, does not speak of God either. For Buddhists, life is unsatisfactory, or has the nature of suffering. Suffering is caused by attachment, and the Buddhist eightfold path offers a way to end attachment and thereby release human lives from that sort of suffering. Christianity, however, does speak of God, and the question for Bultmann is what difference this makes to one's existential concerns and commitments.

Existentialist philosophers like Sartre tend to see God as a rather infantile projection of human needs, who must be abandoned if true human freedom and authenticity is to be achieved. Why does Bultmann not agree with them? There is in fact a deep evaluative difference between the sort of authenticity of which Heidegger speaks, and the freedom of which Bultmann, as a Lutheran, speaks. There is an affinity too – the affinity of those who see the inauthenticity of their own lives and seek a more authentic human possibility of being-in-the-face-of-death. An existentialist might speak of an encounter with 'the Nothing', an encounter in which anxiety is overcome. 'The Nothing', in Heideggerian thought, is not simply the absence of anything. It is a sort of reality which is 'not a thing', not an object in the world, but the boundary condition of all beings. Hegel had said the Nothing is identical with Being, and, however mysterious this is, it catches the thought that there is that of which nothing can be said in objectifying language, but which is the root of but beyond all beings (beyond even a personal God).[10] For Buddhists, *Nirvana* is beyond any linguistic description, and yet it is in a sense that at which liberation from sorrow is aimed, and it is not mere annihilation.

[10] Hegel (1977), section 1, para. 132.

It may be that the idea of God is nearer to such an idea than some think, and the apophatic tradition, which asserts that God in Godself is beyond all description, in Christianity, Islam, and Judaism, resurfaces many times. Yet, to speak of God is to speak of a reality which it is correct to speak of as conscious, personal, and intentional. Whatever 'the Nothing' is, it is not correct to speak of it as personal and intentional. When Bultmann speaks of being open to the future that 'God will give', he is not speaking of an inactive state, but of one who 'gives' in an active and personal sense, however metaphorical and inadequate this description is. He says that 'God calls man',[11] and speaks of a law of 'man's own being'. That law 'has its origin and reason in the beyond'. It is 'the law of God'.[12] 'In the Bible a certain possibility of existence is shown to me not as something which I am free to choose or to refuse'.[13] This points to one of the paradoxes of existentialist thought. On the one hand, one is to seek a total freedom from all conventional morality, to choose one's way of life for oneself. But on the other hand, there is an 'authentic' way of existing, a law of one's own being which is not simply chosen, but which defines what it is to exist truly as a human being. Such a law (like the law of *karma* in Buddhism) may be conceived impersonally, as just written into the nature of things. But we do not just choose it, and we may mistake it through ignorance or attached desire. It is objectively there, and we become what we ought to be when we recognise and follow it.

For Bultmann, however, as a Lutheran, even such an impersonal conception is insufficient. He wants an 'open readiness to personal encounters'.[14] He wants to say that 'God acts on me, speaks to me, here and now'.[15] He insists that this is not 'another general world-view'.[16] But this claim is not plausible. If God encounters me here and now, this entails that there is a God who can encounter human beings to convict them of sin and offer the possibility of authentic life. That is a world-view! It differs from the Buddhist world-view that there is no God who encounters people, even here and now. Many Buddhists in the *Mahayana* traditions do speak of *Bodhisattvas* who are compassionate and can encounter people, and so introduce a note of personal devotion into their faith. But Christians say there is just one personal reality who encounters people. In that encounter, a quasi-personal relationship is established, which is unlike the abandonment of any sense of self, and, therefore, of self–other relationships, that is characteristic of much Buddhist spirituality.

[11] Bultmann (1960), p. 40.   [12] Bultmann (1960), p. 41.   [13] Bultmann (1960), p. 53.
[14] Bultmann (1960), p. 44.   [15] Bultmann (1960), p. 64.   [16] Bultmann (1960), p. 65.

Bultmann's concern is to say that we should not treat the existence of God as a theoretical or speculative issue, as though it is a matter of dispassionately assessing the validity of the 'proofs of God's existence'. We must be 'drawn into the event', be 'confronted with God', have 'real experiences of God'.[17] The difference is like the difference between accepting evidence that another person exists (which really may be a matter of indifference to me) and meeting that person and falling in love. This is a real and important distinction. Falling in love changes me radically, whereas just knowing that someone exists does not. But that does not entail that 'only such statements about God are legitimate as express the existential relations between God and man'.[18] On the contrary, if my experience of God is genuine, that does entail that God objectively exists and is as I experience God to be. There is knowledge by acquaintance with God, and knowledge by description of God. The latter does not entail the former, but the former entails the latter, at least to the extent that it enables me to give some correct descriptions of God, however inadequate to the full divine reality.

Bultmann's analysis does, however, suggest that, while religions presuppose world-views, having such a theoretical view of the reality is not the heart of religion. That heart lies in a personal understanding of what existing as a human being is like (self-understanding), and of what it is to live a good human life. It lies in personal experience and our personal response to it. By that, I do not mean the occurrence of particular and perhaps intense experiences which might be called 'religious'. I mean the way in which, for each individual, there is a sequence of experiences, good and bad, which give rise to a specific understanding of what human existing is like, and which influence one's general approach to the future.

Nevertheless, different philosophies and religions give different interpretations of these existential situations. A Heideggerian or a Sartrean understanding does not seem to be one which is true for all humans everywhere. It is one which arises in very specific historical situations, in Western Europe after the disasters of two world wars and in a rapidly changing technological culture. The sort of '*Angst*' of which Heidegger speaks occurs to those who have lost the sense of a long Christian heritage, who have experienced the horrific evil of war, and who fear for the end of human life on the planet. The sort of 'Authentic life – *eigentlichkeit*' – Heidegger recommends is a heroic embrace of absurdity in face of a life which has no objective goal or external

---

[17] Bultmann (1960), p. 69.   [18] Bultmann (1960), p. 69.

moral constraint. It is, in other words, the expression of one human creative response to experiences which have shaken previous moral certainties in a radical way.

It is ironic that Bultmann finds this analysis appropriate for Christian thinking, which usually does postulate objective moral principles and purposes. But it is not accidental that his Christian tradition is Lutheran, that Lutherans in Germany often rejected Catholic beliefs about natural law and Aristotelian beliefs in 'purposes of nature', and that they tend to distinguish sharply between socio-political realities and inner spiritual life (the 'two kingdoms'). All these influences can lead to a scepticism about confident claims that there is a natural morality upon which all humans can agree, and about an attainable moral goal apparent in history. In Bultmann's case, they led to a stress on the inner life which actually excluded any claims about objective and discernible acts of God in history.

He says, 'faith grows out of the encounter with the Holy Scriptures as the Word of God'.[19] Of course, he is really speaking of Protestant Christian faith. There can be other forms of encounter with God that do not depend on the Christian scriptures seen as the word of God. A Muslim may encounter God through hearing the Qur'an, and this too can be a life-changing response to an experience of God. The existential concern with human finitude, transience, and death may be universal to humanity. But ways of dealing with this concern differ quite sharply, and historical contexts and personal experiences are important influences on the existential way of authenticity that is recommended. Bultmann's treatment already presupposes a personalist Christian understanding of God, and a revelation of this understanding in and through the person of Jesus.

A truly existential understanding of faith, as encountering and overcoming the anxiety of inauthentic being, will have a global dimension. Yet, proposed ways of authentic life differ quite widely, so there is not just one agreed existential truth. Even among existentialists, there are Catholics like Gabriel Marcel, Protestants like Bultmann, and atheists like Sartre. So, perhaps Bultmann has identified one important element of religious belief – its analysis of the human situation as defective in some way, and its proposal of a truly authentic way of living – but his analysis only outlines one Christian proposal, while it implies that this may be a universal feature of human existence. His is not only a Christian view, it is one specific sort of Protestant view. There is nothing wrong with this, but it undercuts any claim

[19] Bultmann (1960), p. 71.

that there is some sort of universal religious view towards which all religions may be moving.

Recommendations of an authentic human way of living depend upon an assessment of the nature of human existence and of the world in which humans exist, which is not just a matter of subjective feeling, not just a self-understanding, but an understanding of the historical situation and of the wider objective reality in which the self exists. It may be significant that existential concerns about the meaning of one's own life are important determining factors in making decisions about the truth of more general world-views. Where the facts are subject to different reasonable interpretations, a decision about which interpretation to accept may depend partly on how one responds to one's own situation and tries to cope in a creative way with it. Religious belief will not so much be about proofs or disproofs of God, as it is about how individuals face up to the problems of their own situation and find, or fail to find, a way of living that gives them a sense of meaning and purpose.

Such proposed solutions may be, especially in the religious case, responses to the influence of exceptional teachers, like Jesus perhaps, who claim to have achieved such a sense of meaning and purpose, and who speak from their own life-affirming experiences and insights. Nevertheless, such teachings will have to be checked against the objective truths to which we have access about the nature of the world and of human life. One feature of our situation today is that these objective truths, provided by science, have changed our world-view considerably, and almost out of all recognition.

Bultmann and many others think the world-view has changed to such an extent that all ancient religious world-views must be rejected as myths. They often try to preserve the existential aspects of religion without any commitment to a world-view at all. This is impossible, and the fact remains that if they cannot provide a world-view that is consonant with religious faith then the faith will wither, becoming just an option for a set of purely personal attitudes which fail to integrate with any scientific knowledge. Religious faith becomes a 'leap of faith', without rational foundation, and, in that situation, it does not much matter which faith one adopts, since they are all options which no longer make claims to objective truth. The gap between faith and reason opens up. It has become a characteristic mark of modern Western civilisation.

I have argued that there is a problem, at least for Jews and Christians, which has arisen because of the existence of radically different knowledge of the nature of the physical universe from that which is presupposed by the Bible. Rudolf Bultmann, one of the major Christian scholars of the New

Testament, responded by proposing that all ontological and metaphysical claims, that is, all claims about the nature of objective reality, must be dropped from religion. Instead, the heart of religion can be seen in the attempt to find personal meaning in one's existence, to escape from fear and despair to find new possibilities of a more creative and fulfilled life. I think this proposal does bring out something important about the nature of religion, its primary concern with overcoming alienation, and finding a more authentic human possibility. But I do not think that can be done by eliminating all concern with the nature of the reality in which humans live and by which their possibilities are defined.

Those religions which speak of God do intend to speak of the basis of objective reality as one that is ultimately personal and purposive, in relation to which human authenticity is to be conceived. Some way must be found by Jews, Christians, and Muslims, of harmonising belief in a morally purposive and personal God with new scientific knowledge of a vast law-governed, often seemingly amoral and non-purposive, cosmos.

That may, in turn, require a revision of some traditional attitudes to sacred Scriptures. At the very least, literalist interpretations must often be rejected – that, of course, would not be new. But the problem would be of how far this rejection might go. Would it, for instance, mean that miraculous exceptions to general laws of nature would have to be abandoned? Or that one would have to give up expectations of an imminent end of the universe? One will also have to be prepared for further revisions as science progresses, and one cannot know in advance what these revisions may be. This suggests that the discovery of religious truth lies in the future, not in some ancient past, before the scientific world-view had arisen.

I have spoken about the Bible and about a particular Christian view. But all canonical sacred texts have had their authority called into question, and responsible expositors have at the very least to be aware of this challenge and accept that the challenge is not irresponsible or impious, but the result of an honest search for truth. This is a new situation, historically speaking, and it almost certainly calls for new sorts of religious response. Many sacred scriptures, insofar as they do state or assume certain statements about objective reality, face similar problems. The Indian scriptures, which speak of a beginningless and endless series of universes, of the underlying unity of all things, and of the dependence of material reality upon consciousness, seem to some to be more in accord with much modern physics than does the Bible. Yet, when the texts and commentaries are examined closely, they contain many statements incompatible with modern science, such as that at death souls go to the moon, and then fall as rain on the earth before they are reborn.[20] The problems raised by questioning the scope of religious authority, the critical study of Scriptural texts, and the possibilities of acceptable revisions of ancient doctrines or interpretations, are common to most world religions. They suggest that religions in the modern world face problems that were not addressed by, and cannot be resolved by, appeal to some alleged primordial tradition. They suggest that religions are liable to change and development, but that, at least for the foreseeable future, such developments will take place within a number of diverse religious traditions. The problem of religious diversity is not resolved, but it is placed more firmly within a number of historically changing processes that exist alongside an increasing consciousness of their wider global context.

[20] Sankara (1977), Ch. 3, Section 1.

16

Immanuel Kant

I HAVE CONSIDERED SOME OF THE PROBLEMS RAISED BY THE development of a scientific world-view and by a critical examination of ancient Scriptures. Another significant change that is associated with the European Enlightenment is the disentangling of morality from religious authority and the call for the freeing of thought in general from ancient customs, traditions, and authorities.

The Enlightenment philosopher who is probably most closely associated with these changes was Immanuel Kant. As well as being one of the most significant philosophers of the Enlightenment, he is also a significant figure in modern thought about religion, even though his own approach to religion would not be acceptable to many orthodox religious believers. Though Kant was raised by parents who were Pietistic Christians, he reacted strongly against any suggestion that religious experiences were helpful or even possible. 'The feeling of the immediate presence of the Supreme Being' is 'the moral death of Reason', he wrote in his book, posthumously published but probably written in 1793, *Religion wthin the Limits of Reason Alone.*[1] He never attended Church services, even when it was his academic duty to do so (ironically, for a philosopher who is famous for holding that one should do one's duty whatever the cost). And he held that any claims to experience the grace of God in one's life must be discounted – 'By reason of the dignity of the idea of duty, I am unable to associate grace with it'.[2]

These quotations re-inforce the idea that Kant was a supreme rationalist and moralist, who had no time for religious experience, and would have rejected Bultmann's talk of 'encounter with God' out of hand. But the facts are much more complicated. In his younger days he had been a rationalist,

[1] Kant (1960b), p. 163.   [2] Kant (1960b), p. 119.

following the philosophers Leibniz and Christian Wolff in thinking that reason could provide intuitive knowledge of ultimate truths about reality. But his most famous work is probably the *Critique of Pure Reason*, and it is a Critique, not a defence, of reason as a source of knowledge.[3]

He said that he wished to be known as a 'critical Idealist'.[4] As a philosophical Idealist, he held that the human mind, in its faculties of sensibility and understanding, constructs the world of appearances which we see as the external world. There is a real world beyond and underlying appearances, but of that world of 'things-in-themselves' nothing can be known. Reason cannot know it, and the role of Reason with respect to that real world is purely regulative, providing Ideas (such as God, freedom, and immortality) which the mind necessarily promulgates, and which regulate our approach to the world, but cannot provide verifiable information about things-in-themselves.

When it comes to Ideas about God, they are so paradoxical and mysterious that we can see that they cannot give objective knowledge. They have a necessary, practical use, but they point to incomprehensible 'holy mysteries'. In 'Religion', he writes that reason must think of humans as created but also as free, and it is impossible to reconcile these ideas rationally. We must think of humans as responsible for their moral actions, yet also as in need of Divine grace, and this too is incomprehensible. We must think that God's purposes will be realised, yet also that humans are free to choose evil. These paradoxes, although produced by Reason, 'transcend all our concepts'.[5]

These are hardly the views of a rationalist. Kant does think that Reason necessarily legislates ideas that we must use, but he does not think that we can understand them in any cognitive sense. He does not think that feelings or experiences will help us to understand them either. Thus, religion within the bounds of reason turns out to be religion which generates cognitive paradoxes, showing what the limits of reason are. As Kant said in the preface to the second edition of the first Critique, 'I have therefore found it necessary to deny knowledge, in order to make room for faith'.[6] For Kant, Reason shows that there are limits beyond which knowledge cannot go, but at the same time it generates paradoxical and mysterious Ideas in terms of which we necessarily think.

This is certainly not an appeal to Divine revelation. Such a thing always remained anathema to Kant. But it is not a claim that Reason provides ultimate truth. It is rather an admission that we must in practice live as if

[3] Kant (1952).   [4] Kant (2004), 'How Is Pure Mathematics Possible?', Note 3, p. 45.
[5] Kant (1960b), p. 133.   [6] Kant (1952), Bxxx, p. 22.

certain things are true – there is God, moral freedom, and immortality – even though we have to admit that they have no possible proof, and that they are beyond human understanding. Kant was nearer to Kierkegaard than is sometimes thought.

Neither was Kant the severe moralist that he has sometimes been thought to be. He did think that, if one had a duty, then it must be possible to do that duty – ought, it seems, implies can. But in the 'Religion' he writes that humans are necessarily and radically evil – 'What we are able to do is in itself inadequate'.[7] Evil, he thinks, consists in the will freely choosing to place its own inclinations above the rational principle of what is right. All human beings do this, and so there is in all a principle of radical evil, which makes moral rectitude impossible. It seems that 'ought' does not imply 'can' after all!

He does believe in autonomy, which he defines as the capacity of the will to determine itself. And he means by this that the rational will, acting on the principle of the Categorical Imperative (in one main formulation, 'Act only on that maxim whereby thou canst at the same time will that it should become a universal law'),[8] determines what is morally right. He is clear that moral duties do not derive from revelation or authority. In a pamphlet, 'What is Enlightenment?', he enjoined everyone to dare to think for themselves – 'sapere aude' – and not slavishly to follow custom or tradition or authority.

'Historical faith ... contains nothing, and leads to nothing, which could have any moral value for us',[9] and faith in the Bible is merely 'faith in Scriptural scholars and their insight'. For a philosopher who taught anthropology for virtually every year of his academic life, this is a strange statement. All humans learn a specific language and are taught values and attitudes very early in their lives which are going to affect their subsequent beliefs in major ways. We are all very much influenced by the groups in which we live, and it is false to think that we can just start from nowhere and make up beliefs and values for ourselves.

'Historical faith', learned from our culture, leads to our most basic moral values, and it is clear to modern readers that Kant was strongly influenced by his early Lutheran training and by his parent's faith, even though he reacted against it in many ways. Even his reactions were reactions to a broadly Lutheran view of religion, and he does not seriously consider non-Christian religions at all.

What he is opposed to is an unquestioning acceptance of moral views we have received from others or from the Bible. In his case, he had come to

---

[7] Kant (1960b), p. 40.   [8] Kant (1959), Second Section, p. 46.   [9] Kant (1960b), p. 102.

question many of the moral principles that can be found in the Bible (like killing the children of one's enemies), and he thought he had found an independent method for deciding on moral truths. This method led him to accept some absolute moral truths, like 'It is never right, in any circumstances, to tell a lie', or 'Murder must always be met by capital punishment', which do not seem so clear to many of us. Many philosophers would not agree that the Categorical Imperative is the one and only supreme principle of morality, or that it leads to the absolutist conclusions that he thinks it does. But when we reflect on the principle, we are learning something from a historical figure, Immanuel Kant, that is certainly morally relevant.

We do need to learn from the past, though we should not be fixedly bound to it. 'Thinking for oneself' in morality, as in religion, is not making beliefs up from nothing. It is learning from the past and learning how to discern what is of lasting value and what is due to lack of vision or imagination. It is learning practical wisdom, which requires the exercise of empathetic imagination and a search for consistency and impartiality in one's moral and religious beliefs. That is very difficult and requires reflection and persistence.

One should learn to think empathetically, imaginatively, and impartially. It is when learned moral beliefs seem to be less than sympathetic to the experiences of others, show less ability to imagine what it is like to be them, and make us less able to adopt a distanced and equitable attitude towards others, that we may wish to amend those learned beliefs. For instance, in thinking about the moral treatment of animals, we should try to imagine what their existence is like, and what pains they may feel, and then we may find that some acts of cruelty to animals are immoral, even if they are commonplace among humans and in our traditions, whether religious or secular.

Moral thinking is a skill, more developed in some than in others. There are moral leaders, like Gandhi or Martin Luther King, who lead us to see things we have not seen for ourselves. They become authorities for us, because they point out to us aspects of existence we had overlooked. Most ironically, Kant himself was a moral teacher when he stressed that we should respect persons for their own sake, just because they were thinking and responsible agents, and not treat persons just as means to an end. We may not have thought of that, or put it like that, but, when we read it, it seems a deepening of moral insight, and we may adopt it as our own, and reflect on what it means for our own conduct.

Is this 'thinking for ourselves'? That is surely too simple a view. When a Christian reads the words of Jesus, 'Love your enemies', that may come as a moral revelation, as a new moral possibility. We have to see how we can apply it in our own lives, but we may see that it has authority because it evokes a new moral insight. What the Enlightenment principle should be is something like, 'Do not just unthinkingly accept tradition even when it seems unimaginative or hurtful or prejudiced in favour of one group over all others'. The Enlightenment was a rebellion against unjust and tyrannical practices in churches and states. But any encouragement that everyone should just decide for themselves what is morally right or wrong, without reference to moral leaders of past and present, who are often, though not always, religious leaders too, is apt to be disastrous. We need reflective, imaginative, compassionate, and impartial moral thought, and that means listening to the moral teachers of the past and re-imagining their insights in the changed circumstances of the present.

In seeking for 'authorities' in morality and religion, we would be looking for people with wisdom, wide and deeply engaged experience, and outstanding moral or mental achievement. We will have to use judgement in this, but some people with such qualities will probably attract us. In religion, it might be said that the Chinese traditions (like Confucianism and Taoism) look for sages, the Indian traditions (like Buddhism and *Vedanta*) look for ascetics who have intense personal experiences, and the Abrahamic traditions (Judaism, Christianity, and Islam) look for prophets with moral insight. Naturally things do not divide up quite as neatly as that, since every tradition contains these strains of wisdom, experience, and moral insight to some extent and in some way.

Applied to religious texts like the Bible, this implies that one should read the words of moral teachers like the prophets and Jesus and their disciples, reflect on them, learn from the best of them, and seek to apply old rules in new situations. We should not just accept whatever they say, usually taken out of context, as though we no longer had to think for ourselves at all. Perhaps the lesson of the Enlightenment is that we need moral guidance, but no guidance is unchallengeable and inerrant. It is not that there is something called reason which can solve all our problems. It is that we should seek to discern the best in our traditions, and discern the best in other traditions too, and apply their principles in ways conducive to what Kant himself says is the ultimate end of morality, 'One's own perfection and the happiness of others',[10] which, when universally applied, entails universal happiness and human flourishing.

---

[10] Kant (1964), Introduction, Section 4, p. 44.

17

The Extension of Moral Concern

*K*ANT IS A RATIONALIST IN MORALITY TO THE EXTENT THAT HE thinks there is just one absolute rational principle, the application of which will reveal what is morally good or right. He did not think, however, that people had to work out the applications of the Categorical Imperative just by the rigorous use of reason. He was impressed by Rousseau, and thought that even unreflective people had an intuitive knowledge of right and wrong. The Categorical Imperative made it clear that there was a rational basis for such intuitive claims to moral knowledge. But Kant always continued to hold the view he expressed in his early work, *Observations on the Feeling of the Beautiful and the Sublime*, that morality is founded on the 'feeling of the beauty and dignity of human nature'.[1] He pencilled into a copy of the *Observations* the note: 'There was a time when I despised the masses ... Rousseau has set me right ... I learn to honour men'.[2]

Kant was not the emotionless dry rationalist that he is often depicted as being. The Categorical Imperative is meant to apply to all humans without exception, and the moral law fills the mind with awe and respect. Kantian ethics, in principle, treat all human beings with equal respect and concern for their welfare, and feelings are important to the moral life, even though Kant argues that they cannot be the foundation of acceptable moral principles. He pleaded for creative and imaginative thought in morality, in opposition to those who insisted on conformity to ancient laws and traditions. Thus, it is in accord with his basic concerns to point to developments in moral thinking such as those that have become much more important in the modern world.[3]

---

[1] Kant (1960a). [2] Quoted in Schilpp (1960), p. 48.
[3] For a fuller account of Kant's ethical views, see Ward (1972).

These developments largely relate to the extension of moral concern to a wider range of objects. Those who think morality is founded upon reason may tend (and David Hume did tend) to view 'the masses' as irrational and primitive beings whose views should not be taken into account. Yet, Kant's support of moral principles as applying to all humans should certainly entail the equal moral consideration of all classes, races, nations, and genders. Yet it has taken decades of passionate debate to establish that women should be included in the human moral community as free self-determining and fully participating agents. It cannot be said that Kant himself saw the full implications of applying his basic moral principle consistently.

Since the early twentieth-century, the voices of women have been heard ever more clearly, and they have made a difference to moral and religious debate. Writers like Sallie McFague and Mary Daly have pointed out that there has been a massive gender bias against women in religion and in moral thinking. Mary Daly moved from a relatively reconciliatory attempt to reform Christian theology in her early book, *Beyond God the Father*,[4] to a view that the Roman Catholic Church was irredeemably patriarchal, and virtually gave up her interest in religion. Sallie McFague, in *Models of God*,[5] adopted a rather different approach and tried to provide a feminist reading of Christian systematic theology. She called for a 'new sensibility', which would be ecological and evolutionary, rather than regarding human beings (and in particular males) as 'the summit of creation', and the truth as having been given once for all at some moment in the past. She commended less patriarchal metaphors for God, seeing the divine as mother, lover, and friend. And she suggested that the world (the whole universe) should be seen as 'the body of God' – 'What we can know of God's transcendence is neither above nor beneath but in and through the world'.[6]

This image is appealing to those who feel uncomfortable with dualistic world-views, views that sharply divide spirit from matter, God from the world, and often make God and spirit superior in value to the world and the body. God and spirit, taken in themselves, are of greater value than the world and body, taken in themselves, but perhaps they should not be taken in themselves. The world and the body are vehicles, expressions, or embodiments, of God and spirit. Without the world, it might be said, God would not be all that God is. Without God, the world would not rightly be seen as what it truly is, the appearance of a spiritual dimension of being.

---

[4] Daly (1973).   [5] McFague (1987).   [6] McFague (1987), p. 184.

Christianity, as a religion of divine embodiment, may seem particularly suited to such an approach. But Christians say the incarnation was in a man, and that has been taken to privilege males as the only humans who can actually stand in the place of Christ (in the Eucharist, for example). Also, largely because of the dependence of Western ideas of God upon Aristotle, Christian theologians have said that the world makes no difference to God, who is impassable.

The thought that the world is the body of God – also powerfully commended by Grace Jantzen[7] – suggests a greater reverence for the world as an expression of the divine, and a greater active embodiment of God in the events and beings of the whole world. It suggests an extension of the range of human moral concern to the whole world. No longer can it be said, as Aquinas wrote, that 'the whole of material nature exists for man'.[8] In McFague's 'ecofeminism', men and women exist in order to guard and tend the earth, as the second creation account in Genesis puts it.[9] Plants, trees, and animals have their own lives and beauty, and they, along with humans, are parts of the divine body, not to be used merely as means to satisfy human desires.

This expansion of moral concern is taken to its fullest extent by movements in 'deep ecology', first formulated by the Norwegian philosopher Arne Naess.[10] Some deep ecologists blame Christianity for reducing nature to a mere means which can be used in any way that humans desire. This seems rather unfair, since the doctrine of creation implies that God cares for the world that God has made, and the doctrine of incarnation implies that God can be truly embodied in the world. But Christianity has also limited moral concern to humans – sometimes especially male humans – as though the rest of the world has little or no intrinsic goodness and beauty. However that may be, there is clearly a possibility that religions which seek to find a spiritual dimension in reality may find it in and through many sorts of beings in the natural world. This should give the natural world a value that does not just depend on subjective human feelings, and that should challenge humans to become the priests of being rather than the consumers of being. Ecofeminist thought is a form of moral thinking that has the power to change human ways of looking at the world and at other and different sentient lives.

[7] Jantzen (1984).   [8] Aquinas (1993), section 148.
[9] 'The Lord God took the man and put him in the garden of Eden to till it and keep it' (Genesis 2, 15).
[10] For a fuller account of deep ecology, see *The Christian Idea of God*, Ward (2017), ch. 12.

Feminist writings vary between very radical calls to replace 'masculinist' thoughts with 'feminist' ones in new ways of organising society, and more accommodating attempts to eliminate gender bias within the framework of existing institutions. They have established the point that most religions have been and often still are patriarchal, and that both religions and moral systems need to develop behaviour and language in ways that avoid privileging one gender (or class or race) over others. Theologians like Daphne Hampson find themselves unable any longer to associate with a Christianity which, in their view, regards God as male, women as ineligible for religious or moral leadership, and divine omnipotence as an exercise of overwhelming and all-determining power.[11] She has moved to a view of God as 'a dimension of reality', but a dimension which is 'a power for healing', making for 'the fulness of our potentialities'.[12] A rather similar approach to God as not an independent transcendent and supernatural being, but a spiritual dimension of an expansively 'natural' world, is taken by the philosopher Fiona Ellis.[13] It is rather unclear to what extent such views might be helpful to a revised Christian spirituality, or whether, as Dr. Hampson thinks, they must move us beyond traditional religious views altogether.

Other feminist writers, like Rosemary Radford Ruether[14] and Elisabeth Schussler-Fiorenza,[15] would wish to reform religious practices that reinforce the domination of women (and of nature) by men, and that associate the good and the spiritual with maleness, while evil, temptation, and the body are associated with femaleness. Writers like Sarah Coakley, who is also an Episcopal priest, find it possible to be both feminist and reasonably orthodox. But they argue that Christian commitment entails active opposition to patriarchy, to global injustice, and to instrumentalist views of nature. Religion, Dr. Coakley insists, should be fully engaged with the reformation of society, not just with hopes for a better afterlife.[16]

In moral thinking, too, the assignment of domestic and familial duties to women, while only men are allowed to engage in politics and business and intellectual pursuits, express principles which it is hard, if not impossible, to justify rationally. As Pamela Anderson has pointed out,[17] Kantian principles ought to call for full moral equality between social classes and different genders, but they have often not been seen in that way, not even by Kant himself. Some regard Kantian morality as 'rationalist', as appealing to an

---

[11] Hampson (2002).   [12] Hampson (2002), p. 250.   [13] Ellis (2014).   [14] Ruether (1993).
[15] Schussler-Fiorenza (1983).
[16] Sarah Coakley is writing a multi-volume systematic theology; the first volume is: Coakley (2013).
[17] Anderson and Bell (2010).

allegedly neutral reason which smooths out human diversity and reduces everything to a matter of obedience to a set of abstract and absolute principles which ignore the complexities of human feeling and desire.

It is certainly true that Kant has not said the last word about morality. He probably did have an over-confident view of what 'Reason' might legislate, and an insufficient appreciation for the diversity and historical contextualisation of human feelings and beliefs. Feminist critiques of this sort of approach to morality re-inforce the point that truly to include many human perspectives in moral and religious debate will lead to profound changes in moral outlook. They do not, however, generally entail that morality can or should be totally disentangled from religion. They rather suggest that religious views need to develop concurrently with moral views, whether, as with Daphne Hampson and Iris Murdoch,[18] this leads to the rejection of traditional views or, as with Sallie McFague and Marjorie Suchocki,[19] they call for a revisionary development of ancient religious traditions.

This body of literature, expressed in the writings of feminists, liberation theologians, and deep ecologists, illustrates new streams of moral thinking that arise when Kant's call to 'think for oneself' is heeded, and qualified by close attention both to ancient wisdom and to new social and physical conditions. For the foreseeable future, conservative beliefs that resist such new approaches will continue to exist, both in secular and in religious environments. Both secular and religious morality have been changed by these developments, but neither has succeeded in establishing one universally agreed view.

---

[18] Murdoch (1970).   [19] Suchocki (1982).

Morality and Religion

$\mathcal{I}$T MAY BE ASKED, THEN, WHAT DIFFERENCE RELIGIOUS BELIEFS make to moral attitudes. To this, Kant has given such a surprising answer that many commentators ignore it as an aberration, perhaps, it has even been suggested, to pacify the worries of his manservant Lampe.

In *Religion within the Limits of Reason Alone*, Kant outlines what he thinks are the necessary conditions of the possibility of a categorical and imperative morality. The main one is that, in his view, Reason is of itself practical and legislative, with absolute moral authority. As such, it is not just a human mental faculty. It is built into reality, and Reason is supreme over the physical, sense-based realm of appearances. In the posthumous writings of Kant, the 'Opus Postumum', he says, 'The proposition: there is a God, says nothing more than: there is in the human, morally self-determining reason a highest principle which determines itself, and finds itself compelled unremittingly to act in accordance with such a principle'.[1] As always in philosophy, the 'nothing more' is unduly excessive. But the important point is that reason is self-determining, in accordance with a necessary principle of action, which aims, Kant says, at the two supreme goals of universal happiness and fulfilment (which he calls the '*summum bonum*').

Speaking of God is speaking of this supremely self-determining practical principle, which is not the principle that every person can make their own subjective choice of what to do. On the contrary, Reason is the same in all humans, and, more than that, it is the reality which underlies the whole world of appearance. Kant views God as like a supreme reality which expresses itself as practical reason, embodied in human beings in the world of appearances. God is not a person, or a personal being who can be an

---

[1] Kant (1920), p. 146.

object of experience or encounter. God is practical reason itself, with which humans are identical when they act morally, but which appears as categorically demanding to the egoistic and individual will. When humans have reverence for the moral law, they are showing reverence not just to some abstract humanly generated rule, but to a creative and necessary active principle of being, which seeks to realise itself in the physical world of desires and inclinations, and with which humans in their deepest reality are identical.

As an Idealist, Kant sees the whole of experienced reality as the self-expression of Absolute Practical Reason, and human beings as destined to be channels of that self-expression. One can see with hindsight that the roots of Hegelian Idealism are already present here. Kant's view is certainly a grand metaphysics. He did not, as some mistakenly think, destroy all metaphysics. On the contrary, he saw himself as laying the ground for all future metaphysics. He did, however, subordinate theoretical cognition of or direct experience of reality to its practical expression in action, to a moral life aimed at happiness, in accordance with virtue (virtue being the realisation of all distinctively human excellences).

It is unfortunately obvious that humans are not in fact channels of pure practical Reason. They have a natural propensity to evil, which corrupts all their actions. Indeed, the actions of conventionally moral persons which are lawfully good, may still be totally evil, if 'the incentives of sensuous nature' predominate over the purely moral motive – as they almost always do! Kant does believe in 'Original Sin', which he calls 'Radical evil', and he sees the Biblical story of the Fall as an allegory for the innate evil of humanity.

The traditional Christian response to acceptance of the absolute demands of morality and the incapacity of humans to meet those demands is to appeal to some form of divine atonement and forgiveness. This is where Kant really gets into trouble. He thinks that the attainment of the moral goal must be possible – 'The impossibility of the highest good must prove the falsity of the moral law also'.[2] It is not possible by human striving, due to human radical evil. So, it must be by divine grace, and yet Kant regards the idea of grace as a 'completely empty notion' which undermines moral striving, and the idea of Jesus' atoning sacrifice on the cross as a mere historical fact which can have no moral value to us.

His proposal is that, in the noumenal world (of things-in-themselves), humans not only fall into radical evil, they also at the same time undergo

---

[2] Kant (1956), p. 118.

a conversion, 'a new creation', which is a reconciliation to God (the moral demand). This conversion appears in time as an infinite moral progress, 'a whole conformable to moral law',[3] in which endless progress is seen as an actual conformity to moral law. In our lives, the punishments due to the 'old man', the radically evil one, are visited on the 'new man', the repentant moral seeker, in the form of the many ills of life. This can be seen as a sort of atoning sacrifice, not of Jesus, but of the new man for the sake of the old man in each of us.

I do not think that this resort to a noumenal fall and conversion has proved convincing to many people. It is the exclusion of any possible experience of God or of the power of grace that leads to many of the paradoxes of Kant's view of religion. He is, to use Bultmann's term, taking a Christian view of a categorical divine command, human disobedience to it, followed by redemption and the attainment of a state of final beatitude, and de-mythologising it. What he rejects is worship of God, which he regards just as favour-currying; experience of grace, which is superstitious fanaticism; and prayers for divine assistance, which encourage servility and impotence. All the concepts of the Christian faith – like a personal God and a personal Devil, Heaven and Hell, Doomsday and Jesus' resurrection – must be denuded of their factual or historical referents and be interpreted as symbols whose only use is to determine the will to moral action.

This may seem like a reduction of all objective claims to a personal and subjective pragmatism. Yet, Kant does believe in a rational ground of the universe, which sets a moral goal for human life and exerts a necessary and categorical moral demand upon humans. This rational ground (the 'noumenal' reality, a Kantian expression which significantly derives from the Greek '*nous*', mind, or reason) is beyond space and time, eternal, present as the same underlying reality in every finite rational will, expressing itself in and through human moral actions. He believes in human moral freedom to choose good or evil. He believes that humans are radically corrupted, and yet obligated to an endless progress to holiness. He believes that there must, therefore, be some 'inscrutable power' which enables us to reach our final goal. And he believes that there is, beyond this space and time, a final moral goal of infinite worth. This is without doubt a metaphysical creed, even if it is founded on what Kant calls faith.

This could form a creed for a 'moral church' of the future, 'a voluntary, universal and enduring union of hearts'.[4] Every ecclesiastical faith, founded

---

[3] Kant (1956), p. 127.   [4] Kant (1960b), p. 93.

on some historical revelation, must fade away. Present churches may be acceptable if they stress the moral element, admit the symbolic character of most religious concepts, and prepare people for the coming ethical commonwealth. As dogmas wither away, they leave only 'a feeling of the insufficiency of the contingent for realising the moral destination of man's existence'. The symbols of religion are mysterious and often contradictory pictures to express such a feeling, and to reinforce the central importance of the moral life.

Kant proposes a future for religion, and in principle his proposal could be applied to all existing religions if they were revised in somewhat the same way in which he has revised Christianity. Since devotion and experience form such an important part of religions, there seems little hope that Kant's 'moral church' could become a universal religion for the future. It must be admitted that it almost entirely lacks emotional appeal, and that its appeal to Reason as a virtually supernatural power has not been well received. The religion of Reason that was instituted in France after the Revolution quickly died out, and Kant's total rejection of any possibility of conscious relationship to a spiritual power seems impractical. Even Confucianism, which in some ways is rather like the Kantian ideal of commitment to an objective moral standard without worship of a personal God – Confucius said 'Heaven is silent' – has temples and sacrifices to Heaven and to ancestors. Regrettably, perhaps, no one has suggested having sacrifices to Kant or to the Categorical Imperative, though there have been attempts in Britain to establish 'atheistic' services with hymns. It may be salutary and valuable to be sceptical of the power of human reason to probe the ultimate mysteries of being, to affirm that a morality of respect for all persons without exception is more important than an acceptance of intellectual or contestable historical claims, and to encourage informed critical enquiry in religion as in other areas of belief. But for most religiously inclined people, some place must be found for the joys and solaces of religious experience.

19

Friedrich Schleiermacher

*I*MMANUEL KANT MAY NOT HAVE REDUCED RELIGION TO A HUMANISTIC morality, as some have thought, but he did deny the importance of devotion to and experience of any spiritual reality. Reverence for the moral law may be a sort of spiritual experience, but it does seem a rather austere one. And it is obvious that Kant confined his attention to the Christian faith, rather than dealing with religion as a universal human phenomenon. It was left to Friedrich Schleiermacher to consider religion as a distinctive area of human experience, to find a more central place for devotion and experience in religion, and to try to account for the diversity of religious traditions in the world.

Schleiermacher, in his 'Speeches on Religion', proposes that religion is not founded on intellectual belief in doctrines, or on the acceptance of specific moral principles. Religion is not primarily an assent to conceptual truths, and not an assent to moral principles. 'Religion's essence is neither thinking nor acting, but intuition (*Anschauung*) and feeling (*Gefuhl*)'.[1] By 'intuition', Schleiermacher means an immediate apprehension of a non-conceptual nature, like the immediate apprehension of visual perceptions before concepts have been applied to them, for which Kant uses the same term. By 'feeling' he intends to refer to the subjective affective tone which such apprehension evokes. He states that intuition and feeling are originally inseparable, though they can be separated by subsequent analysis.

There is an obvious problem with this suggestion. If this is meant to be a form of non-conceptual apprehension, how can anyone possibly say what the object apprehended is? To say anything is necessarily to use a concept, so, while one might be sympathetic to the thought that one can apprehend

---

[1] Schleiermacher (1988), p. 102.

94

something without being aware of what it is, hesitations arise if an attempt is then made to say what it is.

Schleiermacher does, however, use a range of concepts to describe the object of religious intuition. 'We intuit the universe' he says.[2] Other expressions he uses are 'the infinite nature of totality', 'the sensibility and taste for the infinite',[3] and 'to see the infinite'. It seems that this apprehension is not of particular things, but of the infinite, the universe as a whole or totality, or (to anticipate what he says in *The Christian Faith*) the 'absolutely independent'. These expressions are very vague, but they are still concepts. How could anyone possibly know that they had apprehended the universe as an infinite whole? Sometimes he speaks of 'the universe', and sometimes of 'the all-creating world-spirit' – a concept he was to develop in the *Glaubenslehre* (translated into English as *The Christian Faith*) as the 'absolutely independent'. The former seems to refer to the universe of space-time itself, while the latter speaks of something beyond, but possibly including the space-time universe. This reflects a similar ambiguity to the philosopher Spinoza, by whom Schleiermacher was influenced. For Spinoza, God and Nature can be equivalent terms, but on the other hand God has infinite attributes, of which space and time are presumably only two. When Schleiermacher comes to describe God in greater detail, in the *Glaubenslehre*, he writes, 'The feeling of absolute dependence ... is not to be explained as an awareness of the world's existence, but only as an awareness of the existence of God'.[4]

Schleiermacher also revised the second Speech, from which most of these expressions are taken, quite thoroughly in the 1806 and 1821 editions, especially his use of the word 'intuition' and the description of its object as 'the universe'. He tended just to speak of 'feeling' rather than intuition, though he did not drop the term intuition altogether. He proposed a new definition of religion as 'immediate perception (or consciousness) of the universal existence of all finite things, in and through the Infinite, and of all temporal things in and through the Eternal'. Some, not unreasonably, think that this was to protect himself against charges of pantheism (reverence just for the universe as it might appear to a secular mind), and also to prepare the way for the much more openly Christian views that he was to affirm in the *Glaubenslehre*. In the 1799 original he spoke of God as not necessary to religion – 'one religion without God can be better than another with God'[5] – whereas in 1821 he speaks of 'immediate consciousness of the deity', and also speaks more positively about the prospects of immortality.

---

[2] Schleiermacher (1988), p. 102.   [3] Schleiermacher (1988), p. 103.
[4] Schleiermacher (1989), p. 132.   [5] Schleiermacher (1989), p. 137.

What he has in mind is clarified a little in the 'Speeches', when he says that the basic religious feeling is, in a phrase reminiscent of Blake, 'to be one with the infinite in the midst of the finite and to be eternal in a moment, that is the immortality of religion'.[6] Here, it seems that the infinite and eternal is seen in and through things that are finite and temporal. Instead of thinking of an apprehension of a separate reality, the infinite, we can think of finite things, which we apprehend as mediating a sense of the infinite, the whole, the independent, the eternal. The 'sensibility and taste for the infinite' is a capacity to sense the finite as a 'representation of the infinite'.[7] This is an immediate apprehension of something that finite things can express or represent, but that lies beyond our normal conceptual capacities. There is a vague sense of unlimitedness, of unity, of wholeness, of an all-circumscribing and all-embracing reality beyond all finitude and limitation. This is not totally non-conceptual, but the concepts we use are felt to be inadequate attempts to depict something which escapes precise conceptual definition, yet which is a greater reality beyond that of which we can speak plainly. We are not apprehending the universe as an infinite whole, as though this was a definite acquaintance with something precisely describable as such. We are rather seeing finite things as pointing beyond themselves towards an underlying self-existent and unbounded reality from which they are felt to spring and which they express.

In the *Glaubenslehre*, Schleiermacher gets much more definite about this unbounded reality. He clearly states that 'the feeling of absolute dependence is the consciousness of God'.[8] He then says quite a lot about God, though he claims that 'All the divine attributes to be dealt with in Christian Dogmatics ... are only meant to explain the feeling of absolute dependence'.[9] God is eternal, having no temporal attributes at all. God is omnipresent, which he interprets as possessing spaceless causality, and thus being equally present to (or absent from) every place. God is omnipotent, in that 'everything for which there is causality in God happens and becomes real'.[10] There is no potential in God, and it is not possible for God to do anything that God does not do. Everything that there is, both evil and good, is willed by God, and 'God thinks of nothing else ... save what he actually produces'.[11] God is omniscient, meaning that there is no receptive knowledge in God, and no distinction between God's

---

[6] Schleiermacher (1988), p. 140.   [7] Schleiermacher (1988), p. 105.
[8] Schleiermacher (1989), p. 25.   [9] Schleiermacher (1989), p. 198.
[10] Schleiermacher (1989), p. 211.   [11] Schleiermacher (1989), p. 225.

thoughts and God's actions. In fact, 'omnipotence and omniscience are one and the same'.[12]

This interpretation of the divine attributes is, of course, extremely controversial. The list of attributes is similar to what one finds in, for example, Thomas Aquinas.[13] Schleiermacher may well claim that he simply gives a more consistent interpretation of these attributes. It does seem to follow from God's complete changelessness that God cannot think of what to do *before* God does it. If God is necessary and simple, then whatever God does must be done necessarily, and God could not do anything other than God does. God must create the universe in one non-temporal act, so that God determines everything to be what it is, and cannot wait to respond to what happens in the universe before deciding what to do next.

But it may seem presumptuous to say that God actually does everything that God could possibly do, and that there is nothing God thinks of that God does not actually do. These assertions are not part of traditional Christian doctrines of God, for the traditional view is that God creates a contingent universe, no universe had to exist, and God could have created a different one if God had chosen to do so. Again, however, one could argue that a necessary God could not have done anything different, and that there cannot be any arbitrary (contingent) actions in a necessary God.

This is not the place to debate these abstruse matters. The point is that they are abstruse and require much argumentation and reflection. They can hardly be implicit in a simple feeling of absolute dependence, which Schleiermacher thinks is present and innate in every human person. The obvious implication is that Schleiermacher's commitment to a more explicitly Christian idea of divine reality was much clearer in the *Glaubenslehre*, which was after all meant to be a Dogmatics of Protestant Christianity. He does not deny that there could be other interpretations of a general view that God is 'the Original Being and the Absolute Good'.[14] He does not deny that non-theistic religious views exist, and he could ascribe to them the vaguer view of the 'Speeches', that the Infinite – that which is not determined by anything other than itself[15] – can be discerned in and through many diverse finite forms of being. It does seem as though he thinks Christian monotheism is the correct or most adequate interpretation of such feelings of 'piety', which are the core of all religion. He does recognise that non-Christians would not agree, and this is a problem for his view that there is one common feeling underlying all authentic religions. Is there really one clearly most

[12] Schleiermacher (1989), p. 221.   [13] Aquinas (1967).   [14] Schleiermacher (1989), p. 194.
[15] Schleiermacher (1989), p. 231.

adequate interpretation of a universal human feeling, which Christians happen to hit upon?

Some might prefer to stay with Schleiermacher's earlier and vaguer definition of 'a sense and taste for the infinite', and speak of something like a 'sense of transcendence' as 'the piety which forms the basis of all ecclesiastical communions'.[16] This would construe an 'intuition of the universe' as rather like the twentieth-century English philosopher Ian Ramsey's concept of a 'disclosure-situation', in which we see 'the empirical and more'.[17] That 'more' is felt to be of a greater reality (not transient and dependent) and of greater value (worth existing just for its own sake), but it cannot be further pinned down in any literal description. For Ramsey, that evokes 'commitment', which is perhaps Schleiermacher's 'feeling', the response of the apprehending subject, which is one of awe and humility and dependence.

If one grounds religion in such 'apprehensions of transcendence', it may not be possible to exclude anything finite from having the capacity to evoke such apprehensions. Indeed, Schleiermacher says, 'everything that can be is for it [religion] a true indispensable image of the infinite'.[18] All finite things can become symbols of infinity, images of transcendent reality. He writes: 'Let the universe be intuited and worshipped in all ways'.[19]

In his fifth speech, 'On the Religions', Schleiermacher says that he regards the plurality of religions as 'something necessary and unavoidable'.[20] 'Religion', he says, 'is infinite and immeasurable'.[21] But it appears in 'an infinite number of finite and specific forms', each of which exhibits a determinate concept, and each of which the infinite necessarily had to assume.

'Natural religion', divested of all particularity, is not what he has in mind. He regards natural religion as 'an indefinite, insufficient and paltry idea'.[22] It regards religion as a matter of very general intellectual beliefs, and this is not the heart of true religion. He is wholly opposed to distinguishing or identifying religions by reference to their doctrinal beliefs. This is much too intellectualist for him. Rather he thinks that each religion is a 'particular individual entity',[23] a sort of developing organic unity. It may contain many changing strands of belief, interpreted in many different ways. Indeed, he thinks that every religion must contain each form of 'the basic intuition of the infinite in the finite'. But one such intuition becomes basic or central for each religion, and all other beliefs are interpreted with reference to it.

---

[16] Schleiermacher (1989), p. 5.   [17] Ramsey (1957).   [18] Schleiermacher (1988), p. 109.
[19] Schleiermacher (1988), p. 222.   [20] Schleiermacher (1988), p. 190.
[21] Schleiermacher (1988), p. 192.   [22] Schleiermacher (1988), p. 195.
[23] Schleiermacher (1988), p. 191.

That basic intuition can be traced back to a founder or founders who had an original form of intuition of the infinite in the finite. Thus, Judaism, he thinks, has a central intuition of 'universal immediate retribution',[24] and Christianity has a central intuition of 'corruption and redemption, enmity and mediation'.[25] He does not mention Islam, but presumably its central intuition is of unity (*tahwid*). There is an unending multitude of determinate forms, each of which is established by relating all religious experiences and ideas to one distinctive 'central intuition'.[26] This seems a radically pluralist view of religions, seeing them all as necessary and good, especially since he writes, 'new messengers of God are becoming necessary',[27] and that Christianity should rejoice to see new religions constantly arising.

As has been noted, this view is not consistently held by Schleiermacher. Sometimes he says that each religious form is necessary, and sometimes he says that some forms are degenerate or dead or less sublime. Sometimes he inveighs against 'natural religion', or the attempt to find a common core of belief in religions. Yet, he does not hesitate to say that all religions intuit the infinite in the finite, and that such 'feelings' or 'intuitions' are the core of religion, presumably of all religions. Probably one needs not to be quite so inclusive of every possible type of religion. Things like Aztec human sacrifice or militant religious violence are unfortunately not uncommon in religions, and they cannot all be called good or life-enhancing. There must be some criteria of what is acceptable in religion, and Schleiermacher did take note of that, though he did not manage to integrate the view that the more religions the better with the view that some religions are superior to others, despite holding both views, perhaps at different times.

He regards Christianity as religion 'raised to a higher power',[28] so he certainly does not regard all religions and their symbols of infinity as on a par. He notoriously said that Judaism was a dead and 'fetishistic' religion, and that Christianity is 'more sublime, more worthy of adult humanity'.[29] In *The Christian Faith*, he is much clearer that the monotheistic religions are superior to other sorts of religion, that Christianity is superior to the other monotheistic faiths, and even that Christianity is destined to become the universal religion. The other two monotheistic faiths that he recognises are Judaism, which he thinks has been superseded by Christianity, and Islam, which he regards as inhibited by its allegedly fatalistic and unduly sensuous outlook, and its lack of a 'teleology', that is, the aim of realising the kingdom

---

[24] Schleiermacher (1988), p. 212.   [25] Schleiermacher (1988), p. 213.
[26] Schleiermacher (1988), p. 200.   [27] Schleiermacher (1988), p. 22.
[28] Schleiermacher (1988), p. 214.   [29] Schleiermacher (1988), p. 213.

of God on earth.[30] These assessments no longer seem realistic in the contemporary world, but the 'Christian Faith' is explicitly devoted to one specifically Protestant version of Christianity at one specific time in history, so these opinions are not totally surprising. But they hardly seem compatible with welcoming new forms of religion as necessary expressions of the Infinite, with their own basic intuitions and ways of organising religious life around them.

It is also intriguing that he is a Christian ecumenist – he deplores the fact that there are many Christian churches and thinks they should all unite around their basic intuition, founded on Christ. Yet he is a religious pluralist, welcoming what seems to be an infinity of basic intuitions. One problem here is that different Christian churches could well be said to have different basic intuitions. Is the sacramentalism of Catholic churches the same as the primacy of the Word in Protestant churches? And why should not many different Churches have different ways of interpreting the originative teaching of Jesus, ranging from literalist views of severe Divine judgement and strict predestination to highly metaphorical views of a new loving community and libertarian human freedom?

If one is looking for a general idea of religion, as Schleiermacher was, perhaps it lies in positing a spiritual dimension to reality, which is thought by some to have been accessed by a privileged teacher or tradition of teachers, and which has developed rituals for accessing its power, in order to live a morally good and fulfilling life and achieve or work towards some sort of ideal goal. It seems that almost every possible variation of this general schema has been tried in history, some of which have not survived. Those which have survived have tended to privilege their own founders or teachers as inerrant and absolutely unique, to regard their own rituals as uniquely efficacious, to see their own moral rules as binding on everyone, and to see their ideas of ultimate reality and the goal which lies in conscious relation to it as absolutely and unchangeably true.

In such a situation, it may seem more probable to infer that the founding teachers have not been inerrant, though they have had exceptional insights into the nature of Spirit (critical analysis of Scriptural texts may suggest this). There may be, in different religions, various rituals and practices, all of which are intended to promote in various ways personal access to Spirit. The original moral rules often laid down in the founding texts of religions may need to adapt to changing circumstances (as Kant suggests, the goals of

---

[30] Schleiermacher (1989), p. 38.

happiness and fulfilment are basic to morality). One might surmise that all religions only have provisional and inadequate ideas of Ultimate Reality, so that fuller truth can and must yet be pursued (Schleiermacher's stress on the primacy of non-conceptual intuition suggests this). One might learn from many religious teachers but accept none of them as a supreme teacher. One might take insights from many, but construct one's own spiritual view, as well as one can. It is highly unlikely, maybe impossible and probably stupid, to be influenced by no religious tradition. It will be better to have knowledge of a range of traditions if one's own views are to be as comprehensive as possible. One can stand in a general tradition, but hold to many diverse beliefs or interpretations of one's own, whether explicitly drawn from other sources or not (thus, Bultmann stood firmly in the Christian tradition, but used concepts created by the non-religious Heidegger to interpret that tradition).[31] It is likely that one will regard some leading teachers as authoritative guides, though one knows that they are not infallible, and that they may sometimes be wrong.

This is a form of pluralism, but it is a sort of open and provisional and revisionist pluralism, which is not committed to saying that 'all religions are more or less equally true', or that one religion exists at a higher level than all others. It is saying that there is fuller truth yet to be found in every tradition, that there may be much to learn from others, and that revisions to one's own beliefs are to be expected. One might call this 'open belonging', the spiritual practices of which are mainly, though not exclusively, centred in one tradition, and which is open to developments in its own form of understanding, as history progresses.

Such a view would be consistent with one major strand in Schleiermacher's ground-breaking consideration of 'religion' as a global phenomenon. That strand stands in contrast with his writings as a Christian dogmatician, when he clearly writes of Christianity, in its Protestant form, as existing on a higher level than other religious forms. This illustrates a tension that exists between wishing to consider religious phenomena as different species of a basically similar spiritual search and feeling a commitment to one particular religious faith. That tension continues to exist, and in an even stronger form, in a world in which many diverse religious traditions have the ability to understand each other more fully and need to find some positive and creative way of co-existing.

There is a need to shape a philosophical view of religion which might address this tension. Kant had stressed the new emphasis on the autonomy

---

[31] Bultmann (1960).

of human reason and morality that the Enlightenment had evoked. He saw that this required some revision of the ideas of authority and revelation that were commonplace in his day, and he proposed an understanding of religion as providing a background metaphysical context for a firm commitment to a rational and self-legislated morality. But he restricted his written comments to the Christian faith. Schleiermacher sought a broader view of religion which might include more than just the Christian tradition. He found the distinctiveness of religious belief in a specific sort of apprehension of a spiritual dimension, a 'feeling for the infinite', an experience of transcendence. It is in such experiences, as they occur in especially sensitive human lives, that revelation ultimately consists. Thus, Jesus is said to have been wholly 'God-conscious', and to have passed on something of this consciousness to his disciples. But Schleiermacher's treatment left the dimension of doctrinal truth virtually untouched, except insofar as he held truths to be implicit in certain forms of human consciousness.

Hegel, a third major German Protestant writer on religion, wanted to put the issue of truth at the forefront of any enquiry into the nature of religion.[32] Hegel's work exhibits another major change in human thought in recent centuries. That is the change from a basically static view of human existence, in which perfection is looked for, if at all, in the past, and change is often seen as an imperfection and degeneration. Hegel created a philosophical system in which change and progress is good, and an evolutionary and teleological view of human history places perfection in the future, to be brought about through struggle and genuinely new creative effort.

[32] Hegel (1985).

20

G. W. Friedrich Hegel

*I*N COMPLETE CONTRAST TO HIS CONTEMPORARY SCHLEIERMACHER, Hegel considered that the most important element of religion was its doctrines and its concern for truth – not only feeling or experience, which he thought was too subjective and often irrational when taken on its own. Schleiermacher had placed Reformed Christianity at the peak of the religious tree, but the Lutheran Hegel considered Christianity in its Lutheran form to be the nearest to the absolute truth. This opinion is made quite clear in his *Lectures on the Philosophy of Religion,* in which he says, 'The Christian religion is the religion of truth',[1] and later is recorded to have said, 'The Lutheran version is undoubtedly the most ingenious, even if it has not yet completely attained the form of the idea'.[2]

The *Lectures* are a compilation of Hegel's own lecture manuscripts of lectures given on four separate occasions, in different forms, together with various auditor's notes, often very extensive, and various other transcripts. They were first published in edited form in the year after his death, in 1832. A more recent, completely new edition, based on a great deal of subsequent scholarly research, was published in English in 1985, and it is this text to which I will refer. However unreliable in detail it may be as a finished product of Hegel's thought, it, nevertheless, contains one of the shortest and most readable expositions of what Hegel thought of religion, especially in the section on 'The Consummate Religion'. Though the published text contains at least three transcripts of his lectures, it is valuable because it represents a late stage of Hegel's thought, and it shows Hegel to be committed to a strongly Lutheran faith – though admittedly interpreted in an idiosyncratic way.

---

[1] Hegel (1985), p. 64.   [2] Hegel (1985), p. 157, including the relevant footnote.

It must be said that Hegel's thoughts about Indian religions, and about Judaism and Islam, would today be considered prejudicial and ill-informed. He writes of Indian religions as a mass of superstitions and absurd fantasies. What he calls the 'Hindu Trinity' of Brahma, Vishnu, and Siva, is, he says, 'the wildest mode of fanciful imagination'.[3] He thinks Hinduism annihilates human individuality, and pictures the Spirit as appearing in many accidental forms, which are only masks of the Divine. So, even though he holds that the truth of Spirit is present at all times in some form, in its Indian forms he thinks it is a very inadequate picture, especially when compared to the Lutheran faith.

This can hardly be called a deep insight into Indian religion. Hegel seems to miss completely the fact that the philosophy of Vedanta, in some of its many diverse forms, is remarkably similar to his own system. The 'Hindu Trinity' is part of a quite different conceptual web than the Christian Trinity, and it is not at all as typical of Hindu worship as the Trinity is for Christians. What is similar is the thought that there is one absolute Spirit, which generates individuals, particulars, and space-time out of itself, and wills that all finite beings should be re-absorbed (reconciled?) to itself as the cosmos completes its spiritual journey. There is a place for devotion, for mystical union, and for practical action in Indian spirituality, and it is sad that Hegel did not see it. He relegates Indian religion to a lower level of insight than Lutheranism, by chiefly considering the popular religious practices of Indians, without comparing them with the similar popular religious views of Evangelical Lutherans. If he had done so, he might have found that popular Lutheran faith can sometimes be just as fantastic – for instance, in speaking about being washed in the blood of Jesus, sending millions of humans to eternal torture, and believing that the planet earth is the centre of the universe – as any Indian set of beliefs. Hegel provides a very rationalised version of Lutheranism, where it is his own general philosophy that provides the true content of faith, but he fails to do the same for Vedanta.

His views of Judaism are not much better. It is, according to him, a preparation for the Christian faith, and it does express a demand for absolute moral purity. But he thinks that it is a spirituality of humiliation, and that it has become a nationalistic and formalised system of laws without seeing the need of divine reconciliation from human alienation. Islam is a particular problem for his thesis that other religions are all preparations for the fully developed Lutheran religion, since Islam is, of course a later development

---

[3] Hegel (1985), p. 193.

than Christianity (though earlier than Luther). Nevertheless, he writes that 'In the Islamic doctrine there is merely the fear of God',[4] and supposes that it is by nature fatalistic and fanatical. Again, he is focussing on what he sees of Islam in some of its popular and perhaps perverse forms, and neglects the great philosophical traditions of Islam in the tenth Christian century. It is true that Hegel finds the idea of God as Trinity to be one of the defining characteristics of true faith, and that Islam rejects such a conception. However, Hegel's own conception of the Trinity is very unlike that of many important Christian theologians, and displays striking analogies with some forms of Islam, particularly Sufism. What this suggests is that the development of religious understanding is not quite as linearly progressive as he thinks, and that generally Idealist views of religion can be found in many religious traditions, when they are regarded in somewhat the same way in which he regarded Lutheran Christianity.

Be that as it may, Hegel's official view was that 'the consummate religion' is not to be found by comparing the history or teachings of particular religions. It is supposed to develop from an analysis of 'the concept' (*Begriff*) or Idea of Absolute Spirit, and it is known with certainty by pure thought. He says that Spirit has to be considered in three forms: '[first] eternal Being, within and present to itself – the form of Universality. [second] The form of appearance, that of Particularisation, of being for others. [And third] The form of return from appearance into itself, the form of absolute singularity, of absolute presence-to-self'.[5]

In this short formula, the Hegelian philosophy is expressed with remarkable and rare succinctness and clarity. Spirit posits itself in these three forms, and they are inseparably connected. Being in itself is all-inclusive, containing every possibility, both good and bad. Yet in this 'moment' of its being it is potential, and in this form it has not yet come to knowledge of itself. The second form of the divine being, Being manifested – the Word of God – is expressed in the whole temporal existence of the cosmos, which is a progressive realisation of what was potential in Being in itself. It is an Other to Spirit, and yet it is as an expression of Spirit also identical with it. It is Being as Other. The third form, Being as Return, is the negation of that difference, as Spirit takes the cosmos into itself and harmonises it in complete self-knowledge where Subject and Object are one.

Philosophies which place God wholly outside of nature, as an infinite which is opposed to the finite and which does not participate in the finite,

---

[4] Hegel (1985), p. 218.   [5] Hegel (1985), p. 186.

are inadequate. Philosophies which identify God with nature as it is are equally inadequate. One needs a 'history of God', of an infinite Being which goes out into its opposite, which is truly embodied in Nature (the whole material universe), but which then transfigures Nature by raising it from a sensuous and alienated form to a spiritual and reconciled form of the divine Being itself. 'Spirit in itself, which is other than itself as the natural will and existence of humanity, sublates this its other being, and now is for itself in all its glory – issuing forth to be Spirit through this history'.[6] The idea of 'sublation' is central to Hegel's thought. Translated from the German *Aufhebung*, it has the sense of cancelling or annulling, while at the same time raising to a higher level. Thus, the human world and its values are cancelled, yet also raised to a higher level by being reconciled with or incorporated into the life of Spirit. 'It is the essence of God as Spirit to be for another (i.e. to reveal himself) ... God is this process of positing the other and then sublating it in his eternal movement'.[7]

God is essentially a Trinity, but a Trinity which has a history of which the universe is an essential part: 'Spirit is the divine history, the process of self-differentiation, of diremption and return into self'.[8]

This is the unity of divine and human which, for Hegel, is the heart of the Christian faith. It may seem that this is a cosmic conception which has little relation to the particular historical facts of Christian faith. Such an impression is reinforced when Hegel speaks of religions as pictorial expressions or 'representations' of philosophical faith. He writes, 'The truth in and for itself is found in philosophy, and only recent philosophy has attained this conceptual depth'.[9] It is not just philosophy as such which provides the truth; it is Hegel's philosophy of absolute idealism which does so. He has, it seems, improved on traditional Christianity: 'Only by philosophy can this simply present content be justified, not by history'.[10] It is not surprising that, while many theologians have been influenced by Hegel, few have adopted his interpretation of Christianity wholesale.

Yet the relation between philosophy and historical faith is complex. Hegel says, 'What is must be actual on its own account before philosophy comes ... everything true begins in appearance'.[11] In other words, it is not pure philosophy which originates Christian faith. What comes first must be historical facts, and philosophy seeks a conceptual understanding of those facts. Yet, once philosophy has done its job, we cannot any longer base faith on appeal to history alone. We must have a spiritual understanding:

---

[6] Hegel (1985), p. 123.   [7] Hegel (1985), p. 170.   [8] Hegel (1985), p. 186.
[9] Hegel (1985), p. 143.   [10] Hegel (1985), p. 232.   [11] Hegel (1985), p. 144.

'What is to have truth for spirit as spirit, what spirit is to believe, must not be a sensory belief'.[12] Historical faith is not false. Faith says what is true; but it says it in picture form, and philosophy is needed to uncover its deepest meaning. He says of his lectures on religion, 'That was the purpose of these lectures, to reconcile reason with religion in its manifold forms, and to recognise them as at least necessary'.[13]

This, of course, raises the question of whether Hegelian philosophy is the absolute truth, and whether it really has the same content as Christian religion, or whether it penetrates to a truth which underlies all religions, although imperfectly expressed in many of them. But at least it shows that Hegel did not see his thought as in conflict with religion, and that he did see religious belief as necessary, not an option for those who like that sort of thing.

Why is religion necessary? 'The truth of the idea of God ... has this necessary characteristic, that it must be universally accessible'.[14] That is, it must be accessible to those who are not philosophers or who are not primarily interested in metaphysical speculation. Not only that, but 'What is necessary in regard to humanity is that the thought, the idea, should become objective in a single individual'.[15] Spirit essentially manifests itself in Nature, and this must take place truly and in one individual, for the antithesis in which Spirit realises itself, which is then to be sublated, must be manifested in one individual who dies, and whose particular death is the absolute Other to the universality of Spirit. That death is for the whole of humanity, but it is and must be expressed in one individual life which expresses the nature of Spirit in its character of reconciling love.

Hegel, it seems, has here a very high doctrine of incarnation. Ordinary men, even philosophers like Hegel, do not directly express God in their lives and words, but in Jesus history comes to a critical point in 'a single self-consciousness which has united divine and human nature within itself – the divine nature in this human element'.[16] Yet, that historical form, though true, does not as such reveal the spiritual truth to all who simply encounter the historical Jesus. In fact, the pictorial, historical, form 'must be stripped away and the meaning, the eternal, truthful essence must be made to emerge'.[17] That essence is that Spirit itself dies, in the ultimate anguish of self-diremption, which is also, when rightly seen, a moment in the history of Spirit's reconciliation of the world to itself, which is the fulfilled self-conscious of Spirit.

---

[12] Hegel (1985), p. 228.   [13] Hegel (1985), p. 247.   [14] Hegel (1985), p. 189.
[15] Hegel (1985), p. 226.   [16] Hegel (1985), p. 216.   [17] Hegel (1985), p. 226.

This does not mean that we must reject the picture, with its miracles, including the resurrection and ascension of Jesus. It means that one must penetrate beyond the physical facts, which in themselves are always subject to doubt and cannot be completely verified empirically. One must see these facts as expressions of spiritual truth, which is in the heart, and which is the eternal and universal unity of divine and human, where subjectivity is seen as an absolute moment of the divine nature. They are real expressions, and without them Spirit would not have expressed its nature as finitude in its most extreme form, and at the same time the abolition and absorption of finitude.

It is the death of Jesus, which is the death of God, which is the extreme of that contradiction which has taken place in God himself. For 'God has died . . . a moment of the divine nature: God becomes the other and sublates this other; negation is thereby overcome, and the negation of negation is thus a moment of the divine nature'.[18] But it is essential that it is only a moment, which is negated by the resurrection, by the return and reconciliation of all that is most opposed to God, and its reception into the Divine being. Only the death of Jesus shows that to be possible, a death which shows the self-sacrificial expression of the Divine nature, and its triumphant and final reconciliation.

Jesus is, thus, unique among humans, and yet 'in one all are encompassed'.[19] What was actual in Jesus is potential in all humans, but it is destined to become actual, as Spirit realises itself in history.

Humans essentially possess a division between the spiritual self and the natural will. Man is only potentially good, and there the defect of his nature lies. Division or disunion is essentially implied in the concept of man. But just as essential is the fact that humans are eternally reconciled as the negation of evil is itself negated by the power of the Spirit, and each self progressively becomes the vehicle of the self-expression of Spirit in its supreme goodness. The history of the cosmos and the history of humanity are revealed as a history of 'love in infinite anguish',[20] of infinite joy forged from infinite sorrow.

In the course of history, the Trinity appears as a temporal process, though in fact it is a trans-temporal, eternal, reality. Spirit is divine history, and the history of the universe is the history of Spirit as it realises and knows itself and reconciles its estranged self-expression into harmony with itself. All this, familiar to philosophers from the earlier 'Phenomenology of Spirit', is said to

---

[18] Hegel (1985), p. 219.   [19] Hegel (1985), p. 114.   [20] Hegel (1985), p. 143.

be expressed in the doctrine of the Trinity. Jesus is the temporal expression of the unity of divine and human, of Spirit and Nature, and the Church is the expression or foreshadowing of that reconciled unity which includes the whole of creation. The central core of Christian faith is the complete unity of divine and human nature. This unity is eternally attained through the process of the self-objectification of Spirit, the alienated and imperfect form of that objectification, and the reconciliation of all finite realities to absolute union with Spirit.

I doubt if all Lutherans would recognise this interpretation of the Trinity, but it is true that Luther's love of paradox, his theology of the crucified God, and his insistence that humans are at once sinners and reconciled, *simul justus et peccator*, are important background influences on Hegel's philosophy.

Hegel sees Christianity as a 'sensory representation' of a rational system which must be apprehended and realised by Reason alone, and Christian theologians have not on the whole been persuaded that this is the case. Yet it may be thought doubtful whether Hegel would have formed his system of Absolute Idealism if some major Christian doctrines had not formed part of the influences on his philosophy. Forms of Idealism can be found in Plato, Plotinus, Berkeley, and Kant, but in Hegel they have certainly been modified by the Christian doctrine of the incarnation of the eternal Word of God, and the reconciliation of a sinful world to God which is part of the Christian gospel.

Hegel is far from being a pluralist, since Absolute Idealism, and this alone, is the absolute truth. Yet, in a sense all particular religions are more or less imperfect pictures progressing towards this, though in Lutheranism the picture gets as near to the truth as theology can. It is Lutheranism in a particularly rarified form, which can rarely be found in actual Lutheran congregations, I suspect.

Hegel says that it is essential to see that Jesus really is divine, the Son of God. He is 'the consummation of reality in immediate singular individuality'.[21] Nevertheless, it is hard to see whether the sensuous miracles, like the resurrection of Jesus, are essential to the spiritual perception. As sensuous events, they are subject to doubt and uncertainty. But the Spiritual perception, Hegel holds, is absolutely certain, self-verifying, a matter of personal transformation whereby one becomes aware of one's unity with Spirit. Is the miracle then just a representation, a picture, inessential in itself, of the

---

[21] Hegel (1985), p. 115.

spiritual reality? Or is it an expression of Spiritual reality, without which Spirit would not be the reality that it is? Or perhaps an event, not strictly necessary itself, but helpful for people in conveying difficult spiritual truths to them (this is the option of esoteric philosophy)?

In the Hegelian philosophy as a whole, Spirit expresses itself in the Other, and reconciles that other to itself. The Other in itself is, therefore, not independently existent. It is a moment in the process of Spirit. Yet the history is real in its own terms, and a necessary expression of Spirit. Hegel argues that the historical reality is necessary to express the essential spiritual truth. The historical resurrection appearances are sensuously real, even though they are real as symbols of an eternal philosophical truth, which must be realised in believers. What matters above all is the inner (subjective and communal) realisation of reconciliation. This is primarily a process within the self and the community of the church – and, for us today, it is the reason people can reasonably believe the appearances occurred in history. They occurred by necessity, and historical research cannot establish necessities. Only the Concept can do that, and it is our participation in the three-foldness of the Concept which gives access to the absolute religious truth.

Hegel's apparent claim that he knows the absolute truth seems to be in tension with the idea that history is a progressive unfolding of truth. Why should the process stop here, with absolute certainty? Hegel was not, after all, the last philosopher in history, so should we not expect further developments of understanding in the future? Has the Lutheran formula ended the process of interpreting divine revelation? It seems more consistent with Hegel's own theory to think that revelation is known progressively and in part in many traditions, and that it is as still embryonic and partly hidden in Lutheranism as well as it is in, for instance, Vedanta.

Most philosophers have not been convinced by the claim that Reason can of itself come to affirm that there is one supreme self-objectifying Spirit which reconciles all things into a spiritual consummation. Hegel complains that appeal to alleged events like the resurrection can never give rise to certainty, since there are always reasonable objections that can be brought against the reality of such events. But is it true that some philosophical system of an extremely rationalist sort can give religious certainty or absolute truth? If it could, one would expect that all informed and fully rational philosophers would accept that system; but they do not. In fact, Absolute Idealism has almost disappeared from contemporary philosophical thought. I think one just has to admit that Idealism is highly contestable, even if one thinks it is true.

Hegel may be right that there has been a development in human thought over the centuries, both in knowledge of the nature of the universe and in moral beliefs. But that development has not stopped. It is too early to say where human thought may be going. Most past attempts to predict the future have turned out to be wrong. But, at present, Absolute Idealism, like Lutheranism, is just one system of beliefs among others, and not the leading one. I say this as an Idealist, but one who has been chastened by the existence of many competing philosophies, and who is, therefore, less inclined to say that any philosophical system is the absolute truth.

I rather think that Hegelianism is one stage in the development of a philosophical view which is deeply influenced by the Christian tradition, but that it is far from absolute. It contains major insights which set one form of Christian faith in a wider context of understanding. But it depends on one tradition of 'revealed' truth more than it admits, it claims for Reason an authority which reason alone may not possess, and it has not taken seriously the diversity, ambiguity, and continuing and interconnected history of many religious traditions in the world.

One can be an Idealist without being a Hegelian, and the crucial claim of Idealism is that the spiritual is more real than the material, or that something like conscious intelligent awareness is the fundamental nature and originating condition of all reality. If Mind is the basis of cosmic reality, and something more than just some sort of purely external cause, it seems reasonable to suppose that Mind has a purpose in generating a physical cosmos, and that the nature of Mind is changed by the progressive unfolding of this purpose. Thus, Idealists see the cosmos as the progressive unfolding of the nature of Mind, a dynamic process which involves the creation of a material reality which is quite different in kind from Spirit, but which is capable of generating finite minds with their own forms of self-awareness. These minds, if truly autonomous, are capable of adding new creative content to the being of God, and of co-operating in the divine purpose of realising new intrinsically good states. God will be, in Hegel's words, 'The absolutely true, that from which everything proceeds, and into which everything returns, that upon which everything is dependent, and apart from which nothing other than it has absolute, true independence'.[22] That is perhaps a concept of Spirit to which more than one religion could assent. But it is one which can be elaborated in many different ways, not all of them Lutheran.

---

[22] Hegel (1984), p. 368.

21

The Rise of Pluralism

*K*ANT, SCHLEIERMACHER, AND HEGEL WERE ALL SCEPTICAL OF the view that there was an ancient, perennial, or esoteric tradition underlying all religions. In accordance with the early modern belief that there was much new knowledge to be had which would revolutionise human thought and belief, they tended to think that the new was better or more evolved than the old. Thus, religion needed to be changed to reflect the impact of the new, and to escape from the conventions and dogmas of the past. Kant looked for a moral faith, which would not depend on strange religious experiences or dogmas handed down on authority. Perhaps he did not realise how questionable his own understanding of ethics was, and how unappealing and anaemic his proposed church would be. The positive aspect of his thought was that moral principles should not simply be derived from ancient authorities, religious or otherwise, but should creatively seek rational ways to bring about human flourishing and happiness. He also believed that his high view of morality necessarily postulated a transcendent and rational ground of moral demand and of the possibility of the realisation of a moral goal. Though this aspect of his thought is often ignored or derided, it is an important part of Kant's thinking on religion and morality.

Schleiermacher tried to remedy Kant's austerity by stressing the importance of religious experience. He agreed that the traditional emphasis on dogmatic correctness had been undermined by the rejection of old and especially of outmoded Aristotelian ways of thought. Instead, he found a non-conceptual, non-dogmatic, experience of transcendence (the 'feeling for the infinite') at the heart of religion. This enabled him to think of 'religion' in a global context, though he still thought of Protestant Christianity as the highest form of religion. For him, Christianity was the same sort of thing as religions throughout the world, not one absolutely unique and supernaturally revealed set of doctrines. His positive contribution to religion was to interpret religious faith not as acceptance of truths on authority, but as commitment to personal experiences of transcendence – though he emphasised, particularly in his later work, that some persons (especially Jesus) had more intense and authentic experiences than others.

Hegel, on the other hand, insisted that objective truth was of the first importance to religious belief. He too found Protestantism to be the highest form of religion, but it turned out to be a sort of Protestantism that most Protestants had never dreamt of. That form was, amazingly, found in Hegel's own philosophy of Absolute Idealism, and it was only when interpreted in terms of that philosophy that any existing religion was truly acceptable. It is almost a coincidence that Lutheranism happened, he thought, to be the religion nearest to his own philosophy. I doubt if most Lutherans agree with him. Nevertheless, Hegel did show the importance of having a coherent intellectual support for religious beliefs, and the necessity of finding a replacement for the brilliant but out-dated world view of Aristotelian physics and philosophy.

All three writers agreed that the profound intellectual changes that were taking place primarily in Europe after the sixteenth-century called for a new approach to religion. Kant stressed the need for moral thinking to be liberated from old authoritarian traditions. Schleiermacher thought that the intellectualism of Scholastic theology needed to be replaced by a stress on religious experience, and perceived that this led to a more empathetic consideration of religions other than Christianity. Hegel proposed a new developmental or evolutionary approach to religious phenomena throughout the world and devised the philosophy of Absolute Idealism to express this approach. He, thus, epitomised one of the most important influences in religious thought in the early modern period, which was the rise of historical consciousness, of the sense that all cultures and religions are parts of one continuously changing stream of interconnected causal influences.

For such a consciousness, there is not just one unchanging truth, set down in some ancient Scripture or philosophical writing. Different cultures have developed throughout the world, and Christianity, which itself has been in continuous change through the centuries, is part of a wider global history. The basic underlying change is away from a view which thinks that the eternal and unchanging – something like Plato's world of Forms or essential natures – is the truth, whereas history is just a series of half-real and imperfect reflections of those eternal truths. For that traditional view, the particularities of history are not of fundamental importance, and there is no real goal in the processes of history. In the modern world-view, however, change can be for the better. Life has evolved from simpler elements, and in diverse creative ways. The particular is the real, and Platonic forms, if they exist at all, are constructs of the mind. They are the half-real. In the historical world there are no essential natures, just processes of change, though they are always creatively striving towards a better future, towards a future goal.

22

Ernst Troeltsch

*I*T WAS ERNST TROELTSCH, ANOTHER GERMAN PROTESTANT, WHO most firmly set religion in the context of such a transformed historical world view. Troeltsch, in an essay on 'Historical and Dogmatic Method in Theology', set out three main principles of the new historical approach. The principle of criticism subjects all reports of past events to critical scrutiny. Though historians should be sympathetic, they should also be on the lookout for political biases, prejudiced value judgements, and the sheer unreliability of much human testimony.

The principle of analogy states that one should assume the past to be more or less like the present, so it is unlikely that signs and wonders occurred in the remote past that do not occur today.

The principle of correlation proposes that we should see each event as related to many others, so that there are no unexplained supernatural interruptions in history, but events happen because of many preceding causes, and represent new occurrences which do not necessarily fit into any sort of universal pattern or plan. 'A true understanding of history presupposes only ... physical and anthropological conditions and basic psychological drives and social laws'.[1]

Since religions often have a very long past, and since what happened at or near what are believed to be their origins is often taken to be of great importance, these principles of historical study will have a great impact on religious belief. If one is critical of the Bible, one will be on the lookout for biases which spring from the beliefs of the Biblical writers, for inconsistencies in their writings, and for the presence of factors due to their limited knowledge of the world (for instance, that the universe had not existed for

---

[1] Troeltsch (1913), p. 63.

long, and that it would probably end very soon). If the past is thought to be rather like the present, the occurrence of rare miraculous events will be doubted, and the success or failure of various religious movements will be traced to specific cultural situations which encouraged or thwarted their growth, rather than to supernatural interference. And one will see in Scriptural texts many influences from surrounding cultures which have either been incorporated into a set of beliefs or which have been strongly opposed because of particular situations which are unlikely ever to occur again.

The application of this sort of historical method to ancient Scriptures is bound to lead to a rejection of the view that they are inerrant and unchallengeable divine intrusions into a world of human diversity and disagreement. This is of course a challenge to many religious orthodoxies, which assert that their Scriptures are precisely divinely caused and unchangeable truths, and that they are founded on supernatural events (like the incarnation or resurrection) which are totally unique and find no parallel in the modern world.

It is no surprise, then, that Troeltsch opposed 'ecclesiastical theology'. A historical/critical study of the New Testament, he thought, would show that Jesus' simple teaching of the Fatherhood of God and the future coming of a kingdom of justice and peace had been changed by the quickly forming belief that Jesus was a supernatural Messiah, and by Paul's 'Christ mysticism' which turned Jesus into a cosmic power. This led in turn to the invention of doctrines of the Trinity and the supernatural nature of the Church and its sacraments.

The historical method could, he thought, restore Christianity to its original simplicity, as a form of 'personalist redemption-religion'.[2] This was 'the complete individualisation and humanisation of religion',[3] and religion's highest form. It is personalist, because it posits God as a supreme personal reality, to whom one can relate in reverence and love. It is redemptive, because it posits an achievable goal in history, 'a world of ultimate, absolute value' that can be realised.

Rather like Hegel,[4] Troeltsch held, when he wrote *The Absoluteness of Christianity*, that Christianity was the highest form of religion. But it was a Christianity that was opposed to 'ecclesiastical theology', to miracles, to the cosmic Lordship of Christ, to the Trinity, and to any sacramental view of the faith. However, Troeltsch opposed Hegel (whom he described under the heading of 'liberal Christianity', interestingly), because Hegel subjected

---

[2] Troeltsch (1972), p. 16.   [3] Troeltsch (1972), p. 145.   [4] Hegel (1985).

history to a rational system imposed upon the historical process which becomes the necessary unfolding of an eternal Ideal. Troeltsch wanted to derive his theology from the processes of history, not from some preconceived ideal model. History was messier, more contingent, more diverse, often more non-rational than Hegel had supposed.

It was a contingent fact that Christianity was the highest form of religion, and it could be seen to be so because it was the latest development of an evolutionary process towards a universal ethic and an absolute value. It is, he said, 'the convergence point of all developmental tendencies in religion and the elevation of the goal of religion to an essentially new level'.[5]

There was a problem with this view, which Troeltsch clearly saw. On the one hand, each religion had to be seen as part of a long developing and constantly changing process which was only a small part of the history of religions on earth. It had to be placed in its historical context, as a contingent and developing part of a wider stream of world-wide contingent developments. On the other hand, many religions have made a claim to an exclusive truth which cannot develop in its most basic affirmations, since they are absolutely and exclusively true.

Christianity was to be proclaimed the highest religion, precisely because it renounced such claims and was prepared (at least Troeltsch was prepared on its behalf) to revise itself radically to meet the demands of historical consciousness. But could not the same thing be said of many other religions too? If, for example, Hinduism renounced its claim to state the absolute truth about ultimate reality, and if it accepted that most of its Scriptures were based on myths and legends, why should not it too be religion on a higher level? Might Islam not come to admit that the Qur'an was not literally spoken by God, and contained many influences from surrounding religions, and even some misunderstandings of Arabic Christianity? Yet it could be a form of redemptive personalism, since it believes in one Creator who wills to bring all things to union with the Divine. So, is it just a contingent and temporary fact that Christianity is the highest religion?

In *The Absoluteness of Christianity*, Troeltsch held that his form of Christianity was 'not the absolute but the normative religion',[6] the 'purest and most forceful revelation of the higher world'. The two basic elements of this normative religion are that there is an infinitely valuable goal, and that there is an authentic knowledge of God. Personalist religion is committed to

---

[5] Troeltsch (1972), p. 146.   [6] Troeltsch (1972), p. 121.

a moral teleology in nature, and to personal apprehension of a personal God, and 'all other religions . . . have not yet achieved the breakthrough to personalism'.[7]

They have not yet achieved it, he says. But they may do so in the future, and Troeltsch accepts that Christianity may die, though some form of personalist religion will survive. In a later essay, 'The Place of Christianity Among the World Religions',[8] he retracts his earlier view that Christianity was the normative religion. His comments on Judaism, Islam, and Hinduism were not empathetic enough to see that personalism of the sort he recommended could well be an important part of their faiths too, and that indeed in many cases it already was. For example, Martin Buber's 'I and Thou', written from a Jewish perspective, is arguably more personalist than the view of most orthodox Christians, who confuse the issue by talk of such mysteries as the Trinity and atonement.[9]

In any case, it is not totally obvious that personalism is the highest form of religion. Troeltsch admitted that this was a subjective judgement. Buddhists, and many Christians, would insist that the idea of a trans-personal ultimate is a more mature concept than that of a supreme person. Even his allegedly more objective view that history shows a purposive progression towards a truly absolute religion is questionable. If history really is a concatenation of events that are not ordered in accordance with some universal principle, but 'always an encounter between opposed forces',[10] it may not be moving towards any goal. He often expresses the opinion that an 'absolute' may never be realised in history, although it is an ideal goal which gives a tendency or a direction to the processes of history.

What Troeltsch achieved was to show that, after the sixteenth-century, a new form of historical consciousness had become possible. Beliefs and practices had to be given a historical place in the flow of historical events which was in continual change. The present is not just a repetition of the past, or of some privileged past golden age. Each present is new, develops out of the immediate context from which it springs, and its problems are those of its new situation – 'all historical phenomena are unique'.[11]

The historical flow is global, and each religion must also be given a place in the global history of religions. It is not enough to say that God has spoken in one time and place, and nowhere else. God, or spiritual reality, must be present at all times and places, though it seems that it is perceived in different ways. These differences must be explained within a general

[7] Troeltsch (1972), p. 129.   [8] Troeltsch (1980).   [9] Buber (1957).
[10] Troeltsch (1972), p. 64.   [11] Troeltsch (1972), p. 89.

understanding of all human existence as particular and unique expressions of a more general global process.

The methods of historical criticism that Troeltsch enumerated are, of course, not infallible and beyond criticism themselves. They rule out unique spiritually caused events by definition, which may seem rather arbitrary. But they do show that historical study can only give probabilistic assertions about the past, and that very different interpretations of past events are more or less equally reasonable. For many people, this undermines any religious assertion that some past events can be known with certainty and are vital to religious faith. Somehow faith must have a rather more agnostic or probabilistic relation to historical assertions, and that relation stands in need of clarification.

Troeltsch's key question was, 'How can we pass beyond the diversity with which history presents us to norms for our faith and for our judgements about life?'.[12] His tentative answer was that one might 'discern in the relative, tendencies towards the absolute goal'.[13] I doubt whether a historical study that is essentially critical, that judges the past in terms of my limited experience of the present, and that disallows any reference to specifically spiritual causes (the principles of criticism, analogy, and correlation), can possibly discern tendencies in history to an absolute moral goal, or provide us with norms for our judgements about life.

Perhaps our basic values derive from some apprehension of a spiritual dimension, which may be discerned *through* historical experiences, but does not derive *from* them. It is important to see the historical circumstances which evoke our perceptions of moral value and of the transcendent reality that may be mediated though our experiences. Probably our specific moral and existential commitments are influenced by the things that happen to us in our lives. Almost certainly a fully adequate grasp of moral and spiritual values lies ahead of us and is never attained within history.

Acceptance of these things naturally leads to a deeper appreciation of the many different ways of life that one finds in the many religions of the world, and of the ways in which religions are intertwined with other moral and political factors that are peculiar to their own historical circumstances. It may lead to the relinquishing of claims to absolute truth in religion, and to an acceptance that different religions may be reasonable responses to transcendence within different histories and developing cultures. This is a form of religious pluralism, but it still faces Troeltsch's problem of whether one

---

[12] Troeltsch (1972), p. 61.   [13] Troeltsch (1972), p. 90.

can speak of one religion as superior to or higher than another, or, if not, how one is to accommodate some of the major contradictions that seem to exist between religions.

In this section, I have considered a number of factors which suggest that a revised understanding of religion is necessary in the modern world. I have mentioned the rise of scientific method and of a scientific world-view, the critical study of ancient religious texts, the advocacy of a morality of human flourishing and happiness, the acceptance of freedom of critical thought, the growth of an increasingly global outlook, a growing stress on experience as the basis of religious revelation and beliefs, the genesis of evolutionary and Idealist philosophy, and the development of historical consciousness.

All these factors have already had an impact on the understanding of religion. Often that impact has been negative, seeing religions as intellectually obsolete, emotionally naïve, and politically dangerous. Most of the writers I have discussed have accepted that some revision of traditional religious beliefs is necessary. They have in some sense accepted the superiority or normativeness of Christianity in a revised form, and that is a natural result of their place in European history. But some of them have seen similar implications for other religions of the world, without having the knowledge of those religions that would be needed to come to a truly global understanding.

There is virtually no hope that all religions would integrate these factors into their thinking, and those that do so will integrate them in different ways and to different degrees. There is some hope, however, that a number of religions, or sub-classes of religions, will find a common agreement on seeing their faith as needing to be compatible with science, as welcoming constructive and informed criticism, as seeking human fulfilment and happiness, as accepting the limited and historically influenced nature of their claimed knowledge of the spiritual, and as prepared to reformulate beliefs, where it seems right to do so, in the light of increasing awareness of the diversity of religious approaches, none of which has attained a complete grasp of truth concerning the spiritual life.

This is a matter of agreement upon an open and developmental approach to religious questions, rather than a matter of agreement on specific doctrines. It is more likely, for it is more in accord with human nature, that disagreements will always remain, though they will be seen in a more accepting way. This could be called pluralism in a rather restricted sense, as it refrains from making claims to completely adequate and irreformable truth, and attempts to interact positively with other systems of belief, so far as this is possible.

Part IV

The Pluralist Hypothesis

23

John Hick

*J*OHN HICK IS PROBABLY THE BEST KNOWN TWENTIETH-CENTURY philosopher who has defended pluralism in religion. He has written a number of major works on the philosophy of religion, and is an outstanding defender of the sort of open and developmental approach that I have mentioned. His book, *An Interpretation of Religion*, is a defence of the rationality of religious belief, and proposes to give a 'religious, but not confessional, interpretation of religion in its plurality of forms'.[1] His exposition of the views of many religious traditions shows a mastery of the material and a deep insight into how adherents of those traditions would themselves express their views. He develops the view that religion is a response to a transcendent reality or realities, and its various very different forms are all responses influenced by different historical and cultural forces to a reality that transcends the material world and that offers salvation or liberation from the ills of human existence to a radically better state. 'We always perceive the transcendent through the lens of a particular religious culture',[2] he writes, but world religions form a global continuum of culture-relative forms symbolising a mysterious transcendent reality.

He is sometimes misunderstood as trying to reduce all religions to a simple common core. But, in fact, he is clear that there are different forms of experience that 'justify different and often incompatible sets of beliefs'.[3] He suggests that it is rational for people to trust their own form of religious experience, and this implies, he thinks, if we are not simply to discount some religious experiences, that there is one ultimate Real which is discerned in different phenomenal forms (the pluralistic hypothesis). These discernments evoke 'parallel salvific transformations of human life',[4] and the basic

---

[1] Hick (1989), p. 1. [2] Hick (1989), p. 8. [3] Hick (1989), p. 13. [4] Hick (1989), p. 15.

criterion of the truth of a religious belief is its efficacy in bringing about such transformation. Thus, there are many different phenomenal truths which often contradict if taken literally. The Real lies beyond them all as their source. Though this Real is unknowable by us, its many phenomenal expressions are authentic insofar as they succeed in liberating human lives from meaninglessness, egoism, and despair.

In my view, this is a scholarly, informed, tolerant, and insightful proposal. It is a creative attempt to take seriously the many different religious doctrines that exist, to root them in forms of transcendent experience and a desire for moral transformation, and to propose a way in which the many religions of the world can move forward in harmony of purpose. Despite that, I think that Professor Hick's specific thesis of pluralism has some problematic features, and that his general programme can be advanced by amending it to some extent.

He does not merely mean, by pluralism, that one should refrain from claiming to have the whole truth, and that one should look on at least some other religious beliefs and practices favourably. Having rejected the view that all religious experience is delusory, so that all religions are false, and the view that all religions are false except one's own, he proposes his own definition of pluralism. This is, he says, a 'third possibility, that the great post-axial faiths constitute different ways of experiencing, conceiving and living in relation to an ultimate divine Reality which transcends all our varied visions of it'.[5]

This sounds unexceptionable to any person who wishes to see the religions of the world as sincere and informed attempts to relate to a higher spiritual sphere. However, there are two main claims in this proposal that may be missed. One is that there is 'an ultimate divine Reality', and the other is that this Reality transcends all our visions of it. The trouble is that not all religions think that there is one ultimate divine Reality, and not all religions think that it transcends all our ideas of it. There are religious views which hold that there are at least two divine Realities, one good and one evil, and that we can know that this is true (some varieties of Gnosticism and some forms of Zoroastrianism affirm such a thing). Indeed, Hick himself seems to be open to this possibility, since he writes that 'we cannot apply to the Real *an sich* the characteristics encountered in its *personae* and *impersonae*. Thus, it cannot be said to be one or many, person or thing, substance or process, good or evil, purposive or non-purposive'.[6] So, for all we know, there may be two divine realities, one good and one evil.

---

[5] Hick (1989), pp. 235–6.   [6] Hick (1989), p. 246.

Hick can respond that we could not know such a thing, because in fact we can know that such specific qualities as number and moral goodness cannot apply to the Real. But if no concepts at all can apply to the Real in itself, how can one speak of an 'it' at all? How can one even say that it exists, or that it is the cause or creator of the universe? If we take a statement like 'whereof we cannot speak, we must be silent' with full seriousness, we could not say 'there is a God' or 'there is an ultimate Reality'. Reality and existence are human concepts which cannot apply to some thing or things which is or are completely unknowable. Ultimate Reality and nothing at all turn out to be identical, for all we know.

But even if it made sense to say that there is something of which we know nothing, how could we possibly know that none of our concepts apply to it? If we know nothing about it, then as far as we can tell our concepts might well apply to it. We would just never know this. But we would never know, either, that our concepts definitely do not apply.

Immanuel Kant, whose thought is one important influence on Hick's view, struggled with a similar problem. If the Real in itself (the noumenal world) is totally unknowable, because all our knowledge is confined to the phenomenal world, the world as experienced by us, then how can we even say that there is such a Real? Though Kant's answer is hard to understand, it seems to be that we can, and must, speak *as if* there was a realm of free moral agents, a 'kingdom of ends', and one supreme Reason which is the cause of the intelligible and predictable world of phenomenal appearances. But we speak regulatively, and this is a rational faith which is not a form of knowledge. Kant then has to produce an argument to show why we must speak in this way, and he tries to do so by showing that human Reason compels us to use such regulative Ideas, as a condition of truly understanding and living in the world as we do.

For Kant, it is Reason that makes such regulative ideas necessary for human understanding, and Reason makes those ideas necessary for everyone. Hick's view does not have this advantage. Hick admits that it is not necessary for everyone to believe that there is 'an ultimate divine Reality'. It seems that roughly 50 per cent of the world's population do not, and Hick himself argues that, as far as reason goes, the world seems to be ambiguous about a divine existence.

Moreover, it is not clear what might make belief in God a necessary condition of understanding. For many people, God stands in need of explanation, and just gives rise to misleading ideas about the moral government of a universe which seems completely indifferent to the moral concerns of humans. Belief in God might be a necessary condition for worship, and it might give people hope for a better life after death. But worship may be regarded as servile flattery (Kant seemed to think this), and hope for 'pie in the sky when you die' may be just a delusory 'opium of the people'. Belief in God seems to be an option, not, as in Kant, a necessary postulate of faith. And what is the point of saying that your option is between believing there is no God, and believing that there is something of which we know nothing, and of which nothing can be said?

The situation is even worse than this, logically speaking. Suppose two religions each say that the ultimate object of their devotion is some completely unknowable something. If this is true, there is no way of telling that they are talking about the same thing. What is sometimes called the quantification fallacy is this: 'Two footballers scored a goal in the last game, therefore there is a goal which two footballers scored'. The fallacy is clear; they scored different goals. So, in the case of the unknown God, if two religions posit an unknown God, it need not be the same God that they are talking (or not talking) about. What entitles anyone to say that, if two religions worship an ultimate divine Reality, it is the same Reality that they worship? This is a wholly relevant question, because there is a living dispute in Malaysia about whether Muslim worshippers of Allah are worshipping the same being as Christian worshippers of God. Both traditions contain apophatic aspects, saying that ultimately God/Allah is beyond human understanding. Are they, therefore, the same or not?

The only way to answer this question is if we can produce descriptions of that Reality upon which both religions agree. But that is what is forbidden by Hick's definition of pluralism. Now in fact, rather like Kant, Hick does provide some minimal description of ultimate reality. He accepts, quoting Anselm, that it is 'that than which no greater can be conceived'.[7] This, Hick says, is a 'purely formal statement' which attributes no concrete characteristics to the Real, which is 'the noumenal ground of the encountered gods', which are 'authentic phenomenal manifestations of the Real'.[8]

This statement gives away more than Hick seems to think. The Real is something which is at least the greatest reality that can be thought, even if it is also much more than that, as Anselm says. It is true that this definition does not say what the great-making qualities of the Real are. But it does say that there are some, and that there is a greatest, or supreme great-making quality. By 'great', Anselm meant 'valuable' or 'worthwhile', so on this definition there is a most worthwhile possible reality. This entails that one

---

[7] Hick (1989), p. 246.   [8] Hick (1989), p. 247.

cannot think God is evil or not worthy of admiration. One must think that God is supremely good, and, if supreme, then one being which contains the most valuable forms of goodness anyone can think of.

There are philosophical disputes about whether such a being is logically possible. Could there be just one most valuable possible being, when forms of goodness might be so varied and perhaps conflicting? Hick seems to assume that such a being is possible. But to say that there exists just one supremely good reality is to commit oneself to a belief about the Real that would be denied by many religious believers – by all those who do not think that God is supremely good, or that there is just one supremely good God – and some (certainly not all) Hindus would qualify under this head.

Hick adds, presumably as another purely formal statement, that the Real is the 'noumenal ground' of the phenomenal appearances of the gods or absolutes (the personal and impersonal objects of religious belief). The phrase 'noumenal ground' is hard to interpret, especially in view of its Kantian overtones. But it does seem to imply that the Real is the ontological cause of experiences of gods and spiritual realities. One main problem here is that, presumably, the Real is the ontological cause of absolutely everything, of every sort of spiritual phenomenon, from Satan to Seth, Osiris to Demeter, Kali to Krishna. What does it add to conceptions of Krishna that they are said to be caused by a completely unknown Real? If that Real was a supreme Good, then something would be added. Evil, vindictive, angry, and savage Gods would not be 'authentic manifestations' of supreme Goodness.

Here the crucial weakness of religious pluralism is exposed. Adherents of some religions, including Christianity, do want to make a distinction between good and evil, helpful and harmful, religious beliefs. All religious views are not equally good, though perhaps all religions have good and evil potentialities. At this point, we may not want to talk about 'religions', as though a religion could be precisely defined conceptually. We might prefer to talk about particular religious beliefs, or about ways of interpreting religious beliefs, which may often co-exist within the large scale institutionalised phenomena we tend to call 'religions'.

To take an obvious example, two people who both identify themselves as Christian believers in God as revealed in Jesus Christ, may have very different sets of beliefs about God and about what is morally right and good. One may see God as a God of strict retributive justice who condemns large numbers of people to eternal Hell, while selecting a small number of 'the elect' for eternal happiness, if and only if they explicitly profess faith in Jesus while they are alive. The other may see God as a God of unlimited love, who wills all people without exception to have eternal life, and they may have qualms about such things as capital punishment and the idea of strict retributive justice.

This is not a difference between religions. An impartial observer would see that Christian Scriptures and tradition contain both streams of thought. I would think that Popes Pius IX and John Paul II might well stand on either side of this divide, but few would deny that both were Christians. Would John Hick say that one of these views was an authentic and the other an inauthentic manifestation of the Real? He could hardly decide this by appeal to the nature of the Real, since by his own admission he knows nothing about that. Would he make the decision on independent moral grounds? He might do so, if he had doubts about the morality of retributive punishment, and if he thought human welfare for all was a moral ideal. But it would probably be wrong to think that religious belief played no part in such a decision. Jesus taught that we should not insist upon taking an eye for an eye, but should love our enemies. And if God is love, that implies that there is a God who also loves his enemies, and cares for all sentient creation. Those who take a different view might point out that God does punish evil, that the world is filled with evil, and that God's love is reserved for those who turn from evil and repent. Either way, religious beliefs are playing a part in making decisions about what is morally right. It looks as if moral and religious beliefs intertwine, without one having obvious priority. But this implies that we do know something about God or ultimate reality after all, since we claim to know that, and even specifically how, God is good.

This conclusion is reinforced by the fact that, when Hick speaks of religion, he characterises it as sponsoring a 'transformation of human existence from self-centredness to Reality-centredness'.[9] If you thought of Reality as supreme goodness, then you could see this as a change from egoism to a love of the good for its own sake. But if you think of Reality as unknowable, then it is hard to see what centring yourself on the unknown could suggest. Losing yourself in obedience to the 'will of the people', as focussed in a charismatic Fuhrer or Leader, might not be a wholly commendable thing. Self-renouncing devotion to a phenomenally experienced goddess who requires human sacrifice is not any better. If you are going to centre yourself on Reality, then that Reality must be conceived by you as supremely good, as worthy of your devotion. If you say that your phenomenal god is good, but is actually an appearance of a morally neutral Real, which is beyond good and evil, this may well lead to a form of moral relativism or neutrality which undermines some of Hick's central moral concerns.

[9] Hick (1989), p. 240

For that reason, I think it is important to say that we do know something about the Real, namely, that it is supremely good. I think Hick does actually say that, even though his definition of radical pluralism seems to forbid it. His view also implies that we know at least in some respects what goodness is. At least he makes claims about what is good and what is bad with which many other people would disagree, and he tends to evaluate religions by testing them against his intuitions about what is good. For instance, he holds that women should be treated equally with men, that slavery is wrong, and that we should not impose our religious views on others. These views have all been widely contested among religious believers. They conflict with some claims to revealed truth, but are consonant with others. Conflict and contradiction cannot be avoided, even when it is agreed that the Ultimate Real is supremely good.

When it comes to saying what supreme goodness would be, there are many conflicting claims. Many theists think that it is better to be changeless and timeless than it is to be creatively changing and responsive to temporal events; others disagree strongly. Some think that it is good for a supremely good being to be just, and exact just retribution for wrong-doing, whatever the consequences. Others think it is better to be merciful and forgive those who sincerely repent. Some think that a supremely good being would create the best of all possible worlds, while others disagree. In fact, disagreements multiply the more specific we try to get about what a supremely good being would be like. These disagreements are not complementary. Each claim is exclusive of its opposite. The disagreements are not necessarily between different religions. All the positions just mentioned have been held by Christians.

If one examines different religions, one may find that, among Jews, Muslims, Hindus, and Christians, there are some who have held each of these conflicting views. Co-religionists of theirs may disagree strongly, at least with the more specific claims. One cannot neatly compartmentalise truth-conflicts on religious matters into different religions. The conflicts cross religious borders. Pluralism is not just unrealistic as a thesis about differing religions; it is unrealistic as an account of just one religion. There are estimated to be over 30,000 Christian denominations in the world, and nothing is going to reconcile all their conflicting truth-claims. Many of the truth-claims of religious groups must be false, and this conclusion cannot be avoided just by saying that they are all different ways of speaking of the same reality. Thus, one can agree with Hick's initial definition of pluralism, that the great post-Axial faiths are different ways of conceiving an Ultimate divine Reality, but one must add that some of these ways of conceiving will be false.

24

Soteriological Effectiveness

*H*ICK'S INITIAL DEFINITION OF PLURALISM IS EXPANDED TO reveal its fuller intention when he says that different religions 'may each mediate the Real to different groups of human beings; and ... in fact do so, as far as we are able to judge, to about the same extent'.[1] I think it is incoherent to say that two contradictory religious claims mediate the Real to about the same extent and also that at least one of them is false. A false claim about the nature of the Real cannot 'mediate' the Real at all.

Yet the use of the term 'mediate' is telling. What Professor Hick has in mind is that the truth of various doctrines of the Real (that it is Vishnu or the Father of Jesus Christ or *Sunyata*) 'lies in their soteriological effectiveness'.[2] This commits him to a pragmatic conception of religious truth. A religious claim is true if it enables a transformation from self-centredness to 'Reality-centredness'. Any image which does that job is an 'authentic phenomenal manifestation of the Real'.[3] Religious images of the Real are defined by Hick as 'myths', and myths, since they should not be taken literally, do not contradict one another. Hick defines as a 'myth' any statement which is not literally true, 'but which tends to evoke an appropriate dispositional attitude to its subject matter'.[4] True religious myths are those which evoke such attitudes. At this point he produces the circular argument that true myths are those which evoke appropriate attitudes, and appropriate attitudes are those which are in 'soteriological alignment with the Real'[5] – that is to say, which are true. This is not really very helpful, since we cannot check which attitudes are in alignment with the Real, about which we know nothing. It seems that 'appropriateness' must be assigned simply on the moral or psychological superiority of some

[1] Hick (1989), p. 375.   [2] Hick (1989), p. 373.   [3] Hick (1989), p. 247.   [4] Hick (1989), p. 248.
[5] Hick (1989), p. 248.

attitudes over others. It seems that one must judge religious truth claims on the basis of their ability to produce good moral or psychological effects. It sounds as if some religions can then be called more true than or morally superior to others. In fact, this is what Professor Hick does when he condemns views which promote violence, tyranny, or injustice.

All religious views are not going to be equally true or acceptable, and it is going to be possible to rank them in the order of their 'soteriological efficacy'. Professor Hick then claims that adherents of many religions move just about equally effectively from self-centredness to Reality-centredness. He might also have said that many religions are more or less equally prone to promote violence, injustice, and tyranny. This means, on his pragmatic theory of truth, that these religions are more or less equally true. It also means that they are more or less equally false – and religions which claim to have an exclusive view of salvific truth and to consign all unbelievers to a terrible fate are certainly false.

This means that even this form of pluralism cannot say that all religious views are equally authentic and appropriate ways of relating to the Real, and, thus, more or less equally true (in a mythical, not a literal, sense). One may wish to refine this point a little and say that one cannot say of a religion in general that it is more or less true than others (though I guess Satanism might be, even for Hick, of a lower order of truth than Judaism). It is particular claims made within religions that must be considered. Then, Hick would think, Christian views which condemn homosexuals to eternal Hell fire will be less true than Christian views which tolerate or celebrate homosexuality. The necessity of morally ranking religious beliefs is concealed by concentrating just on the tendency of religious views to promote personal non-egoism and 'Reality-centredness'. Hick himself suggests that belief in a literal incarnation can have seriously harmful consequences. But in the Catholic Church, great saints usually have had such a belief. How is one to weigh the capacity to produce saints against the promulgation of doctrines which (according to Hick) are seriously harmful? Ranking of religions as such may be difficult, but ranking of specific religious truth-claims seems to be necessary to any consideration of religion.

In addition to this, there seems to me to be a confusion between the concepts of truth and soteriological effectiveness. If soteriological effectiveness consists ultimately in attaining salvation or liberation, on Hick's form of pluralism it cannot consist in a literal eternal knowledge and love of a personal God, as it does in Christianity, or in the dissolution of the ego into a boundless state of intelligence and bliss, as it does in *Theravada* Buddhism. For these two states are incompatible. It must lie in the achievement of such ethical goals as altruism, compassion, and selflessness, and psychological goals such as having feelings of calm and joy, and a sense of unity with all things.[6]

I am very much in sympathy with the proposal that a life of compassion for others, concern for truth, and the realisation of intrinsically worthwhile conscious states should be a major factor in the practices of religion. Yet it seems to be the case that many religious views claim truth, but do not tend to produce universal compassion, concern for truth, and the creative realisation of many worthwhile states. Sociological surveys of religious believers tend to show that they are, on the whole, conservative in morality, and tend to be suspicious of and even hostile to non-believers or to those who hold different religious beliefs. Many ordinary religious believers will not accept marriage to unbelievers, and in that way religious belief can lead to social tensions and has often led to violence. Many forms of religious belief are also hostile to free critical thought, which is a condition of a serious concern to discover truth. They can oppose the findings of science and refuse even to read material which may lead to religious doubt. That hardly shows a real concern for truth. And religions can be repressive of original and creative thought, insisting on conformity to ancient traditions and communal practices.

Not all religions are like that, though most actual religions often show signs of hostility to others, fear of criticism, and repressive conformity. In fact, religions in general produce very few saints, who are rare almost by definition. So if, as Hick says, 'myths [he means religious doctrines about the ultimate objects of devotion] are valid to the extent that they promote transformation',[7] then very few religious doctrines would be valid.

If the production of saints is meant to be a criterion of religious validity or truth, it is embarrassing that many adherents of religious views that many would take to be definitely false can produce outstanding saints. (If you are not a Jehovah's Witness, they would be a good case. If you are one, then Roman Catholicism would be an equally good case). It could even be argued that sincerely holding some false beliefs, like a belief that you will suffer eternally in a pit of fire somewhere in Australia if you are not altruistic, would be conducive to attaining ethical eminence. If you would not go so far, it still seems that anti-religious humanists can be as good as pious religious believers, and that has no tendency to show that their views are correct. They would not even count as pluralists, on Hick's definition, though they would

---

[6] Hick (1989), p. 278.   [7] Hick (1989), p. 365.

fit his soteriological criterion very well. It looks as though the attainment of extraordinary goodness is not only (even if rarely) a feature of some religions. It is at least as common among non-religious people as among the religious. But Hick could hardly take that as a reason for saying that secular humanism is an appropriate response to a Real which it totally rejects and is just as appropriate as fervent belief in a creator God.

For these reasons, it would be wise not to use as a criterion of religious truth a requirement that it should tend to promote moral excellence. One might hope that the practice of religion would produce some kinds of moral improvement. But one should not set one's hopes for this too high, and one might be aware that for some people the practice of religion will make their mental state and their moral performance substantially worse.

25

Truth, Experience, and Salvation

*M*OST RELIGIONS ARE NOT PRIMARILY MEANS TO MORAL improvement. They involve an existential claim – for instance, that there actually exists a Supreme Good, which humans can to some extent apprehend, mediate, and in which they may ultimately hope to share. The actual performance of many believers will be somewhat lamentable, and they may rely (as even Immanuel Kant did) on some inscrutable power of forgiveness and divine help if they are ever to attain the goal of union with Supreme Goodness. Like St. Augustine, they may hope to be transformed, but not yet. They should certainly not let the truth of their belief in God be proportioned to the extent to which they and their friends actually are transformed. Their hope will be on what God may do, and their faith will be that there is such a God, not that they are visibly becoming more perfect day by day. It is not the case that, if a God is believed to transform one's moral life, then there is such a God. Nor is it the case that, if a God is not seen to transform moral life, then there is no God. Humans may resist transformation, but that will not make the existence of a God less real.

When he comes to consider the question of truth, Hick distinguishes three kinds of question that often arise in religion.[1] One is concerned with matters that are, in principle, answerable, but which we can obtain no conclusive information about (like the claim that Jesus was crucified). One concerns matters of trans-historical fact (like whether we will reincarnate). And one tries to deal with questions about the nature of the Real. He proposes that the first two questions are not really answerable, and, more importantly, an answer to them is not necessary to the process of self-transformation. The third question contains what he calls 'mythological truths', which

---

[1] Hick (1989).

picture the process of self-transformation. But there is something very odd about mythological truths.

They are not supposed to be literally true. If one religion speaks of Shiva as that to which we respond in Reality-centredness, and another religion speaks of Christ as the object of such response, these claims conflict when taken literally. Hick does not deny that, but affirms it. He then argues that all our concepts of the Real are a combination of some input from the Real and some input from human culture and consciousness. This gives rise to different models of the Real. The Real in itself is not like any of our models – not even one or many, good or bad.[2] But since all our models contain input from the Real, the most reasonable thing to say is that all our models enable us to make appropriate soteriological responses to the Real, even though it is apprehended under different phenomenal appearances.

That does not seem reasonable to me. The argument depends upon our knowing that the Real is not like any of our models. But, as I have argued, we cannot possibly know that, if the Real is unknowable by us. So, while it is true that our models of the Real literally conflict, and that this conflict is due to conceptual input from different cultures and histories, the reasonable thing to say is that some models may express the nature of the Real more adequately than others (Hick's own view that the Real transcends all human conceptions of it is itself a claim to a more adequate truth than views which think they can conceive the Real correctly). Maybe no models are completely adequate, but if our models cover just about every logical possibility, as far as we can see, then some models must be more adequate than others. For instance, I think it is reasonable to say that either the Real has some personal properties (like knowledge and will) or that it has no personal properties, so one of these assertions must be true and the other false. That is more reasonable than saying that all our models are literally false, but they are all soteriologically adequate to the Real in itself. We could not possibly know that.

A similar argument on which Hick places a good deal of weight begins with the axiom that it is rational to trust human experience, and in particular any religious experiences that we may have, but it is irrational to deny that others are also rational to trust their religious experiences. Therefore, the argument goes, it is rational to postulate that all religious experiences are phenomenal, culture-relative, aspects of one Real, which is 'differently experienced ... within different cultural ways of being human'.[3]

---

[2] Hick (1989), p. 350.   [3] Hick (1989), p. 14.

This is a *non sequitur*. It is indeed rational for people to believe different things on the basis of the different experiences that they have, and in the light of their available knowledge. But what follows is that, if their beliefs conflict, the available knowledge of at least one of them must be incomplete or even mistaken. It does not seem reasonable to say that they must both be perceiving something correct, though nobody knows what it is. Sometimes the mistakes can be obvious. For instance, people who claim to have experiences of conscious beings on the moon can be shown to be mistaken by subsequent space explorations of the moon, which reveal no conscious beings. People who suffer various psychological disorders, or who are irrational in their general beliefs, will have their experiences largely discounted. But many sorts of experience, possessed by sane, intelligent, honest, and informed people, should be taken seriously. We might want to say that, being human, it is unlikely that experiences can provide detailed, precise, and wholly correct information about spiritual reality. It is likely that the language people have learned, with its basic values and presuppositions, will affect their descriptions of experience. It is also likely that those who reflectively consider such experiences will have background beliefs and values that make some interpretations seem more adequate than others. Many religious experiences may indeed be culture and person relative aspects of one Real. But it seems inevitable that we should rank some experiences as more likely to be adequate to that Real than some others. There does not have to be one set of experiences, occurring within one religion, that is more adequate than all others (the inclusivist postulate). But there will probably be some types of experience that are thought to be more adequate than others, even if those types can be found in more than one religion.

This is just the sort of discrimination that Hick makes, when he discounts experiences of a savage and judgmental God, or of a literally resurrected Jesus. He also makes a value-judgement when he accepts that religious experiences are authentic and show that a spiritual realm exists. The question is, then, what range of experiences one is going to count as communicating truth about reality. The postulate of extreme pluralism, that all religions communicate the truth (that there is an unknowable Real as the source of all phenomenal gods), is not the only possible postulate. Nor does it seem the most reasonable, in view of the conflicts between religious doctrines. Some experiences may be – and I think must be – counted as more adequate to spiritual truth than others. It is difficult to make such decisions, but the criterion of soteriological efficacy or a tendency to promote moral and psychological excellence does not seem enough.

Many religious views would of course deny that 'salvation' or 'liberation' is just a matter of soteriological efficacy or moral excellence. For many Christians, salvation consists in the knowledge and love of an actual Supremely Good personal being. For many Buddhists, liberation consists of seeing that personal individuality or selfhood is an illusion, so they posit no relation to a personal God. Both views do entail that moral excellence will somehow be achieved. But the heart of their faiths is that there is a personal God or that there is not, respectively. If this is the case, then to achieve full salvation or liberation is, for them, to see the truth of the existence or non-existence of God. Soteriology – a doctrine of salvation – may be necessary for some faiths, but it is not the whole of religious faith. Many religions do without it altogether (it is not a central idea in Islam). Those which posit a more robust and specific doctrine of salvation would not take kindly to being told that their belief in a personal God is literally false.

26

Universal Salvation

O NE COULD REASONABLY ARGUE THAT KNOWLEDGE OF THE TRUTH (e.g. that there is a God) is necessary for full salvation, in the Christian sense (i.e. that salvation is perfect knowledge and love of God). But does this mean, as some views suppose, that salvation is impossible for those who hold false views about religion? Not necessarily. The question of truth is different from the question of salvation. It could be that salvation is possible for those who at one time hold false religious views, as long as those views will be corrected at some later stage.

This, I think, is an acceptable position for an orthodox Catholic or Protestant Christian to take. It does reflect a major change in traditional Roman Catholic teaching. The change is very apparent if one looks at Papal pronouncements made before the Vatican Council in the 1960s. On 9 June 1862, Pope Pius IX issued a 'Syllabus of Errors', listing 80 errors that had apparently become increasingly current around that time.[1] The Syllabus is largely concerned with affirming the rights of the Roman Catholic Church, to oppose 'rationalist' or secular philosophy, and to uphold the moral teachings of the Catholic Church. But also opposed are 'progress, liberalism, and modern civilisation' (that is error 80), as well as socialism and biblical societies (described as 'pests'). Error 15 is to think that 'every man is free to embrace and profess that religion which, guided by the light of reason, he shall consider true'. Error 17 is to think that 'good hope at least is to be entertained of the eternal salvation of those who are not at all in the true church of Christ'. It is wrong even to hope that those not in the true church can be saved. And to make clear what the true church is, error 18 is committed by those who affirm

[1] See Papal Encyclicals Online.

that 'Protestantism is nothing more than another form of the same true Christian religion'.

This document, of course, was never infallible, but it does reflect a view that was meant to be authoritative for all Catholics in 1862. Times have certainly changed. In the Encyclical 'Redemptor Hominis' (1979), Pope John Paul II wrote, in paragraph 14: 'The human person – every person without exception – has been redeemed by Christ ... even if the individual may not realize this fact'. In 'Redemptoris Missio' (1990),[2] Pope John Paul II wrote: 'God loves all people and grants them the possibility of being saved (1 Timothy 2,4)' (para. 9).

It is possible to try to reconcile these seemingly very different views by holding that the 'true church' consists of all those who, if they had realised the truth, would have become members of the church (they are, however, invincibly ignorant). Or one can say that it consists of all who would have been baptised if they had had the chance. I very much doubt that this is what Pius IX had in mind, and, in any case, it depends upon the truth of a counterfactual conditional – if people knew the truth or had the opportunity to be baptised, they would have acted in a specific way. There is no way of knowing whether such statements about what people would have done had things been different are actually true. In fact, that rather more seems to be a 'good hope' than a known truth. If people are truly free, who knows how they might have acted in circumstances that never actually existed?

An assertion that all people *actually* have the possibility of being saved, or that they *actually* have been redeemed by Christ, is very different from an assertion that, if things had been different (not actually as they are) people would have had a chance of salvation. Moreover, saying that people have been redeemed already does not seem to be the same as saying that they have the possibility of being saved. If you have the possibility of being saved, that implies that you are not yet saved.

It could be said that God has, in Christ, done all that is necessary for salvation – in Christ, God has united human nature to the divine nature – although it is up to individuals to play their part, and either accept or reject this change of state. In that case, God has not actually already fully redeemed everyone, but God has done something that makes redemption actually possible for everyone, whereas before, or without that, salvation was not a human possibility. Now all humans have to do is accept what God has done, which is very different from achieving salvation by one's own acts alone.

---

[2] These Encyclicals are available online.

Perhaps that does capture the sense of recent Papal statements. On such a view, salvation can only be achieved if you realise what God has done and consciously commit yourself to accepting the new role you have been given. You can hardly be saved if you do not believe there is a God who has done anything, or if you turn down the position God has offered you. Thus, at some point atheists must come to believe in God and accept the offer of God's love, before they can actually be saved. In fact, that is what salvation, in Christian understanding, is – the grateful acceptance of the love of God which has been freely offered, and the fulfilled and happy life with God that will result from this. If this is so, there must at least be a point at which they realise what God truly is, so that they can no longer maintain honest doubts about God's existence. Salvation in the Christian understanding is not a coherent possibility for anyone unless and until they come to know the truth about God and the right relationship to God.

Some Christians think that such a point may be the moment of death. There are Christian theologians who think the moment of death is a point of supreme significance, at which one is finally faced with a choice of accepting or rejecting God, and therefore at which one is confronted with an undeniable knowledge of God, in the sense of an awareness of God's presence. At that moment, one might make the decisive choice to accept life with God or reject it.

That view seems to me to be very implausible. Suppose you are a committed Buddhist, who has no belief in God, but has been devoted for many years to cultivating universal compassion. At the moment of death, you believe that you may obtain release from the round of rebirth and suffering and lose your sense of egoistic individuality altogether. Does it seem likely that at the very last moment a God in whom you have not believed will appear to you and offer you a continuance of your individual self in relationship to this personal Lord? All your beliefs will be upset in an instant, and you are asked to choose something you have never before considered, and that you have regarded with some disfavour, without time for further reflection or consideration – and your whole future, for eternity, depends upon it.

Or consider the case of someone who dies after being in a long coma, or when Alzheimer's has changed the personality to a great extent. It can hardly be thought that clarity of mind will come at the moment of death. It seems, therefore, that if there is to be a real possibility of salvation for everyone, and if this entails awareness of the true nature of God and the ability to accept or refuse God's love, then at some time after death such awareness must exist, together with a real freedom of choice.

I do not think this is a view which is radically different from some Biblical suggestions about life in the world to come. Saul was able to speak to the dead prophet Samuel,[3] Elijah and Moses were able to converse with Jesus on the mountain of transfiguration,[4] Jesus preached to the dead after his crucifixion,[5] and Paul seems to accept without critical comment that Christians baptised dead people.[6] If Christians do live after the death of their physical bodies, I am pretty sure most of them will find that they have been mistaken about some of their beliefs. If so, there must be some sort of learning process in which they can discover the truth, some possibility of finding out what God is really like, so that they can know and love God as God really is.

Looking at the huge range of different views about the afterlife that now exist, it is clear that most of them are either absolutely mistaken, or at best inadequate. If there is an afterlife, one will presumably discover this. There will be a truth about whether the afterlife is timeless or temporal, whether there is development of personality or whether there is a possibility of repentance for those who have hated God, and whether one will be able to act and choose in some way. Most of us, perhaps all of us, will receive new information and be considerably surprised at what we find.

A Christian will hope to know Christ much more clearly and adequately when they die, though I suspect this will take quite a lot of development and change on their part, as they gradually dispel mistaken ideas and learn new truths. But Buddhists will not expect to encounter Christ. They accept, however, that they will have to learn much of which they are now ignorant, about their past lives and the course of their future lives. The truth they expect to see more fully is not God, but an indescribable state of bliss and knowledge, a state beyond individual personality or possibility of change. If all have the possibility of liberation, that entails a stage beyond death when all will come to see the truth. Buddhists think that this can happen in a series of rebirths, culminating in final release. At that stage they will presumably have learned the full truth, though it has taken many lives to discover it. Christians will not expect to be reborn on earth, but they must, on this sort of view, expect some sort of developing afterlife, whether their learning process is short or long. It seems that, when it comes to the nature of life after death, most expectations will be wrong to some extent, but some are more wrong than others. It also seems that, if salvation is to be possible for all, even for those who have no religious beliefs, there must be a form of afterlife in which learning and progress is possible.

---

[3] 1 Samuel 28, 8–15.   [4] Matthew 17, 3.   [5] 1 Peter 4, 6.   [6] 1 Corinthians 15, 29.

To say that all have the possibility of salvation, even those who have never heard of Jesus or of the Buddha or of any other religious teacher, is to say that virtually all will go through a time of learning and development, and gradually come to see the truth about ultimate reality and human nature and destiny. Of course, there is always a possibility, logically speaking, that we may remain in ignorance, locked into hatred, pride, and greed, and perhaps never come to know the truth, which would require a transformation of character we might refuse to accept. Perhaps Hell is filled with souls which refuse to learn the truth and live in a fantasy world constructed by their own perverse desires. But even then, salvation must remain a possibility for them, for it hardly seems compatible with the love of God to say that, once they have had just one chance, they are condemned to misery forever.

The implication is that knowledge of truth is only possible for those who have prepared themselves to receive truth. It requires moral and spiritual preparation. From a Christian point of view, awareness of the true reality of God is not possible for those whose lives are bounded by hatred and pride, for what we see is a function of what we are. Just as a scientist must learn to honour truth and to understand physical laws, so the religious devotee must learn to honour goodness and to discern a presence which can only be seen by the eyes of love.

Within the Roman Catholic Church, the doctrine of Purgatory does give a temporal dimension to the afterlife and entails that there can be development and purification. Perhaps virtually everyone goes to Purgatory, or some similar 'intermediate state', whether they have been baptised or had faith in Christ or not. This would be a change in the doctrine of Purgatory as it has been received in the Roman Catholic church. But it would not be wholly unprecedented. In the sixteenth-century, Cardinal Bellarmine is reputed to have said that Catholics are bound to believe that there is a Hell, but are not bound to believe that there is anyone in it. Perhaps Hell is empty, and Purgatory is full. Or perhaps Hell is just a logical possibility for those who refuse to progress in Purgatory, because they are lost in hatred and ignorance.

Suppose that some Christian doctrine of salvation is true. Some devout Buddhists have practised their religion all their lives, so have they been pursuing a false path, which they will then have to abandon? Or are there enough truths in their Buddhist way to enable them to say that their practice has not been wholly misleading? The evidence suggests that there are. The Buddhist eightfold path requires the cultivation of universal compassion and the avoidance of harm to living beings. It requires a renunciation of the three fires of greed, hatred, and ignorance. It may, in some Buddhist forms, encourage devotion to *Bodhisattvas*, beings of wisdom and compassion. A Christian may well hold that compassion, selflessness, and devotion, even if they are associated with false ontological beliefs (about rebirth and *Nirvana*), are unequivocally good. The Buddhist ideal of care for all life may even seem morally superior to many traditional Christian attitudes to animals. To the extent that moral excellence at least leads towards, not away from, salvation, Christians must think that the Buddhist way is not totally misleading, that it contains some important moral truths.

Christians may complain that Buddhists also hold some false beliefs – for example, that there is rebirth, and that the Buddha attained complete enlightenment without God. But most Christians would admit that holding some false beliefs is compatible with salvation. For they will be aware that, whatever their particular form of Christian belief, there are other Christians who disagree with it. Baptists may think the belief that infant baptism delivers from original sin is false, but they would these days probably admit that even Catholics can be saved. Holding some false beliefs is not a disqualification for salvation.

Perhaps a Christian may say that, unless one accepts Jesus as Lord and Saviour, one cannot be saved. Yet what, after all, is entailed by accepting Jesus as one's personal Lord and Saviour? It cannot be just a matter of purely theoretical assent. Such a thing, if it is honestly made, is not a matter for either praise or blame; it just records what one honestly believes to be the case. Accepting Jesus as Lord must be a matter of accepting his presence as a living power in one's life, as one who actually 'saves' from sin (and a rather good definition of sin is that it consists in the Buddhist 'three fires' of greed, hatred, and ignorance). At this point a Christian can say that Christ is the saving power of God which gives new birth and transformation of personality. But such a power may exist, even if it is misdescribed. A theoretical mistake does not entail the lack of personal transformation by spiritual power.

The Buddhist may deny there is any such objective power and assert that one must achieve spiritual enlightenment by one's own power. That is assuredly a difference (though devotees of *Amida* Buddha do affirm such an objective power of spiritual transformation). We cannot say that Buddhists and Christians believe the same things. Buddhists, to put it crudely, have no God and no grace in their theoretical catalogue. From a Christian point of view, their ontology may be 'gravely deficient', as the Papal document 'Dominus Jesus' said. Nevertheless, a life devoted to compassion, selflessness, and devotion is one that has a firm grasp of some important moral truths. Such lives are not following a totally false path. They are lives devoted to truths, which they often grasp and practice better than their Christian counterparts, and which are of vital importance to religious faith. It is possible that the grace of God may be working in them without their knowledge – anonymously, as Karl Rahner famously put it.[7] But whether or not that is so, if the Christian view is correct, Buddhists will not need, after death, to wholly reverse their spiritual paths. They will rather need to expand it to include the power of the Wisdom of God to enable them to complete their spiritual quest.

Of course, Buddhists will feel the same about Christians who, Buddhists may think, do their best to seek compassion and selflessness, although they are hindered by superstitious beliefs about a personal God which must be cast aside (at some future time) before enlightenment can be obtained. The Dalai Lama is quite relaxed about saying that Christians should continue on their own spiritual path, since he believes they have future lives in which to correct their primitive superstitions, and they are doing many good things. Christians have often been much less relaxed insofar as they have believed that the crucial decisions about salvation need to be taken before death. For them, lack of belief in God makes impossible that loving relationship to God in which salvation exists. However, if one has a belief in continued awareness and freedom in the world to come, then the 'inclusive' view of salvation – that one way leads to final salvation, but many ways in other traditions lead towards salvation, even though they lack a full understanding of what salvation is – becomes plausible and attractive. Truth remains exclusive, but salvation is inclusive – it is possible for all.

[7] Rahner (1966).

27

Truth and Religious Language

*I*N *AN INTERPRETATION OF RELIGION*, HICK OFFERED THREE possibilities for the epistemological status of religions – either all religions are false, or one religion offers the only truth (exclusivism), or the 'great post-axial religions' are all more or less equally true (pluralism).[1] To this list might be added the 'inclusivist' option, outlined by Hick's pupil Alan Race,[2] and often associated with Karl Rahner, which states that one religion offers the full truth, but some other religions do have some truths.[3] Professor Schmidt-Leukel, who strongly supports Hick's pluralistic hypothesis, has argued that these are the only four logically possible positions that one can take.[4] But that does not seem to be the case.

Religions are not, as such, either true or false. They are mixtures of stories, rituals, institutions, ethical rules, experiences, and doctrinal truth-claims. Most religions do contain a set of connected truth-claims, organised around some basic key claims, often to do with the status of their founders. However, the particular truth-claims found within religions can be considered separately from the total sets of which they are parts, and for some purposes it is useful to do so.

The claim that there is a creator God can be considered in itself, apart from the wider contexts (in Islam and Judaism, for example) in which the claim might be set. Naturally, the wider context will determine particular, and probably differing, interpretations of the claim. But the claim itself can be separated from the religion, or from any religion.

---

[1] Hick (1989), p. 235.   [2] Race (1983).

[3] Diana Eck, director of the Harvard Pluralism project, used similar categories, and she espouses a form of pluralism which encourages an 'encounter of commitments', and avoids some of Hick's more questionable theses. See Eck (2003).

[4] Schmidt-Leukel (2017).

The point is that it may not be helpful to consider just the total sets of truth-claims that are found in particular religions or religious institutions. One may find that no set of claims can be considered as fully true (which would exclude the exclusivist and inclusivist options), but that a set of claims can be constructed which might be considered to be true, taking specific claims from different religions, and perhaps also taking claims from various sources that are not religious. Then one would have a true set of claims, but no actual religion would possess it as a set. This would enable one to say that no actual religion has the full truth (nor does one's own constructed set have to make such a bold claim), and it is not the case that all religions are more or less equally true. There is not a word for such a view, but I suspect that many religious believers adopt a position rather like this in practice.

Another possibility is that a few religions might possess a basic set of truth-claims in common. One might then say that a group of religions, not just one, possessed a set of truth-claims that were more adequate, in important respects, than other religions. That, again, is not quite inclusivism, since no claim is made that one religion, or this relatively adequate set of religions, possesses the fulness of truth. Nor is it pluralism, because one is certainly not claiming that all religions are more or less equally true.

Or one might claim that one religion is more adequate than others (more of its set of truth claims, especially the most important ones, are correct), but that no religious institution possesses the fulness of truth, and that virtually all religious institutions make some mistakes.

An interesting possibility has been canvassed by Mark Heim, which he calls 'a theology of religious ends'.[5] Like Hick, he affirms that different religions have different ends or goals. 'Salvation', personal communion with a personal ultimate reality, is the distinctive goal of Christianity. Other religious goals, like Buddhist *Nirvana*, do not attain salvation, nor do their adherents wish to do so. Nevertheless, a range of religious goals are attainable, and they can be truly achieved. Buddhists can and do attain *Nirvana*, *Advaitins* can attain identity with the ultimately real, and Muslims can attain Paradise (but not, Heim says, real personal communion with God). This is like Hick's pluralism, insofar as it is true that there are differing religious goals, and Christianity offers only one of them. Reality is such that it is hospitable to differing religious paths.

Nevertheless, Dr. Heim believes that Christian theism encompasses in the 'most inclusive and simultaneously rich ways the variety of the divine

[5] Heim (2001).

life itself'.[6] Indeed, he sees the Trinity in its complex and varied aspects of 'union-in-diversity' as licensing all these different religious goals, since they represent partial aspects of genuine divine reality. The Christian idea of the Trinity is able to offer a fuller truth, and in this respect Heim's view differs from that of John Hick. Heim's view can then seem like a form of inclusivism, but it differs by denying that non-Christian religions are no more than preparations for Christian truth. They may be such preparations, when treated as transitory steps towards salvation. But they need not be taken as transitory, and he accepts that from their points of view Christianity may well be seen as a partial and transitory step towards their own final goal.

This is a finely worked out proposal, which shows the complexity of speaking of religious truth. It allows that diverse religious traditions are 'part of God's providential purpose'.[7] But it does seem to be uneasily balanced between inclusivism and pluralism, between asserting the absolute truth of Trinitarian theism and affirming the sufficient truth of a number of diverse and apparently contradictory religious ends. It is certainly another item to add to the list of logically possible options in this area. Yet in the end it seems odd to think that there is one absolute (Trinitarian) truth, and yet that humans may achieve satisfying religious final goals without recognising that. Their goals must seem rather like 'super-limbos', wherein, though they are spiritually and morally satisfying, the final truth about the universe is not fully known. If truth is of ultimate value, that will not seem finally satisfying after all.

There are no doubt other more complex possibilities, but they all depend on the fact that particular truth-claims are exclusive in the sense that they exclude their contradictories. Religious truth-claims typically belong to sets of related claims, which are maintained by particular religious institutions or communities. Members of those sets may not all be true, and it is possible or even probable that no set contains all the truths there are about ultimate reality or about how to achieve human fulfilment. If this is so, inclusivism is not finally a satisfactory view, because it implies that one institution contains in a fairly complete form all the truths anyone needs to know in religion. It may be better just to maintain that particular truth-claims are exclusive, but to leave open the question of whether and to what extent some of these claims are made by specific religious institutions or religions.

I have asserted that truth-claims are exclusive. But there are some qualifications to be made. Truth-claims are always made in some human language.

---

[6] Heim (2001), p. 289.   [7] Heim (2001), p. 291.

Human languages differ greatly, and things that can be said in one language are sometimes very difficult to express in a different language. Consider the things that are said in poetry. It would be harsh to say that poems make no truth-claims. Yet a poem would be destroyed if its truth-claims were extracted and listed in clear propositions. There is something about the way things are said, about the way concepts convey something new when they are juxtaposed in new and perhaps surprising ways, when they are placed in different contexts, and when they are parts of a ritual practice (like hymn-singing or a sacrificial ritual). Just think how difficult it is to say exactly what truth-claims one would really assent to, even when enthusiastically singing a Victorian hymn, or how difficult it is to say exactly what is being claimed in the Christian Mass when the words 'This is my body' are pronounced in the correct ritual context and by the right person. Eastern Orthodox Christians tend to be suspicious of Western Latin attempts to put what is being said into a precise philosophical (and Aristotelian) vocabulary (like the definition of trans-substantiation). If language is part of a social practice, its role may be evocative or symbolic rather than straightforwardly descriptive. It does make truth claims, but it becomes very difficult to say exactly what these are, or even whether one should seek to be too conceptually precise about language, which is often used to evoke or convey intuitions or feelings which human concepts cannot literally convey.

When Rudolf Otto used the word 'numinous' to convey a certain sort of religious experience, he sponsored a new insight into that sort of experience.[8] One might almost say that he invented it, though that would be rather unkind. Or when Tillich said that God was not a being, but Being-itself, this sponsored for many people a new insight into the transcendence of God – though others found it just meaningless.[9] Religious language in general is often found to be meaningless by non-religious people. I have often heard people say, 'I do not know what "God" means', or even 'The word "God" is meaningless'. There are uses of language which come to have a use in a specific group, but that use remains opaque or sometimes even objectionable to outsiders.

Not only is it difficult to pin down exactly what truth-claims many religious statements are making, it is also the case that, while individual truth-claims are exclusive, sets of truth-claims need not be exclusive of other sets of truth-claims. It will be hard to define with any precision the limits of a

---

[8] Otto (1959).   [9] Tillich (1951).

'set of truth-claims' which constitute a religion. Believers may disagree on how many such truth claims there are in their religion, and on how important it is to accept various claims. John Locke, for instance, in *The Reasonableness of Christianity*, held that only one truth-claim is essential to being a Christian.[10] That is, 'Jesus is the Messiah'. Of course, that phrase entails many other claims – that there is a God, that God chooses someone to liberate people from sin, that there is such a thing as sin, that there is a specific number of people who are to be liberated, that there is a specific way of liberating them, and that the liberated state consists in worship of God. Each of these claims is subject to various interpretations, so there does not seem to be a definite number of claims in the Christian set, or agreement on exactly what they are.

[10] Locke (1998).

28

A Case Study: Christianity and Islam

I WILL TRY TO ILLUSTRATE THE IMPLICATIONS OF THE INDEFINITENESS OF some basic religious concepts by looking at some of the traditional differences between Christians and Muslims. These differences have been so great that they have led to misrepresentation, ridicule, and persecution, and to some extent they still do. But it could be the case that such attitudes have partly arisen from attempts to interpret religious concepts in an unduly literal and definite way. To the extent that religious concepts are seen to be symbolic and conceptually indefinite, such negative attitudes can be counteracted from within the religious traditions themselves.

For instance, it may seem obvious that one must accept that 'Jesus is Messiah (Christ)' if one is to be a Christian. But this statement may be taken in a symbolic sense – Jesus did not after all literally save Israel from her enemies. And it may be very indefinite – it was never very clear in Jewish thought exactly what the Messiah would be, though the Messiah was to be in some undefined sense a liberator from evil and the founder of a just and compassionate society. One possible interpretation of 'Jesus is Messiah', taken in a symbolic and indefinite sense (nevertheless as stating an important truth) says that God acts through Jesus to liberate from evil those who follow him, and they constitute a new society of disciples. This need not be seen as contradicting a Muslim assertion that God acts through Muhammad and the Qur'an to counter hatred and intolerance and relate those who accept the Qur'an properly to God. Both might be true; God can act in different ways to liberate people from evil and relate them to the divine in obedient love. Conflict arises when Christians and Muslims think that theirs should be the only religion in the world, since theirs is exclusively true. To say that these faiths can be seen as complementary, even though they do reflect major differences of interpretation, would remove one source of that conflict.

One can have more or less restricted views of what being a Christian or being a Muslim is. A more restricted Christian view might say that people must believe that Jesus died on the cross if their sins are to be forgiven, and Muslims cannot believe that. Then there is a contradiction. But a less restricted view might say that God acts through Jesus to liberate from evil, which is brought about through the love of God, whose nature is revealed by Jesus' self-offering on the cross. People do not have to believe or even know about this for it to be true. A similarly less restricted Muslim opinion may accept such a view, with the proviso that the liberating love of God is also communicated by the Qur'an, and that the cross is a symbol of God's self-giving love rather than, say, an actual substitutionary sacrifice.

There would still be the question of whether Jesus actually did die on the cross. Many Muslims think this would be impossible, since a true prophet would not be killed as a criminal. Differences would still exist. But it is not impossible to interpret the relevant Qur'anic text – 'They [the Jews] did not kill him . . . though it appeared like that to them'[1] – to say that the enemies of Jesus thought they had killed him, whereas in fact he descended to the world of the dead and ascended to the presence of God, and this was not a total end of his existence. While differences about the exact meaning of the cross remain (as they often do between Christians), many possibilities of re-negotiation and re-interpretation of some traditionally disputed concepts of different religions also remain.

A similar sort of convergence is possible between Muslim and Christian views on the Trinity. A restrictive Christian view might insist that there are three personal wills in the divine being, and a Muslim would probably reject that – the Qur'an says, 'Do not say three'.[2] But if the Christian held that there are three modes in which God always exists, yet God is one mind and will – as Rahner and Barth both do[3] – a blunt contradiction disappears. It would be clearer that there is only one God, but Christians would say that God exists in three ways – a view a Muslim may not accept, but which does not constitute a denial of the unity and reality of the divine being.

The Qur'an also says, 'Allah begets no son',[4] and this, on a restrictive view, contradicts Christian doctrine. Again, however, the expression 'Son of God', can quite properly be taken as a metaphorical phrase referring to a human being whom God chooses to express the divine will in a special way – and both Adam and David are referred to as 'sons of God' in this sense. Muslims might not be able to agree that Jesus was chosen by God to express in a

---

[1] Qu'ran 4, 157.   [2] Qu'ran 4.171.   [3] Rahner (1979); Barth (1936).   [4] Qu'ran 17,111.

human person the eternal Word of God. But they could agree that the use of this expression does not commit the error of thinking that God has a partner who is a divine separately existing son.

A Christian text which often causes trouble for interfaith conversations is found in the reported words of Jesus in John's Gospel: 'I am the Way, the Truth, and the Life. No man comes to the Father but by me'.[5] A very common restrictive interpretation of this text is to say that, unless people explicitly profess faith in Jesus, they cannot live with God. But it seems just false to say that no-one can worship God unless they believe in Jesus. A non-restrictive interpretation would be to say that what is meant by 'me' is not the human Jesus, but the eternal Christ, the Word of God. The Word was truly embodied in Jesus, but pre-existed Jesus and, therefore, has an existence which is other than the human person of Jesus. Thus, one could take the reported words of Jesus to say, 'In me is embodied the Way ... no man comes to the Father but by this Way, the Way of the eternal Wisdom of God'. Since that Wisdom exists independently of Jesus, it may be embodied in different forms. Jesus is a true form of the Way, and a Christian might say, a decisive and distinctive insight into the divine nature. In that sense he is the Way. But Jesus is not the only form of the Way.

Therefore, Jesus *as a human person* is not literally the only way to God. The Way of Wisdom is the only way to God, and, in the end, if this statement in John's Gospel is true, all will come to realise that Jesus is a fully authentic human expression or embodiment of the Way of Wisdom – 'no man comes to the Father but by the Wisdom of God, which I express so fully that it and I are one'. A Muslim may not see Jesus in this way, as the human embodiment of Divine Wisdom (though the Qur'an does say that Jesus is a 'spirit from Him [God]').[6] But a Muslim could readily accept that only through obedience to divine Wisdom could anyone come to know God truly. A difference remains between Christian belief in Jesus as Divine Wisdom (metaphorically described as 'the son of God' and 'the Word of God') and Muslim belief that Jesus is a great prophet, but no more. They disagree about the authoritative form of God's revelation. But they could agree that both could be taken (by different people, usually) as genuine forms of divine revelation, seen in different ways. Neither says that the other is wholly mistaken, though they may think they are partly mistaken. This would be a great advance in interfaith relations.

These are examples of cases which have caused, or have been important contributory causes of, violent conflict in human history between Christians

---

[5] John 14, 6.   [6] Qu'ran 4, 171.

and Muslims. Convergent interpretations are possible, though they will never be accepted by all Christians and Muslims, and though differences of emphasis and specific belief will remain. At least, though, such differences will be more like differing interpretations of a broadly similar spiritual teaching than like rank contradictions which might lead to adherents of each religion seeing adherents of the other as members of an opposing and hostile faith.

The more restrictive conditions that a set of claims contains, the more it is likely to conflict with different sets of claims. The more latitude that is allowed in interpreting claims, the less conflicts are likely to arise with different sets of claims, and the less such conflicts will be taken as erecting insuperable barriers between faiths. Whether or not one set excludes others will depend on how the set is interpreted, and on exactly what the claims that one takes to comprise the set are. One can see how a form of pluralism could seem plausible, as long as a set of religious claims contains many important claims that are symbolic and indefinite, and so allow a wide variety of interpretations. It is not that specific truths are no longer exclusive. It is rather that contradictions can be avoided between sets of claims if one can find an interpretation which makes differing claims complementary, not blatantly contradictory. Or some might prefer to say that the differences of interpretation are not exactly complementary (such that both could be believed at the same time), but that they express differing perspectives within a common acceptance that in these events, and to some persons within a particular cultural/historical tradition, something important of a supremely good God is really disclosed.

Is this really a form of pluralism? It provides genuinely different concep-tions of a Real which is the same in many major respects (being Creator, Compassionate, and concerned for human well-being). A Muslim and Christian could agree that the way their revelatory source (Bible and Qur'an) has been interpreted has often embodied mistakes made by some groups of scholars. Indeed, it is hard to see how they could deny this, since they both must disagree with interpretations of their Scriptures that have been made by sects of their own religion opposed to theirs. If they are reasonably self-aware, they may go on to admit that their own preferred interpretation may well contain some mistakes, and they might well both agree that the Real-in-itself is beyond full human comprehension.

Differences remain, so this is not a pluralism that holds that both ways are equally true or valid. But it can accept that people see things in different ways, that their own personalities and cultures and histories enable some of them to have perspectives on truth that are not accessible to others. In the being of God, no doubt, all these perspectives can be united or qualified in a whole which is able to place them all within a wider and richer reality that can modify each of them by its fully understood relation to the others. But for humans, with their limited perspectives, such a unity is not possible, and humans continue to see and evaluate things in different ways.

If one thinks of the appreciation of art or music, one can see how different people see different things in a painting or symphony. Some people are unable to see what others see; some people see in deeper and more appreciative ways than others; no-one just sees 'the truth'. One can speak of insight rather than truth, though some insights are more penetrating, more accurate, and more comprehensive than others. Many religious differences are rather like that, matters of insight rather than truth. It is important to try to make our insights deep and broad, truthful to what is there to be apprehended. But we may realise that none of the concepts available to us can capture the whole or the one finally accurate picture of the truth.

On a view like John Hick's, one could see all the founders of the great religions as charismatic figures who share an intense experience of a higher spiritual reality, a revolutionary moral message, and an ability to communicate their experience to others.[7] But their concept of that spiritual reality is formed by their own culture and history. The language they use to describe it is taken from that culture and embodies many of the beliefs and values of that culture, however renewed or transformed their creative reception of that culture is. On this view, claims to a uniquely correct and final vision are renounced, and Muhammad, Gautama, Jesus, and Moses, and others too, are seen as creative reshapers of, as well as protesters against, many of the forms of their existing religious traditions.

A person who takes this view may think that Jesus may have been mistaken in thinking the kingdom of God was just about to arrive with a decisive day of judgement on Rome and Israel. He might well have assumed some sort of Messianic role, though one that was radically revised in a non-violent and non-political direction. Siddartha Gautama may have been mistaken in believing in reincarnation, and in thinking that he had attained liberation from the cycle of rebirth. He might well have taught that final liberation was to be achieved by meditation and the overcoming of all sense of ego. But both teachers may, nevertheless, have had a genuine, if partly misdescribed, acquaintance with the Transcendent, which was able to change and deepen the understanding, the moral concern, and the inner

---

[7] Hick (1989).

personal experiences of their followers. Despite that, the Transcendent in itself is not wholly captured by their descriptions of it. The expression 'Father' is maybe too anthropomorphic, and the expression '*Nirvana*' maybe too negative, to express the Transcendent in anything like a finally correct and adequate way.

The adoption of a view like this may take one outside all existing religious traditions; or one may remain within a religion, often adopting at least a partly symbolic interpretation of it; or one may take thoughts from two or more religions in the attempt to find a more adequate view of spiritual reality and be a 'double' or even 'multiple' religious belonger.

Many, if not all, religions do agree, however, in making the minimal claim that there exists something which is ultimately real without depending on anything else, and which is other and greater in value than any physical things, perhaps even supremely good. They agree that it is possible to cultivate some form of relation to this 'something' which inspires moral effort, enhances personal well-being, and gives an insight into a form of reality which is other than the physical. Perhaps here, at least, is something in common to many major religions. Part of the difficulty in obtaining clarity on these issues lies in the idea of 'a religion', an idea which is extremely difficult to define, and perhaps erects artificial barriers where none need exist.

29

Cantwell Smith

*P*ROFESSOR WILFRED CANTWELL SMITH WRITES AS A HISTORIAN and a specialist in the study of Islam, and as one who has come to think that the very term 'religion' is a reification which is more misleading than helpful. It divides religions into discrete blocks of belief and places too much emphasis on sets of abstract propositions which define different religions. So, it tends to ignore the changing, diverse, and complex processes of religious belief and practice, as they are found at different points of history and in different cultures of the world. He proposes 'the conceptualisation of historical process as the context of religious life, and participation as the mode of religious life'.[1]

There are many sorts of Muslims, Buddhists, and Christians, and what is important about them religiously, Cantwell Smith holds, is that they have a relationship to transcendent reality, mediated through the symbols and rituals of various cumulative traditions. Those traditions do tend to begin with a prominent founder or reformer of tradition, but he rejects what he calls the 'Big Bang' theory of religion, which is that the founder issues a complete teaching or doctrine which is just faithfully repeated in each succeeding generation. On the contrary, the life and teachings of tradition-founders is itself amplified through myths and legends, and it changes as time goes on. For instance, how the disciples saw Jesus is different from how Thomas Aquinas saw Jesus, and the Christianity of the Council of Trent is different from the early Christian gatherings of disciples.

What matters is the present mediation of transcendence through the present local and probably transient interpretation of a cumulative tradition. As the process goes on, major thinkers provide new revisions of the

---

[1] Cantwell Smith (1981), p. 33.

tradition, and the process carries on into the future in unpredictable ways. To be a believer is not to accept a static set of doctrinal truths, but to participate in a continuously changing tradition of religious practice.

This view requires a new historical awareness of the process of one's own cumulative tradition, and it requires a new awareness of the truly global context of which all cumulative traditions are part. Professor Cantwell Smith wants the study of religion to be a study of the religious history of humanity, in which people of different faiths will all share. Once they see the 'religions' as diverse processes of continuous change – diverse within traditions as well as between them, and inter-related in many ways – they may come to see their traditions as parts of a global history, which is advancing into a new future.

This view is the opposite of the 'perennialist' view that there is one ancient and continuous tradition of thought that underlies all religions, often in an esoteric or hidden way. For Cantwell Smith, the unity of religions lies in the future, as a goal to be aimed at. It will not be the recovery of an old tradition. It will be the formation of a truly global view of religions, which has only become possible at this moment in history.

Cantwell Smith holds that 'each person's faith has been particular, personal, has been of a specific historical form'.[2] As a personal faith, it is 'one's existential engagement with what one knows to be true or good, obligatory'.[3] That knowledge comes through a particular and local interpretation of a cumulative tradition. 'The locus of revelation is always the present, and always the person'.[4] But that faith, that commitment to transcendence as mediated by one cumulative tradition, is in the case of all such traditions one that leads to 'salvation' – devout believers are 'saved from nihilism, from alienation, anomie, despair',[5] and from egoism, greed, and delusion.

At this point it becomes clear that the view is a quite radical form of pluralism. He wants people to stop thinking of religions as sets of largely incompatible truths, and to start thinking of many different traditions (diversely many even within the large blocks we have thought of as 'religions') in which people participate because they sense the possibility of personal transformation to a new meaning, purpose, and wholeness of being, mediated to them by the symbols and rituals of a particular tradition, or possibly of more than one tradition.

If we see religions in this way, then the thought of a future convergent spirituality becomes possible, in which many traditions, recognising their

---

[2] Cantwell Smith (1981), p. 167.   [3] Cantwell Smith (1981), p. 119.
[4] Cantwell Smith (1981), p. 175.   [5] Cantwell Smith (1981), p. 168.

own fluidity and the salvific efficacy of many other traditions, begin to coalesce into a truly global tradition. This would not eliminate diversity, but it would be a sort of global unitive ecumenism, relating different religions in somewhat the same way as different churches can ecumenically be seen as diverse expressions of one religion without losing their diversity, but also and crucially without seeing others as aliens excluded from true faith.

This vision is an attractive one, but it does present some intractable conceptual problems. For instance, he says that 'the religious history of the world is the record of God's loving, creative, inspiring dealings with ... men and women'.[6] The trouble is that Buddhists and Taoists and Confucians would have trouble with using the concept of 'God', and this gives rise to the suspicion that Cantwell Smith really thinks theism is true, in a sense in which non-theistic views are not. He even says, 'My proposal is unabashedly theocentric'.[7] It is not just that different groups use different symbols of transcendence, but that some groups think their symbols are actually true, even if in a metaphorical or analogical sense.

Cantwell Smith prefers the word 'transcendence' to the word 'God'. But do all religious traditions have a similar idea of 'transcendence'? Casting around for an alternative to 'God' he at one point speaks of a 'surpassingly great Other',[8] but 'surpassingly great' would entail omnipotence for some, and not for others; it would imply personal will for some, but not for others. Perhaps at a very general level one could say that most religious do posit a 'spiritual dimension' which is other and, in some sense, greater than the purely physical, but this general agreement is quite consistent with huge areas of disagreement when one tries to be more specific. The highest level may succeed in demarcating an area of interest, but it does not carry enough content to constitute an actual tradition of thought and practice.

To be more positive, what it may do is motivate a search for positive interpretations of the idea of 'God' which are less anthropomorphic and which admit the inadequacy of all human descriptions of Ultimate Reality. But it will almost certainly not lead to the complete replacement of some idea of God by a term which will be wholly acceptable to Confucians.

When Cantwell Smith says, surely provocatively, that in every religious tradition, salvation is by faith, he has to redefine both 'salvation' and 'faith' in new and unusual ways. He thinks of salvation as transformative and fulfilling experience, and of faith as commitment to what one believes to

---

[6] Cantwell Smith (1981), p. 171.   [7] Cantwell Smith (1981), p. 177.
[8] Cantwell Smith (1981), p. 186.

be good and causally powerful. I think one could plausibly say that different traditions can give a sense of transformative experience and call for whole-hearted commitment to some greater reality that can evoke such experience. That is an advance on the view which holds that followers of religions other than their own are deluded, invincibly ignorant, or culpably wicked. But what of those who think that faith is trust in the promises of a personal God, and that salvation is a conscious relationship of love to such a God? Martin Luther, who insisted misleadingly that the Bible says salvation is 'by faith alone' (it does not), would not be impressed to be told that people can gain a sense of fulfilment by total commitment to what they think of as a greater cause. The definition covers too many things, many of them positively evil, like fascism, to be useful.

Nevertheless, one could see faith as a passionate commitment to the best accessible and practical possibility, where theoretical certainty is unavailable. And one could see salvation as happiness in the contemplation of the good, where the good is increasingly known as one moves towards it. Even if one was badly mistaken about the best possibility, if the mistake was made without a disguised evil intent it might be counted as genuine faith in objective goodness. This might be enough to start a person off on the way to salvation, even though there would be much to learn as the process continued. In that sense, it could be said that people can be ultimately saved by honest moral and spiritual commitment, given that they still have much to learn about the true object of such commitment. Perhaps, after all, that could be said of almost all of us.

It is good to look for interpretations of a religious tradition that do not demonise alternative traditions, but that look for positive affinities between traditions. The Confucian concern to live in a way that justly reflects the 'Way of Heaven' does have a positive affinity with a Christian view that one should obey the will of a personal God. To see and stress this may to some extent broaden or modify one's interpretation of one's own tradition, but it will not lead to complete agreement on what such a way of life is like, or what its ultimate goal is. To say that both are 'saved by faith' disguises the depth of disagreement.

This becomes clear when Cantwell Smith says 'Theology [should] abandon the use of concepts that give rise to statements such as 'God is fully revealed' or 'God was revealed in Christ'.[9] True, as he says, God is never fully revealed to anyone. On the other hand, Christians mostly think that God

---

[9] Cantwell Smith (1981), p. 175.

was revealed in Christ in a way that was distinctively and definitively true. Muslims mostly think that the Qur'an is the Word of God, not just that God has spoken to Muslims through the Qur'an.[10] It does help the cause of religious understanding to think that God inspired the Qur'an and that Muhammad is a great prophet, rather than thinking that the Qur'an is totally false and that Muhammad is anti-Christ (as has been said by some Christians). It does help to see that the Qur'an is to Muslims what Jesus is to Christians, a finite disclosure of the nature and will of the infinite God. But it does not really help religious understanding to think that the Qur'an and Jesus are equally appropriate symbols of transcendence whose only function is to help people to live better.

I also think it is not true that 'the locus of revelation is always the present, and always the person'.[11] On this definition, almost anything can be a channel of revelation and transformation, and that is precisely the trouble! The reduction of revelation to something contemporary and local means that there are no decisive revelations given anywhere in history, that my present experience takes precedence over the revelatory events or texts upon which my faith tradition was founded and by which it lives. It is true that traditions are diverse and changing, a flow of interpretations, but the interpretations are of some basic revelatory core, whether text, teaching, person, or event.

That basic revelatory core does not have to be regarded as a full and final revelation of the true inner nature of spiritual reality. If it was so regarded, then all alleged revelations would simply contradict each other. If that conclusion is to be avoided, the idea of 'revelation' or 'inspired teaching' needs to be nuanced. One way of doing this is to think of revelations as partial disclosures of the nature of the spiritual dimension, in ways that develop existing patterns of knowledge, thought, and evaluation, but do not simply cut across them as a set of inerrant truths. Revelation is perhaps something more allusive and poetic, more intermingled with the knowledge and evaluations of particular individuals, as they participate in their own historical traditions.[12] It is, as John Hick held, as if there is a synergy or interplay of human and the objective Spirit, a process of discovery which is subject to many blind alleys as well as positively transforming insights, and which is not necessarily progressive in every respect.[13]

Do Cantwell Smith's reflections, even when qualified, support his argument that 'the concept of a religion is recent, Western and Islamic, and

---

[10] Cantwell Smith (1981), p. 164.   [11] Cantwell Smith (1981), p. 175.
[12] This view of revelation is elaborated in Ward (1994).   [13] Hick (1989).

unstable'?[14] He asks whether perhaps 'these terms [Christianity, Buddhism and the like] will not in fact have disappeared from serious writing and careful speech within 25 years'.[15] For 'God . . . does not reveal a religion, He reveals Himself; what the observer calls a religion is man's continuing response'.[16]

It is more than 25 years since he wrote those words, and still books continue to appear about 'the religions of the world' (including this one!). It is illuminating to be reminded that the word 'religion' was before modern times largely used to mean 'piety', and that phrases like the Qur'anic phrase, 'Verily the [only] religion in the eyes of God is Islam',[17] might be better rendered as 'true piety in the eyes of God is the submission of the self to God'. It is salutary to accept that religions are not self-contained blocks of exclusive intellectual doctrines, that can be compared and ranked as better or worse, true or false. But a problem is exposed when he speaks of 'God' revealing 'Himself'. This view of revelation would not even be accepted by all Christians, many of whom think God does reveal propositions, and truths about things other than God's own being, and it is too theistic for many cumulative traditions.

Religions may be more fluid and flexible than many suppose. But in the modern world they do self-identify as owing allegiance to some distinctive founder or tradition. I suspect that 'cumulative tradition' is old 'religion' under another name, and that it is often useful to refer to many traditions by referring to their canonical Scriptures. The word 'religion' remains useful in designating a sphere of human thought and practice that is not, as such, either politics, ethics, philosophy, science, or art, but that many take to be of great importance.

Oppositions, on rational and moral grounds, will and must exist, but they will not be between religions as such. They will often be between negative and destructive tendencies in religious life and positive and creative tendencies. Both negative and positive tendencies exist in all religions, and religions are rarely wholly negative or wholly positive. There will usually be differences between overly certain and exclusive interpretations and more intellectually tentative and open interpretations of the same religious doctrines within larger cumulative traditions of religion. The development of religious traditions in the whole history of humanity can become a datum for spiritual reflection, and one such development is one that seeks convergence, so far as is possible, in such a way that each tradition, remaining distinctive, reflects

---

[14] Cantwell Smith (1978), p. 120.   [15] Cantwell Smith (1978), p. 195.
[16] Cantwell Smith (1978), p. 129.   [17] Qu'ran, 3: 19.

others in a non-aggressive and empathetic way. Religious traditions must change and develop, and one motor of such change is increasing understanding of differing traditions, and the discriminating evaluation of the positive insights they express.

What is of great value in Cantwell Smith's position is the suggestion that one should not speak of religions as true or false, better or worse, blocks of beliefs. We should not speak of religious beliefs as unchangeably solidified in a finally adequate way. We should not claim undue certainty and clarity for our views. But we can, and perhaps must, be passionately committed to practices and beliefs we think to make for human authenticity, the good of humanity, and the preservation of the world. We should be concerned not to embrace practices that cause harm. Religions may endure, but they change, and they should change towards a greater convergence and acceptance of a mutually honest and informed search for a life-enhancing relationship with an objectively existing Good.

Part V

Catholicism and Pluralism

30

Karl Rahner

I HAVE EXAMINED THE WORK OF A GROUP OF MAINLY LIBERAL Protestant Christian thinkers as they proposed revisions to traditional Christian beliefs which encourage some form of pluralism, or acceptance of many forms of religious belief as moments in the global process of a general history of religions. I noted that Troeltsch, who began by holding that Christianity is the absolute or at least the normative religion, changed his mind and, like John Hick and Cantwell Smith, preferred to see a range of religions as diverse, partly flawed and partly insightful and creative vehicles in which experiences of transcendence could occur.

There is, I think, little hope that this view could become universally adopted by all members of all religious traditions. In the case of Christianity, there will surely continue to be many who think that Christianity is the absolute religion, the fulness of truth which no other religion can match. This is true of many Evangelical Christians, and it is also true of the Roman Catholic Church, the largest Christian Church in the world, in its official teachings.

One of the most eminent Catholic theologians, Karl Rahner, who was influential in drafting or inspiring some of the documents of the second Vatican Council, has been an important voice in formulating the response of the Roman Catholic Church to the phenomenon of religious pluralism. In contrast to most liberal Protestant thinkers, he says that 'pluralism ... in part at least, should not exist at all'.[1]

Christianity, and specifically the Roman Catholic Church, is 'the one and only valid revelation of the one living God'.[2] It 'understands itself as the absolute religion, intended for all men, which cannot recognise any other

---

[1] Rahner (1966), p. 115.   [2] Rahner (1966), p. 116.

religion beside itself as of equal right'.[3] The coming of Christianity entails 'the abolition of the validity of the Mosaic religion and of all other religions which may also have a period of validity'.[4] Their period of validity, however, has passed as soon as its members come to realise the claims of Christianity, after which, if they do not convert, they incur a 'personally guilty refusal of Christianity', which is 'the only still valid religion ... a necessary means for his salvation'.[5]

These are uncompromising words, which probably exclude all Protestants and Eastern Orthodox believers as well as people like Buddhists and polytheists. The awkward thing is that other religious groups, like many Muslims, Evangelical Christians, and Jehovah's Witnesses, make exactly the same claims for their own faiths. There are a number of religions which do not recognise the rights or validity of other religions and think it would be better if those other faiths did not exist. This is not in itself socially intolerant, but it easily leads, and has led, to the banning and persecution of other religions, and in that sense it is a dangerous view, from the point of view of members of other faiths or none (that is, the greater number of the world's population). It is sad if religions like Catholicism, which profess to be based on universal love or compassion, and on respect for human life, for justice, and mercy, espouse views which can very easily become dangerous to society and to many individuals. I think one reason for querying Rahner's stated view is that even the smallest possibility of encouraging this danger is in strong tension with the concern for love, even of one's enemies, which is supposed to characterise Christian faith.

Rahner is keenly aware of this, and he modified his view considerably in the second thesis of his paper. There he insists that 'God desires the salvation of everyone'.[6] This, he thinks, entails that all humans must have the possibility of 'a genuine saving relationship to God' ... 'One and the same Absolute may manifest in the most varied forms',[7] and these forms may, to various degrees, be 'positive means of gaining the right relationship to God'.[8] Of course, some religions may be so immersed in falsehoods and immoral practices that they must be opposed. But in many religions one may find the grace of God operative, as it must be if God desires the salvation of all. Many religions may be salvific, in the sense that they are paths towards salvation.

---

[3] Rahner (1966), p. 118.   [4] Rahner (1966), p. 119.   [5] Rahner (1966), p. 120.
[6] Rahner (1966), p. 122.   [7] Rahner (1966), p. 128.   [8] Rahner (1966), p. 125.

Rahner takes Judaism as an example and says that the teaching of Jesus shows it to be a mixture of divine revelation and grace with some error and corruption. 'It does not at all belong to the notion of a lawful religion intended by God for man as something positively salvific that it should be pure and positively willed by God in all its elements'.[9]

In this way he allows that there can be, and are, salvific religions with revelations that are mixed with human error, and in these religions its adherents 'have the right and limited possibility to criticise' and to try to correct errors that they may come to perceive. However, he exempts the Catholic Church from such a possibility. The Catholic Church is 'the explicit expression' of the hidden universal reality of God's saving action, and when people are fully confronted with Catholic truth they must join the Church, in which they have 'a greater chance of salvation'.[10] Since more and more people are today in a position to hear the teaching of the Church, 'the possibility [of personal criticism and improvement of the faith] is gradually disappearing today'.[11] The Catholic Church has a magisterial teaching authority, and its adherents are obliged to accept what that authority pronounces.

In Rahner's third thesis, he postulates the idea that members of non-Christian faiths are 'anonymous Christians'. They are 'touched by God's grace and truth',[12] but the absolute truth and a greater chance of salvation lie in the Roman Catholic Church.

The admission that many religions can be salvific and contain much truth, even though mixed with some unclarity about salvation and with some errors about God's nature and purpose, marks a clear difference from those, mostly Conservative Evangelical Christians, who think that only Christianity is salvific and true. But it maintains the belief that only Jesus Christ is the saviour of all people, by holding that Christ is present in a saving, but hidden, way in many places, including many religions, other than the Church which possesses the absolutely true faith. More conservative believers are probably right in suspecting that, once one makes this move, it is a short and natural step to say that the salvific presence of Christ in any Church, including the Roman Catholic, is compatible with some uncertainty and error. Perhaps the full understanding of salvation, and the absolute comprehension of the nature of God, lies in the future, or even lies beyond any merely human understanding for the foreseeable future.

---

[9] Rahner (1966), p. 129.   [10] Rahner (1966), p. 132.   [11] Rahner (1966), p. 130.
[12] Rahner (1966), p. 131.

This is a theme that has been explored by more recent Catholic theologians, though Rahner's view is probably nearest to the present official teaching of the Roman communion. That teaching changed, partly because of Rahner's influence, at the Second Vatican Council, and so it is theoretically possible that it could change again, if it comes to be thought that some development of doctrine is possible that does not simply reject the past teaching of the Church.

31

Hans Kung

$\mathcal{A}$ NUMBER OF ROMAN CATHOLIC THEOLOGIANS HAVE BUILT ON Rahner's[1] work, and have taken it in more radical directions, with varying degrees of critical response from the Vatican. Hans Kung objected, as many others have, to Rahner's concept of 'anonymous Christians', finding it patronising and unhelpful to interfaith relations. Kung does want to say that Jesus is the 'full realisation' of human potential, and the normative case of divine revelation, which other religions need to learn from. Nevertheless, he thinks that other religions can be proper paths to salvation, and he tries to move the Catholic view from 'ecclesiocentrism' to 'theocentrism'. God, not the Church, is the one who saves, though the revelation of God in the person of Jesus has absolute validity. The church is not the company of those who are saved. It is the symbol of salvation for everyone.

In his book, *Christianity and the World Religions*, he engages in a conversation with scholars of Buddhism, Islam, and Hinduism, to show how Christianity has many things it can learn from those traditions.[2] But, though he does not see such traditions just as a sort of preparation for joining the Catholic Church (so they are not anonymously Christian), he is clear that in his view Jesus Christ sets a standard that they must learn to meet. Jesus might not be 'constitutive' of salvation (so that only his death and resurrection makes salvation possible), but he is 'normative' for salvation (his life shows what salvation, available to all, is really like).

When Kung speaks of Islam, he calls for the beginnings of a critical study of the Qur'an and of the diverse historical origins, influences, and developments of Muslim faith, acceptance of religion as part of a secular society, and acceptance of the full equality of women and of universal human rights.

[1] Rahner (1966).   [2] Kung (1993).

He lauds the distinctiveness of the Christian insight that God is 'love' and contrasts the voluntary suffering of Jesus with some of the acceptance of violence in the Qur'an. While he is clear that Islam and Christianity are different, that Islam is an independent path to salvation, and that 'each religion recognises the others as dialogue partners of equal value',[3] nevertheless he finds a normative and over-riding value in the Christian stress on the love of God and the suffering of Christ.

There is a slight irony in Kung's position here, since critical study of texts and historical origins, and a stress on the equality of women and human rights, are very recent features of Christianity, and are still opposed by many Christians. Some would say they are due to the Enlightenment rather than to the Christian faith, which lived without them for a millennium. Moreover, critical study of the Bible has thrown doubt, or at least uncertainty, on what one can justifiably say about the character of Jesus. It can seem that what Kung is really suggesting is that all religions need to be reformed in the light of the Enlightenment values of informed critical enquiry, concern for universal human flourishing, and toleration of diverse religious beliefs. And he is recommending, for Christians, that Jesus should be seen as a preacher and embodiment of unlimited divine love and the possibility of universal salvation – a view that is certainly compatible with, but not securely derivable from, historical research alone. So, the distinctions he makes between Christianity and Islam are not really remarks which are unequivocally true of the religions considered as if they were blocks of beliefs that are relatively unchanged over the years. They show the influence of Enlightenment factors on religious thought – and such factors have indeed had more impact on part of Christianity than on most of Islam. And the claim that historical research will establish certain facts about the person of Jesus underplays the role of faith in Jesus as the incarnation of the divine Logos in making historical judgements about his person.

Similarly, when he speaks of Hinduism, Kung emphasises the historicity of Jesus in contrast to the largely mythological status of Krishna. Yet, historians differ as to whether Jesus was an eschatological and rather judgemental and exclusively Jewish prophet or a reforming and reconciling proclaimer of a universal kingdom of love. For instance, Kung thinks that Jesus, like Paul, was very critical of religious law, speaking rather of the freedom of the Spirit. Yet, Matthew's Gospel presents Jesus as upholding a rigorous interpretation of Jewish law.[4] And did Jesus not threaten that

---

[3] Kung (1993), p. 180.   [4] Matthew 5, 17–18.

the way to salvation was narrow, and that the many who did not find it would be destroyed?[5]

My point is not to say that Kung is wrong about Jesus. It is that there are different ways of interpreting the historical Jesus, and it seems that all historical judgements made on so little evidence, all of it biased, can at best give rise to probable judgements. Truly critical historical study must leave us more agnostic about what Jesus, as a historically accessible figure, was really like, so it can hardly be a definitive point about Christian faith that it is founded on a historical figure about whom we have secure historical knowledge. The best we can do is to say that the Jesus-figure that Kung prefers – the preacher of the Sermon on the Mount as an elevated moral ideal, who gave his life in trusting obedience to God's will – is a faith-inspired picture which a historian as such could not provide. It is quite possible to see the Sermon on the Mount as commending an impractical and impossibly rigorous lifestyle for people facing an imminent end of history ('Take no thought for tomorrow'), and to see the crucifixion as the failure of Jesus' prophetic mission to bring in the Kingdom of God (which is partly why many Muslims cannot accept that Jesus, as a true prophet, can have been crucified).

Appealing to the historicity of Jesus is, as Harnack said, more like actually appealing to one's own image of human perfection or fulfilment. That image will be influenced by reading Gospel accounts of Jesus, but one's reading of those accounts will also be influenced by moral insights, understandings of human nature, and general world-views derived from many sources which may be independent of historic Christianity and have formed the background of one's own development. It is not just a matter of history versus myth. The belief in Jesus as incarnate Logos is more closely tied to the historical records of Jesus than beliefs about Krishna are tied to more or less reliable histories. Yet, in both cases, the commitment to a certain image as representative of the divine is needed to provide an interpretation of the historical facts. There is a difference, but it is not one that makes an absolutely polar distinction between these two religious traditions.

In discussing Buddhism, Kung points out that it privileges monastic life, has often not been socially transformative or involved, and can involve a rather pessimistic view of human existence from which release is to be desired. He says that 'Christianity has perhaps perceived more clearly and interpreted more adequately' the social needs and structures of human life.[6]

---

[5] Matthew 7, 13–14.   [6] Kung (1993), p. 360.

Further, 'Christian thought can perhaps . . . develop a deeper understanding of the uniqueness of the human person'.[7] He does say 'perhaps' and admits that these are the personal judgements of a Christian, but he is in fact citing them as reasons for valuing Christian faith as normative, that is, as of greater value than religious judgements which fail to emphasise them and as expressions of absolute truth. He has not moved far from Rahner.

I suspect that Kung's observations do not provide a compelling reason for seeing that Christianity is of greater value or more normative than Buddhism. There are too many varieties of Buddhism and Christianity to make such a judgement, and anyway 'value' is too vague a term to be useful. It does provide a reason for saying that social issues should be important to Christianity and Buddhism. Christians, as well as Buddhists, have often held that their faith is concerned more with life after death rather than with political and social realities on earth. Christians could think more deeply about the relational nature of the self, and though Christians may wish to stress personal moral responsibility (and Buddhists, after all, certainly do that), they could well see insights into selflessness and universal compassion in Buddhism that they might have overlooked. From the Buddhist side, since most Buddhists are not monks, there is in fact a serious concern in Buddhism with the structures of social life, and with the serious demands of morality. And human persons are mostly regarded by Buddhists as of crucial importance, since only they can obtain enlightenment, and what they do has serious consequences for many future lives.

It seems to me that it could well be said that, in its early days, Christianity almost entirely lacked any social teaching at all, and Jesus expressed no view on how society in general should be organised. As for thinking about the human person, Christian views can vary between thinking that we enter into a timeless eternity after death and thinking that our bodies will one day rise from the grave. 'Official' church views have emerged from time to time, but there are many Christian churches, and many of them have very different views of human nature and destiny.

It is not that there are no differences between Buddhists and Christians. It is rather that these generalisations are so broad, and so susceptible to historical changes and developments, that one should perhaps not try to compare 'religions' as if they were self-contained blocks, and then produce general value-judgements about them. They are neither all of equal value, nor is it necessarily the case that one religion as such can be assessed as of

---

[7] Kung (1993), p. 381.

greater or less value than another. One has to be more specific and address particular problems of very different sorts as they arise in each tradition. In the modern world, part of our cultural situation is the fact of conscious co-existence with many different religions. This might lead one to say that Christianity is not, as such, the full realisation of what all religions strive for. Just as not all Buddhists really have a hidden desire to be members of the Catholic Church, so they do not all have a hidden desire to follow a Jesus the particular historical interpretation of whom is not as clear as Professor Kung suggests.

Professor Kung accepts Friedrich Heiler's general distinction between prophetic and mystical religions.[8] Hinduism, Kung says, belongs in the mystical camp, and Kung characterises it as a 'natural-cyclical' religion. As natural, it lacks a social dynamic, and as cyclical it lacks a purpose or goal for the cosmos and the process of history. Christianity, on the other hand, is a prophetic faith, positing a moral goal in history, and a moral demand to pursue it. Like most generalisations, Heiler's division, while in some ways helpful, overlooks the many sorts of different approaches to religion that exist in the world – mythical, teleological, world-renouncing, moralistic, gnostic, devotional, socially committed, aniconic, sacramental, to name only some. It also overlooks the fact that some Hindu systems, like that of Aurobindo, do look for a future moral goal in history, and some Christian systems, like that of Augustine, deny that there is any moral goal to be achieved in the history of this planet, since things are only going to get worse, and the world will come to an end in a dreadful Day of Judgement quite soon.

Hans Kung has made an invaluable contribution to inter-religious understanding in the modern world, but he is still ambivalent about whether the Christian faith, in one of its forms, is the standard or norm for all religious truth, or whether there are different paths of salvation that are valid for their adherents without being preparations for the Christian Gospel. Other Catholic writers have probed this ambiguity, which basically arises from the official Catholic position (at the time of writing) that the fulness of truth and the paradigm path to salvation is found in the Roman Catholic Church.

Kung tries to place that path in the historical Jesus rather than in the institution of the Church, but the historical Jesus needs to be interpreted, and that requires some tradition of interpretation upon which one can rely. Whether it is the Catholic Church or not, the Catholic Church has

---

[8] Heiler (1932).

certainly developed and preserved a tradition of interpretation that has
become part of the defining background to contemporary Christian thought.
The question for some Catholic theologians now is how far that tradition
can or should change in response to various factors of our historical situation. I will mention three Catholic writers who have gone a little further
than Hans Kung in querying the normative or exclusive uniqueness of the
Church.

32

Raimon Panikkar

$\mathcal{R}$ AIMON PANIKKAR WAS A CATHOLIC PRIEST WHO ONCE SAID OF himself, 'I left Europe as a Christian, I discovered I was a Hindu and returned as a Buddhist without ever having ceased to be a Christian'.[1] He argued that a central insight of Christianity is what he called the 'cosmotheandric reality', that is, the ideal of a complete unity between the divine and the human. In his book, *The Unknown Christ of Hinduism*,[2] he held that this unity was found uniquely in Jesus, but that the eternal Christ was also present in hidden ways in other religions, and especially in the Indian tradition of Vedanta. In his later work, he went further, and suggested that the eternal Christ could be embodied in different forms. No historical form could be the full and final expression of the Christ, and the presence and reality of Christ cannot be restricted to the historical person of Jesus. 'Jesus would be one of the names of the cosmotheandric principle, which has received practically as many names as there are authentic forms of religiousness'.[3] Panikkar does regard Jesus as 'for him' the ultimate form, and as a historically *sui generis* epiphany of Christ.

Unlike Kung,[4] Panikkar does not begin with the historical Jesus, but with the eternal Logos or Word of God. From that point, it is a short step to saying that the Logos could be embodied in many finite forms. Aquinas apparently thought there could have been more incarnations of the Word on earth, but as a matter of fact there had only been one.[5] Anyone who thinks Christ could be incarnate on other planets or in other galaxies also seems

---

[1] Panikkar (1993), p. v.   [2] Panikkar (1964).   [3] Panikkar (1969), p. 101.   [4] Kung (1993).
[5] Aquinas (1967), Part 3, Question 3, Article 7. The point made is that God could have assumed more than one human person to the divine nature. Generalising this point, there could have been more than one divine–human nature, although Thomas Aquinas thought such a thing was not needed.

committed to saying that there could be many forms of embodiment of the one Christ. This is not an outrageously radical move.

It is hard to see, however, that the same cosmic Christ has actually been embodied in many different religions. How could a *Theravadin* Buddhist, who does not think there is a God, see the Buddha as an embodiment of the cosmotheandric principle? It would be easier for a *Mahayana* Buddhist to regard the Buddha as an embodiment of cosmic mind, the *Dharmakaya*, and this would be near to Panikkar's principle. But that seems to involve picking out similarities or close analogies between diverse religions, rather than making a claim about all or even most religions.

Another close analogy to a faith based on divine–human unity can be found in Vedanta, which often incorporates a view that the Supreme Lord appears on earth and sometimes in a human form, like Krishna, to save humans from evil disasters. It is, therefore, no surprise to find that Panikkar was able to identify as the sort of Hindu who accepts Siva as a personal form of Brahman, the ultimate reality of consciousness and bliss, and to interpret this as another manifestation of the Christ.

Even then, one is not speaking of an identity of doctrines, but of close analogies to incarnation, though framed in a very different cosmology involving many rebirths and appearances of the divine in non-human forms. One can find such analogies fairly readily, and they can be ranged on a scale of decreasing similarities. The most similar would be forms of *Mahayana* Buddhism and *Avataric* Hinduism. Rather less similar would be non-theistic movements, like Jainism, which posit a spiritual reality composed of many liberated intelligences, who can be revered and function as ideals for living a detached life. Here the identity of human and divine would be conceived as an inner identity of embodied souls with those souls in the liberated state. Further along the scale might lie Chinese movements like Taoism and Confucianism. The 'spiritual reality' there is an indescribable Way of Heaven or cosmic balance of the complementary forces of Yin and Yang, which can be expressed more or less fully in a human life either in accordance with nature (in Taoism) or of positive, formally structured and harmonious social relationships (in Confucianism) or in some combination of both. And towards the outer limit of the scale would be the local nature deities of tribal religions who can be temporarily embodied in the trance-states of Shamans and Oracles.

I do not think it is misleading to see all these different forms as expressions of or strivings towards a spirit–human unity, which a Christian might see as partial human embodiments of eternal Wisdom and/or Goodness, embodiments which find a historically *sui generis* and ultimate human epiphany in Christ. However, one would have to admit that, from the viewpoint of a Taoist, the identification of the Tao with a personal Creator would be an infantile and anthropomorphic projection of a mind which could have specific personal relationships with human individuals. Thus, as Panikkar confesses, seeing Christ as an ultimate epiphany is a rather subjective valuation which only Christians might be disposed to accept. Nevertheless, this view would enable Christians to see other religions not as inimical enemies or demonic realities, but as partial and divinely inspired moves towards true life in God.

Some Roman Catholic theologians, like Gavin D'Costa, while not going as far as Panikkar, are prepared to refer to the Spirit of God as a presence in many religions. The eternal Word and the Spirit are very closely united, and almost certainly always act indivisibly, in a Trinitarian view of God. In this sense one could speak of Christ, or of the Spirit of Christ, as present in many faiths. But could one see the Spirit as, for instance, inspiring *Theravadin* Buddhists to deny the existence of a personal God? Obviously not. Then we would have to say that the Spirit is just one partial influence, though a divine one, on the thoughts and decisions of human beings. Independent human thought and experience, developed over many years of reflection and action, apparently responds to the promptings of the Spirit in many diverse ways, and is only able to apprehend those promptings in ways shaped by their culture and history.

Once this idea of a co-operative influence of the divine Spirit, 'tuned to' the thoughts and feelings of humans, has taken root, it is reasonable to apply it throughout the global history of religions. One natural implication is that all religious traditions would be a mixture of divine inspiration with human thoughts and experiences. To this one must add the almost universal tendency of humans to corrupt and turn to egoistic purposes all influences, whether divine or not, on their thinking. This could raise a question-mark against any claim that just one religion is normative or contains the fulness of truth.

Professor D'Costa, however, is a staunch defender of the view that the Roman Catholic Church is the only truly salvific and divinely revealed structure in history, that it is normative for all religions, that it contains the fulness of truth, and that there is no 'salvific structure or ... divine revelation' in any other religion.[6] Yet, he also says that all humans can be 'saved', that the Holy Spirit is active in other religions, and even that other

---

[6] D'Costa (2000), p. 105.

religions may have things to teach the Catholic Church. It is difficult to see how these statements are compatible. The difficulty is that there seem to have been quite a few mistakes made by the Magisterium of the Church – the 'Syllabus of Errors' seems to be one, and the past insistence that Matthew was the first Gospel to be written, now rescinded, is another. It is, thus, difficult to say exactly which statements made by the Magisterium are guaranteed to be true. This does not mean that God is not acting in a salvific way in the Catholic Church, but it does mean that a total and unique grasp of the truth is not necessarily the possession of any one religious institution, even the Roman Catholic Church.

In any case, if the Spirit is active in many religions, they must be 'salvific structures' in that such divine activity must be seen as conducive to salvation. D'Costa says 'This is not supernatural revelation in the technical sense, although it is assisted by grace and leads to salvation'.[7] This entails that the Baptist church and the Muslim faith, for example, have no divine revelation, 'in the technical sense'. Whereas it seems clear that, if the Spirit is effectively working to increase knowledge of God and the necessity of worshipping God, then it must indeed, as D'Costa says, be conducive to salvation, and it must be brought about by an activity of God which is revelatory of the nature and existence of God. I am not sure what 'in a technical sense' adds to the argument, since the activity of the Spirit which increases knowledge of God is a real, not just a technical, causal factor. Non-Catholic religions may not present salvation in a complete sense, a Catholic might say, but there does seem to be some form of revealed truth in them, and some pointing to the fulness of salvation.

To that extent, non-Catholic forms of religion must be considered to have some legitimacy. Yet, Dr. D'Costa holds that other religions have 'no independent legitimacy'.[8] That statement is very worrying to those who believe in freedom of religious thought and practice. If it is admitted that there are some mistakes in the Catholic tradition, however trivial, and some truths in other religions; if there are many Catholic sinners and many non-Catholic holy and heroically moral people; if people honestly following their consciences cannot see that the Catholic creeds are true; and if Christ or the Spirit is at work in various religions, how can one say that non-Catholic religions are not legitimate?

Where does the idea of 'legitimacy' come from? If a belief is legitimate, that means it is permissible to hold it. If it is illegitimate, it is not permissible

---

[7] D'Costa (2000), p. 104.   [8] D'Costa (2000), p. 113.

to hold it. But in religion it is simply not clear to all intelligent people that Catholic beliefs are correct, so why should Catholic beliefs alone be permissible to hold? 'Error has no rights', D'Costa says. But no-one ever said that error has rights. It is people who have rights, and people have the right to believe what others consider to be errors, as long as those errors do no obvious harm and are conscientiously held. True, this is a 'liberal' opinion, and liberalism was condemned in the 'Syllabus of Errors', but that makes me more uneasy. Has that not been repudiated by the Second Vatican Council? Are we still to say that, in predominantly Catholic countries, Protestants have no right to exist? That has certainly been held in the past (Anglicans and Protestants have held that sort of illiberal belief too in the past, even though the Protestant Reformation was a major factor in establishing the right to religious dissent). The duty of the state to refrain from coercion in the practice of religion does not just establish a 'negative civil right', as D'Costa claims,[9] it entails the correlative positive right of people to practice their religion freely. And this entails that such practice, the practice of acting on conscientiously held religious beliefs of many sorts, is legitimate.

This is perhaps the most important practical question about pluralism – whether conflicting religious truth-claims have a right to exist in society. From Plato's 'Laws' onwards, moralists have tried to repress views that conflict with their own. One of the lessons of the Enlightenment is that such repression is bad, that it eliminates the possibility of gaining greater truth from open criticism and discussion, and even from a religious point of view it conflicts with Christian ideals of charity towards the beliefs of others and humility about the certain and unquestionable truth of one's own beliefs.

Is one to treat religion as a matter of the sole legitimacy of a particular religious institution, or rather see each religion as one claimant among others to highly disputed truth-claims? It is not surprising that Panikkar seems ambivalent about whether Christ is the normative expression of divine truth, or whether God appears to different humans and societies in different and possibly incomplete and complementary ways – in which case Christ would not be normative for everyone, and perhaps a more purely theocentric view would have to be developed.

---

[9] D'Costa (2000), p. 137.

33

Paul Knitter

*P*AUL KNITTER IS A CATHOLIC THEOLOGIAN WHO GRASPS THIS nettle and tries to present a less institution-centred and more theo-centric view. Of course, in a global context, even a theocentric view would be too limited, as one has to take account of many non-monotheistic religions. It seems that the more one tries to include all religions in one's account of the phenomena of religion, the less content one can require in constructing a personal statement of religious belief.

When Paul Knitter considers his own religion, Christianity, he is influenced by critical Biblical scholarship to view the resurrection of Jesus as 'not essentially different from what Christians can and should experience today'.[1] It is an experience of the living Lord, and stories of an empty tomb and a walk to Emmaus are later mythologisations of that experience. He is also prepared to see talk of incarnation in terms of the charismatic teaching and intense experience of God that were seen in the life of Jesus, rather than implying the descent of a pre-existent Logos to earth from heaven. Jesus is an eschatological prophet who later came to be seen by the Church as an incarnation of the divine Logos.

These are certainly views that can be held by Christians, but they represent a denial of occasional and dramatic supernatural or miraculous acts of God, and they place the central emphasis on the experience of forgiveness and new life that Jesus brought to his followers. It is when this is done that it becomes possible to see diverse religions as places where similar sorts of experiences have occurred, where the transcendent mystery is apprehended through some finite person or event. Knitter writes: 'Is not ... a faith experience essentially what countless men and women have felt in their

---

[1] Knitter (1985), p. 199.

experience of other archetypal religious leaders [than Jesus]?'[2] The central
notion is that of a 'faith experience' (shades of Schleiermacher), an experience which 'moves the human heart', 'broadens the horizons of understanding', and 'promotes the psychological health of all people'.[3] These are wholly
commendable factors, it seems to me, but they do allow a broad range
of very different objects of faith. A Confucian could well have such an
experience, believing that it fulfils all these criteria, and still have no notion
of a supremely good personal Creator God.

'There can be, and most likely are, other particular mediators of this
divine mystery, a mystery that can be captured, definitively, by no one
mediator'.[4] However, it is not just that the mystery cannot be captured
definitively, which is no doubt true of all religious definitions, it is that our
definitions are in conflict, a conflict which appeal to ultimate mystery does
not resolve. Knitter says he is persuaded that Christians should testify to the
'uniqueness and the universal significance of what God has done in Jesus',[5]
and that they should also respect claims made for the uniqueness and
universal significance of 'what the divine mystery may have revealed through
others'. But respecting the claims of others is not accepting those claims or
holding that they are as true as the claims of the religious tradition one
accepts.

Knitter goes on to say, 'I propose the recognition of a common ground
and goal' of all religions.[6] This has been called 'unitive pluralism'. Yet, that is
where the problem lies. Can the common ground be both a loving God who
wills unending life for all, and a cosmic principle of harmony and balance
which has no personal will at all? Can the common goal be both a heavenly
communion of love and a purely earthly society in which filial piety is
sacrosanct? These grounds and goals are not shared. In fact, it is precisely
because they are not shared that it is worth attentively and empathetically
listening to what others who differ from us have to say.

Paul Knitter sees this point when he says that religious 'maps of reality'
are 'really different and . . . these differences are necessary in order to know
the territory'.[7] We need to see the point of positing a Trinity and the divine
oneness; of stressing the nonduality between human and divine and the
radical distinction between finite and infinite; of seeing that the prophetic
stress on social justice must be balanced by the teaching of the contemplative
life. We must also see that no-one can hold all these views at the same time,
and that we are not trying to construct a new religion which somehow holds

[2] Knitter (1985), p. 200.   [3] Knitter (1985), p. 231.   [4] Knitter (1985), p. 203.
[5] Knitter (1985), p. 203.   [6] Knitter (1985), p. 209.   [7] Knitter (1985), p. 220.

them all together. We are trying to set our own faith in a broader, and ultimately in a global context.

In response to Knitter, one might say that no-one, of any faith or of none, can avoid evaluating the specific truth-claims present in religions. If all religions were to accept the more naturalistic accounts that Knitter commends, they would of course be much closer together, but they are not going to do so; even most Christians would disagree with Knitter's accounts of the incarnation and resurrection of Jesus. If it really is a good thing to hold different views in tension, then liberal and traditional views of religion must also be held in tension. Then it becomes clear that they cannot all be true, and that we must personally evaluate specific truth-claims as more acceptable than their contraries or remain agnostic about them.

Perhaps it is for this reason that Knitter ends his book 'No Other Name?', one main point of which has been to say that there is no one normative religion, with a hesitation: 'Perhaps Jesus the Nazarene will stand forth ... as the unifying symbol, the universally fulfilling and normative expression, of what God intends for all history'.[8] If, by a normative expression, what is meant is something that is just absolutely or definitively true, then it has to be the case that either no-one has the absolute truth, or there are some truths about spiritual reality that are definitively true, and they exclude their opposites. Those truths might not be all in one place, one 'religion'. They could be spread through a number of religions or world-views. It could be that some interpretation of Jesus, perhaps as an example, unique because of its unrepeatable context in history, of the cosmotheandric principle, turns out to be absolutely true. In that case one could commit to being a Christian, and to the normativity of Jesus Christ, while also affirming that no Christian Church has a monopoly of all the truth, and that some other religions also possess different absolute truths that Christians have not seen or emphasised enough.

[8] Knitter (1985), p. 231.

34

Peter Phan

*I*T IS A POSITION LIKE THIS WHICH INFORMS THE WORK OF THE
Roman Catholic theologian, Peter Phan. He writes as an Asian Catholic.
Beginning from an informed Catholic viewpoint, he is keenly aware of the
situation that Asian Catholics face, as small minorities in predominantly
Buddhist, Hindu, or Communist countries. After many years of missionary
activity, Catholic Christianity has not attracted more than a tiny minority of
Asians. That is partly because they already had access to sophisticated and
well-loved traditions older than the Christian, and because their general
attitude to religions was not one that made exclusive claims to complete
truth, but one that often combined different religious practices and concepts
in various ways. So, a new religion associated with a Western colonialist
culture and making exclusive claims to superiority seemed alien to their
natural ways of thinking.

In this situation, Phan uses a definition of pluralism that concentrates on
the idea of salvation rather than of truth: 'All religions are valid paths
leading, each in its own way, to salvation'.[1] Rahner had written, rather
ambiguously, that many religions may have temporary validity, and may
be paths towards salvation, though ideally they ought to accept the fulness of
redeeming truth in the Catholic Church.[2] But Phan goes further than this,
and suggests that one should no longer say that the Roman Catholic Church
possesses the fulness of truth, but one should say that many religions are
valid paths to salvation in themselves, and that the existence of more than
one religion is a positively good and divinely willed thing. This supposition
raised the ire of conservative Catholic Bishops in the USA, but their criti-
cisms partly miss the point, since Phan is not actually speaking of ultimate

---

[1] Phan (2017), p. 115.   [2] Rahner (1966).

truth, but of the possibilities of salvation, and claiming that many religions do lead to salvation.

There is a problem, however, which is that some religious paths are not interested in what Christians call 'salvation', and would deny that such a state is their goal. Some Buddhists think that the idea of personal immortality is not a desirable one, and that it should be renounced as a goal. If salvation is construed as personal immortality in conscious relation to a personal God, such a Buddhist path, it may seem, could hardly be said to be a path towards salvation.

Does this mean that such Buddhists can be saved despite their religious beliefs, or because of them? Phan opts for the latter alternative, and that is probably what worried the American Catholic bishops. How can Buddhists achieve a goal which their path denies is a desirable one?

if 'salvation' is construed as personal relationship to a personal God, most theologians would admit that the sense of 'personal' and 'relationship' in this statement is either analogical or metaphorical or both. That does not mean that the statement is not true, but it means that the statement is almost certainly an inadequate and partly symbolic way of stating an objective truth which the human mind is unable to grasp in its fullness.

This is why Phan objects to the claim that the 'full and complete truth' about God is revealed in the church, or even in Jesus. It is wholly orthodox to say that no purely human mind can ever grasp the full and complete truth about God. Phan puts this forward by saying that the full truth may indeed be revealed in Jesus, but probably nobody has understood it fully. I am sure he would say that what is absolutely and finally revealed in Jesus is that God is love, but that is after all a very vague statement, even for those who believe it is completely true, and what such 'divine love' is and implies remains as a project to be worked out through perhaps centuries of human reflection and practice – and the church has not been very good at it.

The thing about analogies and metaphors is that, when they differ, they do not necessarily contradict. If a Christian says that we will be bound in a mutual union of love with God for ever, and a Buddhist says our sense of self will pass over into a boundless state of compassion and bliss beyond individual personhood, then if taken literally these statements will be contradictory. But if we take these as inadequate symbols of a state beyond the present comprehension of most of us, things are not so clear. Both statements deny that individuals are annihilated after physical death. Both commend the practice of love, compassion, and selflessness as ways to attain some final state which is thought to be of supreme value. Both condemn egoism, pride, hatred, and greed, and say that in the ultimate state such tendencies will cease to be. Both postulate a goal of supreme value, to be attained through disciplines aiming at a state of being beyond our present suffering and sorrowful existence. They are obviously not identical, but it would be correct to say that both aim to foster spiritual welfare, as Phan puts it.[3] It is in that sense that both may be 'paths of salvation', increasing awareness of a spiritual reality of supreme value that both exists now, and also lies ahead as a goal of spiritual practice.

Phan's aim is to say this while maintaining the traditional Christian position that Christ is the only saviour of the whole world. This is a coherent position, as I have suggested in Chapter 26. One can say that many (not all) different religious paths increase awareness of a supreme spiritual reality which fosters 'justice, peace, reconciliation and love'.[4] But (probably some-time after death), it will be seen by all that the most adequate symbol for humans of this reality is the Trinitarian model of one supreme Spirit who is transcendent creator, incarnate redeemer, and sanctifying Spirit.

This looks like the 'inclusivist' thesis that one religious view has a more adequate conception of God as self-giving love and of salvation as a communion of love than any religion which lacks such concepts, although many other religions contain important elements that are true. It is not like the form of 'pluralist' thesis that says all religions are more or less equally conducive to salvation, even when salvation is seen in its final and fully achieved form. It is pluralist on Phan's definition because it claims that many religions are paths to salvation – which does not entail that any of them have a wholly adequate and correct understanding of what final salvation is. Thus, at one point, following Jacques Dupuis, he calls his view an 'inclusivist-pluralist' thesis.[5]

Writing as a Roman Catholic theologian, Phan thinks that such terms as 'unique, absolute, and universal', when used of the Christian set of truths, must be very sensitively handled.[6] If no human is capable of knowing the fullness of truth about God, even a 'true definition' of salvation will be inadequate in some ways and liable to being misunderstood. So, if one speaks of 'absolute truth', one must be aware that all language about the divine is inadequate and symbolic in some ways. The form of words we use, with the best of intentions, is probably not 'absolutely' true – truly conveying exactly what God is in Godself. The best that might be said is that it is the most adequate formulation that we humans can understand. Nevertheless, a truth concerning God could be described as absolute, even if it does not adequately or fully state what is objectively the case, if within the limits of

---

[3] Phan (2017), p. 130.   [4] Phan (2017), p. 157.   [5] Dupuis (2002).
[6] Phan (2017), pp. 97–98.

human language, and without laying down a fully specific interpretation, it says something accurate about God. An absolute truth about God, in this sense, might be, for instance, 'God is the creator of the universe'. It hardly tells one everything about God. Nor does it make clear exactly what 'creation' is. But to deny it, for an adherent of an Abrahamic tradition, would be to say something false. While the statement would be in some ways indefinite and perhaps symbolic (we ordinarily understand creation as a temporal process of making something out of an existing material), there is no sense in which, taken without further interpretation, it is false.

As for the word 'unique', it might suggest – and has suggested to some – that only explicit knowledge of Jesus conveys truths about God, but one can hold that there are other great spiritual teachers who convey important truths about a spiritual reality of supreme value, and there are other Scriptures which do the same, and are surely inspired by what Christians may call Holy Spirit. Nevertheless, it could be the case that Jesus is unique in being the only case on earth of a complete union between human and divine, and also historically unique in having the vocation of bringing into being the rule of the Spirit (the Kingdom of God) in a new communal form (the 'new covenant'). Jesus is not the only way to know God, but for many Christians Jesus is the only case of divine–human union and founder of the community of the Spirit of God on earth.

Christians generally believe it is true that Christ is the Saviour of everyone, and in that sense the universal saviour. But if it is said to a Jew or a Buddhist that their views about spiritual fulfilment are 'gravely deficient' and that they can only be saved if they turn to Christ during their lifetimes, then that sounds offensive and patronising. Phan insists that we should not regard all religions as 'preparations' for the Catholic truth, which fulfils and supersedes them, rendering them obsolete. They are 'ways of salvation', by which their followers are saved. Those ways are not and should not be replaced by Christianity, nor should we attempt to convert all their followers to Christianity. Nevertheless, Christians may reasonably believe that it will become clear at the last that all are saved (related to a loving God) by the Wisdom of God, which was incarnate in Jesus.

There is a sense, then, in which the words absolute, unique, and universal can be used of certain religious truth-claims, and Phan does not deny this. But his concern is to stress that this does not mean that absolute truths leave nothing important to be said about God. The assertion of some unique truths does not entail that Christians need learn nothing from other faiths. The claim to have universal truths does not mean that other faiths have nothing of value to add to Christian apprehension of the divine. This is especially important when the assertion of truths is linked to the existence of a specific religious institution, or church, as though all the absolute, unique, and universal truths of faith are possessed by just one institution.

What is important in this life is for people to follow their consciences in seeking a good and spiritually fulfilled life. If they are Jews or Buddhists, this will usually mean following their own path towards such fulfilment. Any claim like, 'My saviour is superior to your enlightened teacher' will sound hollow when uttered by a comfortable well-fed priest to a Buddhist monk who has renounced all worldly goods. Christians must show by example what a God of self-giving love is like, rather than announcing that everybody ought to agree with their beliefs. Jesus Christ is the universal saviour because he serves the world in love, not because he sought to impose a specific set of truths on everybody.

It could be misleading to say, as Rahner did, that ideally speaking only the Roman Catholic Church should exist (something that Pius IX seems to have believed). Against such a view, Phan claims that the existence of many religions is part of God's plan for the world. The reality of God is so rich and unlimited, and the understandings of humans are so limited and liable to corruption by the manifold temptations of power and domination, that many diverse ways of understanding are needed to criticise, correct, and complement each other.

I suppose some Roman Catholics would say that the development of a hierarchical church centred on the sacrifice of the Mass was a necessary correction and development of the Jewish priesthood. Some Protestants would say that the Reformation criticism of such a church was necessary if the purity of the Gospel message was to be preserved. Perhaps, since Vatican II, a time has come when Catholics and Protestants seek to learn from each other, for instance about the importance of reading Scripture in the vernacular, and about the centrality of the Eucharist to Christian spirituality.

If there is any providential direction in history, and if the many religions are not just evil or perverse, one would think that God must in some way include a diversity of religions in the divine purpose for the world. It is indeed hard to see what this purpose is, in any detail, but it is not hard to see that the many religions, as they actually exist, have much to learn from each other. As Phan says, 'each in their own way contribute to the kingdom'.[7] We can, thus, see a positive reason for the existence of a number of religions and general world views, insofar as we can see human understanding developing

---

[7] Phan (2017), p. 114.

by means of a creative interaction of viewpoints. We might even see such a thing as suggested by the fact that, within Christianity, there are many diverse religious opinions. Christians have four Gospels, not just one. The differing viewpoints of the four Gospels cannot be collapsed into one another, but together they provide a picture of Jesus wider than that which only one Gospel would depict. There may not be major contradictions there, but there are certainly differing perspectives on the person of Jesus. We could see in this the need for human knowledge to be expanded by critical and reflective encounter with others, as we grow nearer to that fullness of truth which still lies ahead of us.

What Christians can do in the complex multi-faith world in which we live is to offer the positive vision of a spiritual reality of self-giving love, which can be seen in Jesus, and which can live, as Spirit, in the hearts of those who submit to it in love. This is not saying, 'My set of truths is correct, and yours is wrong', it is saying, 'Here is a way of living in love that is a response to a supremely attractive divine love'. Christians think this persuasive assertion is based on truths, the truth that God is self-giving love, seen in the life of Jesus, whose Spirit of love can be present in human hearts. Those truths are, although central and important, in many ways rather general and unspecific, allowing of various interpretations, and capable of many sorts of overlap and influence with other spiritual traditions. They do not necessarily support the claim that there is one human institution which possesses a wholly correct set of truths, which has the authority to censor thoughts it disagrees with, and to impose belief in the truth by decree, by pressure, and sometimes even by force.

One might, then, be sceptical of claims that any religious tradition possesses the fullness of truth. One might think it unhelpful to regard traditions other than one's own just as preparations for one's own, which fulfils them all. Perhaps our own tradition too is a preparation for something greater and wiser and more loving (Christians call it 'the kingdom of God') for which our tradition is a seed or imperfect foreshadowing. One could still believe that, absolutely speaking, there is just one truth. One might believe that one's own tradition states some of the central truths about ultimate reality and final human destiny in a way that seems to us most likely among the alternatives we know to come somewhere near the truth. But one could still think that other traditions exist, in the providence of God, to lead us into a deeper understanding of truth. The underlying thought is that no one is ever excluded from the love of God, that no one ever has a complete grasp of the truth about God, that many religious paths lead towards God, and that the Christian perception of God as self-giving and invincible love does say something that is, however vaguely, absolutely true.

Part VI

Buddhism and Christianity in Dialogue

THE PHENOMENA OF RELIGION ARE EXCEEDINGLY COMPLEX. Nobody knows everything, even about their own religion. There are huge areas that we know little about, and real knowledge is confined to rather a small set of topics which have arisen or have become debated in recent thought. Scholarly debates are ongoing, and differences of opinion are essential in the study of religion. There is no one uncontested body of truth. Opinions get revised, some rejected, and others preferred, but these decisions can and do change over the years.

To take just one example, one can think of the Trinity as three forms in which God, who is one mind and will, exists. But many Christians think of the Trinity as three substantial entities within the divine being – the so-called 'social Trinity'. There are other ways of thinking of the Trinity as well. So it is unrealistic to speak of 'the' Christian doctrine of the Trinity, as though there was just one. The vast majority of Christians do think God is Trinitarian, but different ways of interpreting the Trinity exist, even within specific Christian churches, and new interpretations are likely to come into existence as time goes on.[1]

There are indeed claims sometimes made that only one view is 'really' Christian. But since people differ about which view this is, it seems more reasonable to accept that a number of different views have been held by well-informed Christians. One might arrange these views along a spectrum of belief, or along a number of spectra which one can invent for different purposes. For example, one could have a spectrum of Trinitarian views which are similar to a greater or a lesser extent to typical Jewish or Muslim views of God.

---

[1] I discuss this more fully in Ward (2015).

Jews and Muslims do not accept that God is Trinity, but Jews and Muslims are as diverse among themselves as Christians are, so their rejection of a Trinity can also be placed on a spectrum of degrees of rejection of Trinitarian ideas of God. At one end of such spectra are views in total conscious opposition. The view that God is absolute unity without division stands starkly opposed to a view that God is a society of mental subjects. At the other end of that spectrum, the view that God has ninety-nine beautiful names (in Islam), or that God, though essentially one, has many emanations (in Kabbalistic Judaism), is not totally opposed to the view that God, while being Trinitarian, is essentially one and that, when we speak of different properties in God, we are actually referring to just one simple but incomprehensible Divine nature (a view held by the impeccably orthodox Thomas Aquinas).

A Christian might accept a Trinitarian account of God because of the way the idea of God has developed over many centuries in the Christian church. That development is not closed, but the belief is the result of historical developments that have taken place in the Christian tradition, and that continue to develop as the tradition seeks to relate to new knowledge and new changes in moral belief.

In other words, one stands in a tradition with a long developing history. One does not simply set a whole lot of religious truth-claims alongside one another and choose those one likes best. One starts from the set of concepts that have been learned from a specific culture and then one seeks to expand or reformulate them as that culture, and one's own personal experience, gives rise to new ideas and forms of thought.

35

A Case Study: Christianity and Buddhism

*A*S A CASE-STUDY WHICH WILL SERVE AS AN EXAMPLE OF THIS process, I have chosen to consider the relation of Buddhism and Christianity. This is partly because in many countries these two faiths co-exist and interact in many ways, and partly because they seem to be so different in many ways. I will consider a specific book, *Buddhism and Christianity in Dialogue.*[1] This is a collection of papers first given at a series of lectures at Glasgow University by Buddhists and Christians, edited by Professor Perry Schmidt-Leukel. The essays provide an excellent basis for approaching the issue of how interaction with a different religious tradition can affect one's own beliefs. It will also provide useful data for trying to decide whether there is a common core to Buddhist and Christian beliefs, whether they are just contradictory, or whether there is some third way that offers progress for the future.

The reason one might think they are contradictory is that Buddhists do not believe in or care about the existence of an omnipotent creator God who wants some or all humans to enjoy an eternity of loving relationship with God. Christians have tended to think that Buddhists are pessimists who think 'all is suffering', and who look forward chiefly to their own non-existence as individual persons. The facts are much more complicated, and this volume of essays shows how.

Elizabeth Harris is a Christian who has been influenced by her first-hand knowledge of *Theravada* Buddhism.[2] She writes that she has found helpful the teaching of the Pali Canon of Buddhist texts that human suffering and evil has been largely brought about by egotistical striving and is the result of the human construction of a continuing 'I' or ego which seeks to possess and

---

[1] Schmidt-Leukel (2005).　　[2] Schmidt-Leukel (2005), pp. 29–53.

is attached to such things as pleasure, fame, and wealth. A central Buddhist teaching is that there is no such continuing self. Each of us is a flowing succession of perceptions, feelings, thoughts, and sensations, and there is no underlying unchanging substance which is 'me', the possessor of that succession. If we can learn that the Self is illusory and empty, we will be freed from attachment, and experience the compassion and wisdom that is *nirvana* (literally, a 'blowing-out' of attachment to objects and to the self). When greed is defeated, compassion arises.

Harris writes that this is very similar to, and helps to deepen, her Christian view that greed or the promotion of self is the root cause of suffering and evil in the world, and that compassion, the empowerment of the poor, and the defeat of egotistical greed can be attained by disciplines of morality, meditation, and wisdom. Insights that are present in one religious tradition can be deepened by seeing them treated in a different way, and perhaps as more central to another tradition.

She is clear that there are differences between Buddhist and Christian thinking, especially about the existence of God and grace, and about the doctrine of rebirth. She is not arguing that these religions are the same. Indeed, it is clear from the Pali texts that the Buddha (the enlightened one), Siddharta Gautama, disagreed with ascetics, Jains and Brahmins, and many other religious teachers of his time. There is no suggestion that all religions are true. For a Buddhist, only the way of the Buddha leads to enlightenment, which is the ultimate goal (if it is correct to speak of the transcendence of a sense of self and personal purposes as a goal).

She remains committed to central Christian doctrines that there is a personal God who was known in a uniquely self-revealing way in Jesus, and that individual and social resurrection is the goal of the religious life. Her expressed view is that she has learned, from her study of Buddhism, much about the human person and its passions and sufferings, and the importance of compassion and an overcoming of self. This is a case where religious understanding can be expanded or deepened by knowledge of a different tradition, though a core of basic beliefs remains distinctive if not quite unique.

Dr. Harris' dialogue partner is Kiyoshi Tsuchiya, who adopts what he calls a more confrontational approach.[3] He asserts that Christian views are essentially relational and personal; they look for a fulfilment of the finite self in relation to a supreme personal God. The Buddhist view he accepts,

[3] Schmidt-Leukel (2005), pp. 53–79.

heavily influenced by Taoism, denies that there is a continuing personal self or a supreme personal God. There is nothing permanent. All things flow, and what we call the self is 'a brief series of rather insignificant accidents'.[4] There is 'an incessant movement of the Yin and Yang spirits', and though there is a reality which is formless and changeless (the *Tao* or the *Dharma-kaya*) it has no will or judgement, and it exercises 'no contrivance or effort'. It may be called a 'thing', but it is certainly not a person. Union with it may be experienced when one comes to see all things, including oneself, as part of a disinterested flow which is chaotic and beyond the grasp of reason or logic.

In a brief response, Dr. Harris suggests that this total opposition is not the only option. As Buddhists stress the 'interconnectedness and fluidity of the cosmos',[5] so Christians can stress that the dissolution of the egotistic self and the breaking down of barriers between 'self' and 'other' is vital for spiritual insight. She agrees that the craving for personal survival after death is not a wholesome motivation, and that God as the ultimately real is not adequately conceived as a person.

There is here no denial that many typical Buddhist and Christian views are different, but there is a suggestion that all human language about the ultimate is inadequate, and this goes for statements about a continuous flow of Yin and Yang as well as for statements about a personal God. After all, if Buddhists call for a renunciation of attachment to particular views, then they can hardly be attached to any specific view of what is truly ultimate. There is something important that Buddhist and Christian views have in common, and that is that attachment and egoism must be renounced, that it is possible to achieve freedom from anxiety and suffering, and that the way to such freedom lies in a transcendence of egotistical existence in union with a reality beyond any human language to describe, though it has the character-istics of wisdom, compassion, and bliss.

The beliefs of some Buddhists that there is no continuing self, therefore no ultimate hope of personal survival, and that there is no personal will in ultimate reality, certainly conflict with some Christian beliefs that there is an immortal soul, that our greatest hope is to live eternally, and that God is a person who can, if God wishes, create and manipulate the natural order. However, Christians can agree that attachment to personal survival is not the mainspring of spiritual practice, yet envisage membership of a commu-nity of loving persons as a worthy spiritual goal. And they can also agree that the nature of God is necessarily what it is – not an arbitrary willing, but a

---

[4] Schmidt-Leukel (2005), p. 54.   [5] Schmidt-Leukel (2005), p. 80.

rational ordering to goodness and a reality of supreme wisdom, compassion, and bliss. The spectrum of belief is wide and flexible. It includes both extreme oppositions – self versus no-self and personal creator versus impersonal ground of being – and convergences of a spiritual quest to transcend alienated existence and achieve union with a reality of wisdom and compassion.

Liberation to a life beyond egoistic attachment by moral practice and meditation is not contradictory to transfiguration (salvation) by an objective power of love. They are different paths from the unsatisfactoriness or alienation of ordinary human existence to the attaining of a supreme and unshakeable wisdom and compassion which radically transforms human consciousness. That goal is believed to have been achieved by the founding teachers of their respective traditions. The figure of the crucified Jesus is very different from the figure of the meditating Gautama. But a life of self-giving love (and some prefer the image of Jesus as the risen and cosmic Lord) is not so very different from a life of universal compassion (and here one might think of the *Mahayana* development of the idea of *Bodhisattvas*, who defer final enlightenment for the sake of suffering beings).

When one sees the many possibilities of creatively reshaping the basic concepts and images of religious traditions, and when one accepts the inadequacy of all human thought about ultimate reality and the folly of thinking that one's own language expresses the absolute, final, and complete truth, then one may see that diverse religions do not always simply contradict each other. They also outline different paths towards and understandings of what is recognisably the same concern for human moral and spiritual fulfilment. The differences will remain; the paths are many. But the concern is shared, and each path can be enriched by the understandings of others, as they progress to a goal that is fully comprehended by none.

In a second discussion, the Catholic scholar Karl Baier writes from a perspective influenced by neo-Platonic negative theology.[6] He wishes to stress the non-duality of Being and the motive of kenotic self-giving in God. He holds, partly following the fifteenth-century writer Nicholas Cusanus, that God is beyond all concepts, and yet that paradoxically God communicates the Divine being which is essentially Trinitarian, a self-emptying flow of life. There is indeed in the Christian tradition a strand that stresses the hiddenness of God, although it is in tension with the claim that God is Trinitarian in the essential Divine nature.

---

[6] Schmidt-Leukel (2005), pp. 87–117.

Then Baier writes that Buddhist doctrines of an indescribable reality which is of 'something unborn, unbecome, unmade, uncreated'[7] refer to 'the same indivisible Ultimate'.[8] Thus, even though Buddhists do not speak of creation or of Trinity, both Christianity and Buddhism can speak of 'the self-emptying of Ultimate Reality ... answered by a spirituality of selflessness and compassion, undifferentiated love'.[9]

Baier's Buddhist respondent, Minoru Nambara, speaking from a Japanese *Mahayana* tradition, will have none of this.[10] He says that the teaching of the Buddha is 'absolute liberation from theories and gods ... the concept of emptiness ... and the central concept of Buddhist wisdom, cause and effect, or *karma*, joined in sweeping away all gods'.[11] There is only the impersonal law of *karma* and the spontaneous arising of events. There is no underlying 'eternal reality', much less a personal or Trinitarian one. 'This very world is the ultimate reality'.[12] 'In Buddhism there is no transcendence'.[13] There is only '*Kong*, empty, contentless, pure activity with neither goal nor cause ... on the way no metaphysical flowers blossom ... the beings are just there, without reason ... Being is appearance and nothing else'.[14] 'Events well up and appear from the bottomless abyss without explanation'.[15]

It seems to me that both these perspectives are paradoxical to the point of incomprehensibility, but, whatever exactly they mean, they clearly differ. Baier thinks that Nambara is adopting a 'kind of Taoist version of Buddhism',[16] which sees the natural world as an unceasing interplay of Yin and Yang, without any underlying transcendent. Nambara is adamant that 'love would only disturb a Buddhist',[17] who sees desire for relationship with another as just another form of attachment. There is a definite opposition of attitudes here, but they are not between Christianity and Buddhism as such. They are between very specific and distinctive viewpoints within more general traditions, and they display two different attitudes to faith, one of them looking for convergences between different spiritual paths and the other for incompatibilities between them.

This is even clearer when Schmidt-Leukel, a Christian pluralist, debates with John Makransky, a Tibetan Buddhist lama.[18] Schmidt-Leukel sees Buddha and Christ as mediators of a salvific relation to the same transcendent reality. *Dharmakaya*, the 'cosmic body of the Buddha' is 'functionally

[7] Schmidt-Leukel (2005), p. 106.   [8] Schmidt-Leukel (2005), p. 116.
[9] Schmidt-Leukel (2005), p. 116.   [10] Schmidt-Leukel (2005), p. 117–37.
[11] Schmidt-Leukel (2005), p. 120.   [12] Schmidt-Leukel (2005), p. 126.
[13] Schmidt-Leukel (2005), p. 129.   [14] Schmidt-Leukel (2005), p. 131.
[15] Schmidt-Leukel (2005), p. 134.   [16] Schmidt-Leukel (2005), p. 139.
[17] Schmidt-Leukel (2005), p. 145.   [18] Schmidt-Leukel (2005), pp. 176–200.

equivalent' to God, the source of salvation or liberation. He argues that anything is functionally equivalent to God if it does not confuse finite and infinite, and if it is linked to the evocation of selfless love. *Dharmakaya* meets both criteria. The descriptions are not identical in all respects, of course, but there is enough overlap to justify the claim that 'they refer in different ways to the same reality that transcends them both'.[19]

Schmidt-Leukel refers to the work of the Zen Buddhist scholar Masao Abe, who accepts the *Mahayana* doctrine of the 'three bodies' of the Buddha. The *nirmanakaya* can refer to any historical religious figure like Gautama or Jesus. The *sambhogakaya* can refer to any personal supra-historical being, whether Amida or Jahweh, and the *dharmakaya* can be described as 'form-less emptiness', the ultimate ground of being. In Pure Land Buddhism it is even clearer that Amida Buddha, the living and eternal Buddha of boundless compassion, is a personal form of the ultimate ground of the cosmos.

Makransky agrees that Gautama was one 'who became perfectly transparent to the unconditioned reality', and as such fully embodied 'its qualities of unconditioned freedom, all-inclusive love and penetrating insight'.[20] He sees a real liberating power within Christian communions, but he sees some clear differences too: Buddhists do not seek relational communion with a God; they seek non-dual complete oneness with Buddhahood. Buddhists rely on their inner powers of enlightened resolve, not on the death of Jesus, for liberation, and Buddhists do not rely on any historical facts for salvation, but on the present and inner liberating power of 'aware emptiness'.[21]

In some forms of Buddhism there are devotional practices such as calling on *Kuan Yin*, the *bodhisattva* of compassion, for help. Devotees can offer themselves to a Buddha or *Bodhisattva* and rely on the liberating power of the company of those who have attained nirvana. This looks very similar to Christian devotion to Christ or to the saints, but the context of these practices is very different. It is true that, to 'realise emptiness' is 'to open up supernal, radiant dimensions of existence ... to commune with the Buddhas there in deep faith'.[22] Nevertheless, what one has realised is that 'all things in their intrinsic emptiness have always been in nirvanic peace, that *samsara* is ultimately undivided from *nirvana*', that all phenomena are empty of substantial, independent existence.[23] The ultimate reality is not a creator God, but 'the empty, radiant, all-pervasive, undivided ground of being'.[24] The idea of an autonomous continuous self, in either humans or

[19] Schmidt-Leukel (2005), p. 170.   [20] Schmidt-Leukel (2005), p. 177.
[21] Schmidt-Leukel (2005), p. 180.   [22] Schmidt-Leukel (2005), p. 187.
[23] Schmidt-Leukel (2005), p. 186.   [24] Schmidt-Leukel (2005), p. 193.

in God, is the result of 'deluded emotions of self-grasping, aversion, and fear'.[25] The goal is to realise 'the insubstantial nature of all aspects of ordinary experience, to be realised in non-dual awareness'.[26] From that viewpoint, Christians still grasp at duality and substantiality. They are in touch with liberating powers from the unconditioned, and they are each 'genuine mediations of the same ultimate reality'.[27] For them, Christ is a powerful manifestation of Buddhahood through whom they can embody many liberating qualities, but they have not yet understood its true nature.

To all this, Schmidt-Leukel protests that Buddhists are meant to be aware of the emptiness of all conceptual constructs, so they should not affirm the superiority of their own conceptual construct. Both traditions bring about a liberation from egoism to a life of love and compassion, so they are 'equally valid as different expressions of salvation/liberation'.[28]

Makransky is unmoved and is not prepared to say that Christians can attain the fulness of enlightenment. Even if *dharmakaya* and God refer to the same ultimate reality, they do so in different ways. They cannot both be true; either there is a self which will exist for ever in its own individuality, or the idea of the self is an illusion. Either we will exist forever in communities of loving beings, or we will realise 'a non-conceptual non-dual realisation of emptiness'.[29]

From these illuminating discussions, it becomes evident that there are many possible Christian views, and many possible Buddhist views, and that there are major disagreements both within and between religious traditions. What distinguishes one tradition from another is reliance on a supremely authoritative figure, whose teachings are recorded in a founding Scripture. But even then, this figure is interpreted in different ways. The eternal cosmic Buddha of *Mahayana* found in the 'Lotus Sutra' is very different from the austere figure revered by *Theravadins*. The Christ who is represented as the *Christos Pantokrator*, the stern judge of the world who has to be persuaded by his mother to be merciful, is very different from the gentle figure who is represented in some Protestant Victorian art as one who welcomes children and animals to his side.

Around those founding figures a core of doctrines have developed, like, in the Christian case, resurrection, atonement, the kingdom of God, and judgement and salvation, or, in the Buddhist case, the ascetic path of self-renunciation, the possibility of personal enlightenment, the cycle of rebirth,

[25] Schmidt-Leukel (2005), p. 193.   [26] Schmidt-Leukel (2005), p. 195.
[27] Schmidt-Leukel (2005), p. 211.   [28] Schmidt-Leukel (2005), p. 205.
[29] Schmidt-Leukel (2005), p. 210.

and the release into a realm beyond change and becoming. These concepts remain central to historical traditions, though again there are diverse inter- pretations, often embodied in different Buddhist societies or in different Christian churches.

The impression is one of endless difference, with most religious believers making claims to membership in a group which generally accepts a certain set of doctrines, practices, and sorts of desired experiences. The borders of such groups are often fluid and ill-defined, though the denial of concepts central to one group is often followed by the formation of a separate group. Some groups have a more rigid and precise set of doctrines, but others are looser and more flexible.

So, it is possible to be a Buddhist and a Christian, if one interprets God in a negative way as the 'ground of all being', if one accepts that *Nirvana*, as a realm of wisdom and compassion and a 'radiant ground of being', is in some sense mind-like (wisdom and compassion are both personal qualities), and if one interprets the denial of a continuing self as a denial of one unchanging nature which can and should and perhaps one day will exist without any body, and which is not essentially interconnected with other minds and with the whole natural world of which it is part. There can be an almost complete interpenetration of central concepts, but that view will be opposed by others for many different reasons.

This is hardly a 'transcendent unity of religions', or some sort of primor- dial truth which is at the heart of all religions. It is a revisionary possibility, that may only be adopted by few, that can provide a new creative formula- tion of the central concepts of more than one tradition.

The revisionary possibility is to say that different paths can be combined in creative ways. But is such a combination always fruitful or necessary? It cannot cover every possible tradition. There would have to be enough similarity and flexibility in traditions to make a revised unity possible, and who would want such a unity? It might mean a 'flattening-out' of valued practices, rituals, and social identities. So, for many, remaining firmly in one tradition will seem the right thing to do, though there will still be many things to learn from a deeper understanding of other religions. It should be possible to see religious commitment at its best as a search to find an overcoming of the egoistic self and the realisation of a conscious relationship with a spiritual reality of supreme wisdom, compassion, and bliss, that leads to human fulfilment and happiness. Even humanism can be concerned with true human fulfilment and harmony with some transcendent truth. There is much here to evoke understanding of and sympathy with the spiritual striving of those who disagree with one's own specific religious commitment.

Ideology often divides; but if empathy and understanding is part of one's ideology, then there is hope for a peaceable and creative future.

Others might think that, in view of the diversity of religious views, there is a low probability that any of them can have the whole and self-sufficient truth. It might be possible to see that many differences are not simple contradictions, though they appear like that when they are put in the form of precisely formulated concepts. They might see a whole range of diverse insights into the truth of human being-in-the-world in the light of a transcendent reality, and various possibilities of pursuing human fulfilment by relation to that reality. No human persons stand in a neutral position, but all stand from birth and by early training, within a specific tradition and practice. From that initial position, one might be led to revise or develop or perhaps reject that tradition in ways which come to seem compelled by problems that arise from within one's lived historical and changing situation. The only views which could not be included in a revisionist project would be views which claim to have absolute and unchangeable truth, or whose views of other religions are completely oppositional, or whose central views seem to others to be immoral or irrational (these being contested ideas too). The revisionist project may be attractive to those who are sensitive to the new problems facing all ancient religions, and who are looking for new and creative ways of being religious in the modern age. It will not eliminate diversity, but it may take the religious quest a stage further than simple toleration of others.

36

Conclusion

ELIGION IS STILL AN IMPORTANT AND WIDESPREAD FEATURE
of human life. An investigation into the nature of religious belief
and practice is, therefore, of great human interest. Why should anyone be
religious at all? Or why should anyone be concerned about other religions, if
one is already a member of one, and one believes that it has salvific efficacy,
or at least takes one towards ultimate salvation or liberation?

The simple answer is that, if anyone is seriously concerned for truth, one
must search as far and as widely as possible to find truth. Even if one thinks
one knows the truth, once one becomes aware that one's view is disputed by
others who are intelligent, intellectually serious, and well-informed, one will
wish to know what accounts for the great differences among religious claims,
and whether one has the right to be certain of one's own highly disputed
beliefs, whether they are religious or non-religious.

Further, on examination of any specific religious tradition, one will find a
historical record of sometimes quite major changes, of new creative suggestions, and of reactions to a supposed earlier truth. One comes to see religious
beliefs as part of a historical process, and to be aware that in future many
present views will be put in question. If one is part of a process of change,
one cannot simply leap out of it, or pretend to have a totally unprejudiced
and impartial view of truth.

In this situation, there are four methodological principles that it would be
wise to adopt. It will be important, first of all, to locate oneself accurately
within the process of history. One needs to know where one stands in
society, where that society stands in relation to the wider world, what the
values and beliefs are that seem to be of vital importance, how consistent and
comprehensive they are, and how they relate, positively or negatively, to the
values and beliefs of others.

Then, secondly, it will be important to discover how, when and, if possible, why one's own views originated in the course of history. What writings or events or experiences led one to have the beliefs and values one has, and how has one accepted or rebelled against them?

Thirdly, it will be important to understand how these views are being challenged or influenced by other factors in one's immediate environment, and to identify the major problems that present themselves in this historical situation.

Fourthly, it will be important to ask how one's beliefs can be expanded in a good and fruitful way in the light of these new factors. One must make a creative decision at this point, but such decisions ought to be guided by what have been called the three transcendental values – the ideals of truth, beauty, and goodness. These ideals correspond to the three dimensions of religion that I distinguished at the outset, doctrine, experience, and practice.

The ideal of truth relates to the dimension of doctrine. It is desirable to incorporate one's religious beliefs into a coherent, plausible, and comprehensive world-view. But a survey of past efforts to construct such a world-view suggests that no attempt will be completely successful. The full truth lies in the future, and, though there is no doubt an absolute truth, it is highly unlikely that human efforts will ever grasp it adequately. Nevertheless, the striving for truth is incumbent on all intelligent human persons.

The ideal of beauty relates to the dimension of experience. In human life there are many experiences of transcendent value, which can and should be objects of contemplation and appreciation. Such experiences are by no means confined to religion, but for religious believers they are parts of a general response to experienced reality seen as disclosing an objective ground of all intrinsically worth-while states. There are many different sorts of value, and they may be integrated into organic wholes in different ways. These correspond roughly to the four major streams of religious thought which systematise the relation between objective values and purposes and the physical world – the idealist (e.g. *Vedanta*), dualist (e.g. *Theravada* Buddhism), monist (e.g. Taoism or Zen), and theistic (e.g. Judaism) streams.

The ideal of goodness relates to the dimension of moral practice. The basis of moral practice is to realise well-being, fulfilment, and happiness so far as is possible for all sentient beings. In religion this can give rise to a sense of objective moral demand and some basis for the hope that the goals of moral practice can be realised. But it also typically evokes a sense of human inadequacy or even incapacity, and often of some need for trust in a higher power which can generate true justice and compassion. Morality is autonomous in the sense that the ideal of goodness is independent of specific religious beliefs and does not depend on some arbitrary divine command. Yet it is closely related to the religious postulate that there actually exists a supreme Good which can bring about the realisation of a moral purpose and goal for the world.

These transcendental ideals should govern the responsible human search for religious truth. It is clear, however, that such a search has been, and is, pursued in many diverse ways, and this problem of diversity is the central concern of this book.

David Hume's argument with which this book began is that the diversity of religions, and the contradictions between them, mean that the vast majority of religions must be false. After all, only one view of the truth or falsity of religion can be true, and all others that contradict it must be false. Since it is more likely that one's own view (whether religious or non-religious) is part of that vast majority than that it is the only true one, this makes it unlikely that any religious belief (or any belief about religion) is true or can be known to be true.

One can now see, perhaps, that this presupposes a misunderstanding of the human situation. It supposes that we can stand outside the flow of history and make purely dispassionate judgements on the truth or value of various beliefs and practices. Reason has no historical location. Then, when one sees that most human beliefs – about politics, morality, philosophy, and the arts, as well as about religion – are false (that is, one disagrees with them), it seems that one's own beliefs are probably false. The fact of diversity puts every possible view in question.

But the human situation is not like that. Each human person is located within the historical process. There is no dispassionate view. All are located within a changing, flowing, continuum of values and beliefs, and are taught, or imbibe, an initial set of values and beliefs, which is the place they start from. The process is one of continuous dialectical interaction. Each person receives influences from their cultural environment and responds either by integrating these influences into an overall pattern, or by reacting against them. This process of integration or rejection is a complex mixture of convergence and confrontation, as people move to include the beliefs they come across or reject them as not fitting the developing pattern.

Each personal experience is a new integration of past beliefs and values, and the problems of belief that arise are raised by the historical situation. They are not just unchanging problems that arise in some timeless and ahistorical realm. Thus, creative responses to such problems are not, as the Humean postulate suggests, purely value-free, ahistorical, and dispassionate choices. They are specific personal responses to unique historical situations. They are parts of a dialectical process that is going to continue as long as time exists.

All possible religious and non-religious beliefs do not appear simultaneously as real possibilities for thought and action. One starts from a unique initial position, and makes some sort of creative response to it, as a small contribution to a continuing process, influenced by the thoughts and beliefs of many others who form the society of which one is part. There is an absolute truth. But human understanding of it is always going to be partial, imperfect, and transient. It is not that all sets of truth-claims but one are false. It is rather that in any given historical situation there is a set of truth-claims that are subject to various interpretations, some of which seem obviously true, and others seem disputable and disputed, to various degrees. Some of these claims will seem able to be readily integrated into one's general knowledge-pattern, others will be more difficult to integrate, and some will be rejected as incompatible.

No-one will think their own belief-pattern is likely to be false, though the fact of intelligent and informed dispute should lead people to accept that their view is historically conditioned, unlikely to be a full and final statement of truth, and will always be seen by some as controversial. It is completely rational to hold such beliefs, and to act on them with passionate commitment. Since this is the inescapable human situation, religious diversity is both inevitable and acts as a spur to the creative expansion of human understanding.

A major factor in most countries in the world today is the existence of different religious traditions living alongside one another. One needs to know what to do about major differences that seem to exist between different religions, and what might be the best (or least harmful) way of relating these differences of faith. There are challenges both to very exclusive and intolerant religious beliefs because they seem to neglect knowledge of the historical and cultural changes that affect all religions, and to the practical issues of multi-cultural living in one country, which are concerned with how seemingly very different conceptions of how human life can be fulfilled and how human societies should be justly organised can co-exist.

Such problems are not peculiar to religion. They are glaringly present in politics, in ethics, and in philosophy, in fact in any area where evaluations enter into questions of truth. In all such areas, one has to take a definite position, and there will almost always be opposition to it from others. When it comes to religion, most people will say that there does exist an objective and absolute truth about the nature of ultimate reality and the right human relationship to it. But where opponents are informed, intelligent, and morally concerned, it seems unlikely that all other views than one's own can simply be ignored or dismissed as incorrect, and it seems impossible that all views could be correct. It also seems unlikely that any one view could be wholly true and contain every truth that other views contain. So, it seems most likely that many traditions, insofar as they are not plainly immoral or irrational, contain important perspectives on truth.

An intelligent believer cannot be content simply to accept religious truths on authority, without reflection. Reflection is needed to test received beliefs against one's highest moral insights and knowledge of the best-evidenced factual knowledge to which one has access. One must be prepared to revise one's beliefs, whether in opposition to or in convergence towards the beliefs of others, in the light of increasing understanding of other strands of human thought and practice. This calls for an acceptance that one stands at a particular place in one continually changing historical tradition, and one must respond to particular problems that arise in that place in the light of knowledge and understanding of the global context of all religions and ideologies. That which is good from the past must be conserved, and that which looks to future good must be embraced. That, and not appeal to some supposed absolute authority of abstract Reason, is the lesson of the European Enlightenment.

Between the view that there is a common core of all religions, and that they all simply contradict one another, there is a third way. That is a way of dialectical interaction. At a particular time and place, each set of religious beliefs and practices can seek to reflect in some uniquely creative way its understanding of the other beliefs it encounters. These sets are not window-less. They are in a continual exchange of experience and understanding. This journey towards a truth that always, for limited and imperfect human minds, lies ahead, is in itself a great good. When this good is seen and appreciated, the problem of religious diversity dissolves. What remains, for those to whom religious belief is important, is an endless journey upon which human persons are drawn further into the infinite life of the Good.

Appendix

Since I have stressed the importance of historical situation and personal psychology, it seems only fair to confess where I myself stand religiously.[1] I have always been an academic, trained in philosophy and theology, and have been a British University Professor in both subjects (successively). I am a priest of the Church of England, and, therefore (though not all might agree), a Christian.

Religion is primarily a practice, constituted by prayers and rituals which train the mind to cultivate specific values and ideals and to pursue personal and social goals.

I believe there is a basic threefold structure to most religions: belief in a core ideal or set of ideals; in a causal power that helps to make them realisable; and in a goal which realises them as fully as possible. For instance, in Judaism and Islam one might say that the ideal is justice and mercy, the causal power is a personal God, and the goal is loving submission to the divine will. In Buddhism, the ideal is universal compassion, the causal power is the law of *karma*, and the goal is release from sorrow, or *Nirvana*. In Taoism and Confucianism, the ideal is a life of balance and harmony, the causal power is the Way of Heaven, and the goal is a fulfilled human life.

In the version of the Christian religion I accept, the ideal is a love which is both self-giving and self-realising, and it is inspired and formulated by reflection on the person of Jesus, who taught both verbally and by his life that God was unlimited love. The causal power is the Holy Spirit, believed to have been given by Jesus to his disciples, which helps to realise these ideals in practice. The goal is a community of loving and creative individuals, and it is achievable, with God's help, though in its fulness it will only exist in the world to come, a world in which all who have ever lived can share.

---

[1] I suppose the best fuller statement of my position is in Ward (2017).

These are my core beliefs. Around them, like a conceptual web, are grouped many subsidiary beliefs and ideas of many different sorts – for instance, what God is like, how the goal will be established, or exactly how Jesus helps to realise it. I accept the core beliefs in one interpretation, but I believe that, within the more general web of typical Christian beliefs, including those of my own Church, there have been many mistakes, and there still need to be many revisions, as new sorts of human knowledge become available. I also accept the legitimacy of many diverse interpretations, especially of the more peripheral beliefs in the web, though obviously I cannot agree with all of them.

I do not accept that only one Church or one religion is legitimate or has a monopoly of truth. If my core beliefs are true (that God is concerned that all should reach the ideal goal), that leads me to believe there will be truths and insights in other religious traditions that I should attend to. So, I think my faith is committed (I believe that my goal is knowledge and love of God as revealed in Christ); open (I see the need for revision in the light of new knowledge); and tolerant (I accept that many views that differ from mine are legitimately, reasonably, and sincerely held, that they may be freely expressed, and that I can and should often learn much from them). I have personally been influenced by the teachings of the *Bhagavad Gita* and of Ramanuja, the twelfth-century Indian *Vedantin*, by the *Dhammapaddha* and Buddhist meditation practice, and by humanist insistence on the importance of human flourishing. Nevertheless, my core beliefs, and much of the conceptual web that surrounds them, remain firmly Christian.

Bibliography

Allen, Kenneth, *Explorations in Classical Sociological Theory* (Los Angeles, CA: Sage, 2013).

Anderson, Pamela and Jordan Bell, *Kant and Theology* (London: Bloomsbury, 2010).

Anselm, *Proslogian*, trans. M. Charlesworth (London: University of Notre Dame Press, 1979), chapter 2.

Aquinas, Thomas, *Summa Theologiae* (Oxford: Blackfriars, 1967).

   The Light of Faith (Mancheste: Sophia, 1993).

Augustine, *The Literal Meaning of Genesis*, trans. J. H. Taylor (Mahwah, NJ: Paulist Press, 1982).

Barth, Karl, *Church Dogmatics*, Vol. 1, The Doctrine of God, ch. 3, part 1, trans. G. T. Thomson (Edinburgh: T and T Clark, 1936).

Buber, Martin, *I and Thou* (1923), trans. Ronald Gregor Smith (Edinburgh: T and T Clark, 1957).

Bultmann, Rudolf, *Jesus Christ and Mythology* (London: SCM Press, 1960).

Calvin, John, *Institutes of the Christian Religion* (1536), trans. Henry Beveridge (Grand Rapids, MI: Eerdmans, 1989).

Cantwell Smith, Wilfred, *The Meaning and End of Religion* (London: SPCK, 1978).

   Towards a World Theology (London: Macmillan, 1981).

Coakley, Sarah, *God, Sexuality and the Self* (Cambridge: Cambridge University Press, 2013).

Daly, Mary, *Beyond God the Father* (Boston, MA: Beacon Press, 1973).

D'Costa, Gavin, *The Meeting of Religions and the Trinity* (Ossining, NY: Orbis Books, Maryknoll, 2000).

Dupuis, Jacques, *Christianity and the Religions* (Ossining, NY: Orbis Books, Maryknoll, 2002).

Durkheim, Emile, *The Elementary Forms of the Religious Life*, trans. J. Swain (London: Allen and Unwin, 1963).

Eck, Diana, *Encountering God* (Boston, MA: Beacon Press, 2003).

Ellis, Fiona, *God, Value, and Nature* (Oxford: Oxford University Press, 2014).

Gellman, Jerome, *Experience of God and the Rationality of Religious Belief* (Ithaca, NY: Cornell University Press, 1997).

Hampson, Daphne, *After Christianity* (London: SCM Press, 2002).

Hegel, Georg Wilhelm Friedrich, *Lectures on the Philosophy of Religion*, vol. 1, *The Philosophy of Religion*, Part 1, and vol. 3, *The Consummate Religion*, ed. Peter Hodgson (first published in German, 1832, English edition, Los Angeles, CA: University of California Press, 1984 and 1985).

The Science of Logic, trans. A. V. Miller (Oxford: Oxford University Press, 1977).

Heidel, Alexander, *The Babylonian Genesis* (Chicago, IL: University of Chicago Press, 1951).

Heiler, Friedrich, *Prayer* (Oxford: Oxford University Press, 1932).

Heim, Mark, *The Depth of the Riches: A Trinitarian Theology of Religious Ends* (Grand Rapids, MI: Eerdmans, 2001).

Hick, John, *An Interpretation of Religion* (London: Macmillan, 1989).

Hume, David, *An Inquiry Concerning Human Understanding*, ed. Charles W. Hendel (New York: Bobbs-Merrill, 1955).

Huxley, Aldous, *The Perennial Philosophy* (London: Chatto and Windus, 1947).

James, William, *The Varieties of Religious Experience*, Lecture 16 (London: Fontana Library, 1960).

Jantzen, Grace, *God's World, God's Body* (London: Darton, Longman, Todd, 1984).

Kant, Immanuel, *Critique of Practical Reason* (1788), trans. L. W. Beck (Indianapolis, IN: Bobbs-Merrill, 1956).

Critique of Pure Reason (1781), trans. Norman Kemp Smith (London: Macmillan, 1952).

Fundamental Principles of the Metaphysic of Ethics (1785), trans. Thomas Kingsmill Abbott (London: Longmans, 1959).

The Metaphysic of Morals, Part Two; the Doctrine of Virtue (1797), trans. Mary Gregor (San Francisco, CA: Harper Torchbooks, 1964).

Observations on the Feeling of the Beautiful and the Sublime (1763), trans. J. T. Goldthwait (Berkeley, CA: University of California Press, 1960a).

'Opus Postumum', in *Kant's Opus Postumum*, trans. E. Adickes (Berlin: von Reuther and Reichard, 1920).

Prolegomena (1783), trans. Gary Hatfield (Cambridge: Cambridge University Press, 2004).

Religion within the Limits of Reason Alone (1793), trans. T. M. Greene and H. H. Hudson (San Francisco, CA: Harper, 1960b).

King, Ursula, *Spirit of Fire* (Ossining, NY: Orbis Books, Maryknoll, 1996).

Knitter, Paul, *No Other Name?* (London: SCM Press, 1985).

Kung, Hans, *Christianity and the World Religions* (London: SCM Press, 1993).

Lipner, Julius, *The Face of Truth* (London: Macmillan, 1986).

Locke, John, *The Reasonableness of Christianity* (1695) (Washington DC: Regnery Publishers, 1998).

Lovejoy, Arthur, *The Great Chain of Being* (Cambridge, MA: Harvard University Press, 1936).

McFague, Sallie, *Models of God* (Philadelphia, PA: Fortress Press, 1987).

Murdoch, Iris, *The Sovereignty of God* (London: Routledge, 1970).

Naess, Arne, *The Ecology of Wisdom* (Harmondsworth: , Penguin Modern Classics, 2016).

Otto, Rudolf, *The Idea of the Holy* (1961), trans. John Harvey (Harmondsworth: Penguin, 1959).

Panikkar, Raimon, 'Christianity and World Religions', in *Christianity* (Patiala: Punjabi University, 1969).

The Cosmotheandric Experience, Emerging Religious Consciousness (Ossining, NY: Orbis Books, Maryknoll, 1993).

The Unknown Christ of Hinduism (London: Darton, Longman, Todd, 1964).

Phan, Peter, *The Joy of Religious Pluralism* (Ossining, NY: Orbis Books, Maryknoll, 2017).

Race, Alan, *Christians and Religious Pluralism* (London: SCM, 1983).

Rahner, Karl, 'Christianity and the non-Christian religions', written in 1961, in *Theological Investigations*, vol. 5 (London: Darton, Longman, Todd, 1966).

The Trinity, trans. J. Donceel (London: Burns and Oates, 1979).

Ramanuja, 'The Vedanta Sutras', trans. George Thibaut, in *Sacred Books of the East*, vol. 48, ed. Max Muller (Delhi, Motilal Banarsidass, 1962).

Ramsey, Ian, *Religious Language* (London: SCM Press, 1957).

Ruether, Rosemary Radford, *Sexism and God-Talk* (Boston, MA: Beacon Press, 1993).

Sankara, *Brahma-Sutra Bhasya*, trans. Swami Gambhirananda (Swami Vandananda, Mayavati, Pithoragarh, 1977).

'The Vedanta Sutras', trans. George Thibaut, in *Sacred Books of the East*, vol. 34, ed. Max Muller (Delhi: Motilal Banarsidass, 1962).

Schilpp, Paul, *Kant's Pre-Critical Ethics* (Evanston, IL: Northwestern University Press, 1960).

Schleiermacher, Friedrich, *The Christian Faith* (1830), trans. H. R. Machintosh and J. S. Stewart (Edinburgh: T and T Clark, 1989).

On Religion (1799), trans. Richard Crouter (Cambridge: Cambridge University Press, 1988).

Schmidt-Leukel, Perry, editor, *Buddhism and Christianity in Dialogue* (London: SCM, 2005).

'Religious Pluralism in Thirteen Theses', *Modern Believing*, **57**(1) (2017).

Schmitt, Charles, 'The Perennial Philosophy from Agostino Steuco to Leibniz', *Journal of the History of Ideas*, **27**(1) (1966).

Schuon, Frithjof, *The Transcendent Unity of Religions* (Wheaton, IL: Quest Books, 1984).

Schussler-Fiorenza, Elisabeth, *In Memory of Her* (New York: Crossroad, 1983).

Sen, Sushanta, 'The Vedic-Upanisadic Concept of Brahman', in *Concepts of the Ultimate*, ed. Linda Tessier (London: Macmillan, 1989).

Sharpe, Eric, *Understanding Religion* (London: Duckworth, 1983).

Smart, Ninian, *The World's Religions* (Cambridge: Cambridge University Press, 1989).

Smith, Christian, *Religion* (Princeton, NJ: University of Princeton Press, 2017).

Smith, Huston, *The Forgotten Truth* (San Francisco, CA: Harper, 1976).

The World's Religions (San Francisco, CA: Harper One, 1958, revised ed. 1991).

Stout, G.F., 'The Object of Thought and Real Being', *Proceedings of the Aristotelian Society*, **11**(1) (1911).

Suchocki, Marjorie, *God Christ Church* (New York, NY: Crossroad, 1982).

Teilhard de Chardin, Pierre, *The Phenomenon of Map* (London: Collins, 1959).

Tillich, Paul, *Systematic Theology* (Chicago, IL: University of Chicago Press, 1951).

Troeltsch, Ernst, *The Absoluteness of Christianity* (1929), trans. David Reid (London: SCM, 1972).

'The Place of Christianity among the World Religions', in *Christianity and Other Religions*, ed. John Hick and Brian Hebblethwaite (Philadelphia, PA: Fortress, 1980).

Über historische und dogmatische Methode der Theologie, Gesammelte Schriften 2 (Tubingen: J.C.B. Mohr, 1931), pp. 729–33.

Ward, Keith, *Christ and the Cosmos* (Cambridge: Cambridge University Press, 2015).

Concepts of God (Oxford: Oneworld Press, 1998).

The Christian Idea of God (Cambridge: Cambridge University Press, 2017).

The Development of Kant's View of Ethics (Oxford: Blackwell, 1972).

Religion and Revelation (Oxford: Oxford University Press, 1994).

Index

Of key words, names, and themes